ISSUES

2002

The Candidate's Briefing Book

edited by

Stuart M. Butler
and
Kim R. Holmes

I look around me and I see it isn't so.

Published by
The Heritage Foundation
214 Massachusetts Avenue, NE
Washington, DC 20002–4999
800-544-4843
www.heritage.org
www.heritage.org/issues

ISBN 0–89195–102–4

Front cover design by Mark Hurlburt
Imagery © 2000 by Comstock;
military images courtesy of the U.S. Department of Defense

TABLE OF CONTENTS

About The Heritage Foundation

The Heritage Foundation is a unique institution—a public policy research organization, or "think tank." We draw solutions to contemporary problems from the ideas, principles, and traditions that make America great.

We are not afraid to begin our sentences with the words "We believe," because *we do believe*: in individual liberty, free enterprise, limited government, a strong national defense, and traditional American values.

We want an America that is safe and secure; where choices (in education, health care, and retirement) abound; where taxes are fair, flat, and comprehensible; where everybody has the opportunity to go as far as their talents will take them; where government concentrates on its core functions, recognizes its limits and shows favor to none. And the policies we propose would accomplish these things.

Our expert staff—with years of experience in business, government, and on Capitol Hill—don't just produce research. We generate solutions consistent with our beliefs and market them to the Congress, the executive branch, the news media, and others. These solutions build on our country's economic, political, and social heritage to produce a safer, stronger, freer, more prosperous America. And a safer, more prosperous, freer world.

As conservatives, we believe the values and ideas that motivated our Founding Fathers are worth conserving. And as policy entrepreneurs, we believe the most effective solutions are consistent with those ideas and values.

We believe that ideas have consequences, but that those ideas must be promoted aggressively. So, we constantly try innovative ways to market our ideas. We are proud of our broad base of support among the American people and we accept no government funds.

Our vision is to build an America where freedom, opportunity, prosperity, and civil society flourish.

About Issues 2002

As candidates begin their campaigns for office in 2002, they will need to be able to define the key issues quickly and then present their clear policy recommendations, supported by facts, for addressing those issues. *Issues 2002: The Candidate's Briefing Book* provides these issues, facts, and solutions in language every voter will understand.

FEATURES OF THE BRIEFING BOOK

Each chapter on one of the 24 key issues—like Social Security and welfare reform, missile defense, and terrorism—offers the candidate clear analysis in four sections:

- **The Issues**—This section provides straightforward statements of the primary problems facing Congress and the executive branch, and how the candidate should frame the debate.
- **The Facts**—Candidates will find a straightforward presentation of facts to support the Issues statements. The Facts statements offer the supporting data that the candidate needs to clarify the problems, formulate the right solutions, and push the debate in the right direction.
- **What to Do in 2003**—Heritage analysts have examined the issues and facts in depth and provide the candidate with the most important near-term priorities for action in 2003.
- **Experts**—To help the candidate find more information on any issue, *Issues 2002* lists complete contact information for both Heritage and outside experts who specialize in these major issue areas.

WHAT'S NEW IN ISSUES 2002

Issues 2002 is so much more. In addition to *The Candidate's Briefing Book*, the *Issues 2002* package includes:

1. **A CD–ROM**, which contains a searchable version of the entire *Briefing Book* for quick access by the candidate and the campaign staff, whether preparing policy papers, speeches, or

notes for a media interview or debate. In addition, the CD–ROM includes everything candidates need to argue effectively: a searchable library of Heritage policy papers and books, including those mentioned in each chapter, and a searchable bank of useful charts and tables.

2. **An Up-to-Date Campaign Web Site**, at *www.heritage.org/issues*, featuring on-line versions of the *Issues* chapters. The site will be continually updated with breaking news, new studies, talking points, and other items of interest to campaigns. A great resource for candidates who need to keep abreast of developments in a wide range of issue areas, it will include:

   - **A "Briefing Room" for each issue in *Issues 2002*:** A constantly changing Web page that addresses breaking developments on the issue—talking points, new studies (by other organizations as well as Heritage), and experts in each area.

   - **Resource Pages:** A comprehensive library of links to papers, organizations, and non-Heritage studies related to each issue.

ACKNOWLEDGMENTS

With *Issues 2002*, The Heritage Foundation provides candidates with the facts they need to know about the key issues facing the country, as well as with practical policy solutions. We provide this in an easy-to-read, constantly updated, multimedia format. Any project of this magnitude involves many people, and this is especially true with this unique product. We are grateful to the members of the Heritage staff for their many contributions to this year's *Issues*—from the authors of the chapters and their diligent assistants, to all the editors, designers, production staff, and those who shepherded the project through to completion.

We would like to give special mention to the members of Heritage's editing staff, Janice A. Smith, Collette Caprara, William T. Poole, Richard Odermatt, and Andrew Olivastro; to our Coalition Relations staff,. Bridgett Wagner and Timothy Lobello; to our Web personnel, Michael Spiller, Jon Garthwaite, John Hanley, and Melissa Kaiser; to our Publishing Services staff, Jill Colella Bloomfield, Michelle Fulton Smith, Mark Hurlburt, and Harris Byers; to project coordinators David Cole and Daniel W. Fisk; and to all the department directors, research assistants, and college interns who contributed their expertise and talents to make this book a top-quality resource for candidates in 2002.

—Stuart M. Butler

—Kim R. Holmes

ISSUES 2002

Domestic Policy

THE FEDERAL BUDGET
Getting Spending Under Control

Brian M. Riedl and Christopher B. Summers

THE ISSUES

The federal budget climate has changed significantly since the 2000 election, when America was at peace and the economy was booming. Then, the central budgetary debate concerned how to allocate the predicted 10-year $5.6 trillion budget surplus to tax reductions, debt reduction, or new spending. By the close of 2001, peace had been replaced by a war that could last several years, the economy had fallen into recession, and the President's budget director was predicting deficits for at least the next four years.[1]

Though the budget situation has changed, however, commonsense fiscal principles have not. Just as before, the federal government should reduce taxes, cut wasteful spending, reform the massive entitlements, and fully fund America's national defense priorities.

1. **Billions of dollars continue to be wasted on federal pork projects unrelated to the recession or the war on terrorism.** As quickly as the money arrives, Congress has spent the remaining surplus on programs that have nothing to do with the war or the recession, such as massive farm subsidies and corporate welfare. Some are using the war as an excuse to spend more money on their priorities or to concentrate more power in Washington. Others see the economic stimulus bills as opportunities to pay back special interests. Every dollar needlessly spent on wasteful or unnecessary programs is one less dollar that can be allocated to the war on terrorism or used to reduce taxes and speed up economic recovery.

---

1. Mitchell Daniels, Director, Office of Management and Budget, speech to National Press Club, November 28, 2001.

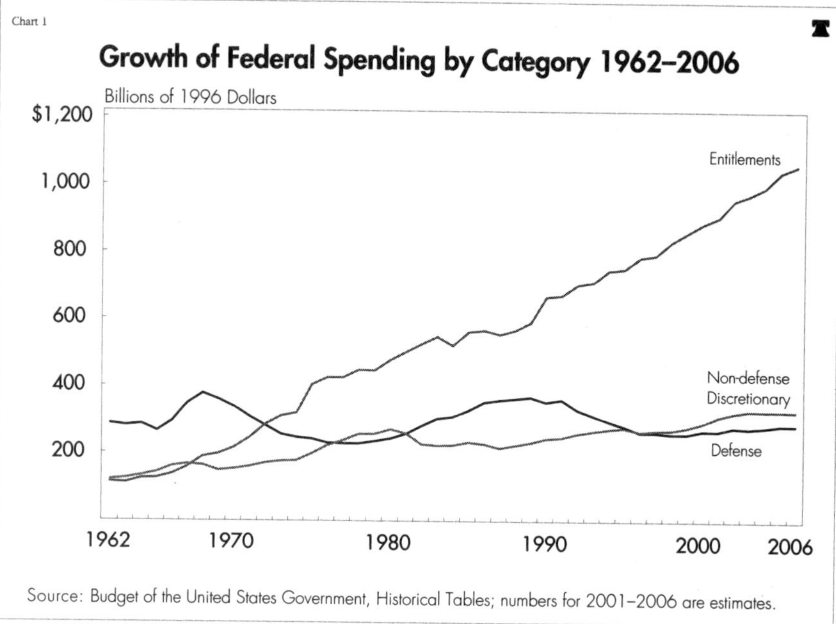

Source: Budget of the United States Government, Historical Tables; numbers for 2001–2006 are estimates.

2. **Rapidly expanding entitlement programs like Social Security and Medicare threaten to bankrupt our children and grandchildren.** Uncontrollable mandatory spending programs like Social Security and Medicare are growing at unsustainable levels. Unless these programs are reformed, the coming retirement of the baby boomers will further increase their cost to society, threaten the fiscal solvency of the federal budget, and necessitate massive tax increases. The sooner these programs are reformed to control their costs, the less painful the reform will have to be. (See Chart 1.)

3. **Government's own watchdogs provide examples of waste, inefficiency, and redundancy that are prime opportunities for reining in spending.** The U.S. General Accounting Office (GAO) and Congressional Budget Office (CBO) have identified hundreds of billions of dollars that each year is allocated to agencies and programs that are wasteful, mismanaged, or unnecessary. Eliminating or consolidating such programs could substantially reduce the size and cost of government without endangering programs that are vital to the national interest.

4. **The budget process must be reformed to curb Congress's pro-spending bias.** It will never be possible either to get

spending under control or to have spending reflect real priorities until something is done about the budget process—the arcane rules that determine how taxpayers' money is spent. No family or business would function well under the process Congress now uses to establish a budget. It simply declares some spending "off-budget," so lawmakers ignore it. Other spending, including spending on most entitlement programs, is on autopilot and only occasionally subject to control. Under this budget system, a Member of Congress can vote to increase a program's budget by 6 percent and still be accused of "cutting" its funds. The budget system also effectively discourages tax reduction while making it easy to increase spending. It is time for a sober rewrite of the budget process rules.

THE FACTS

FACT: Neither the war on terrorism nor the recession is reason to increase spending on programs that are wasteful, unnecessary, or unrelated to the current problems.

Washington continues to waste taxpayers' money despite the demands related to the recession and the war on terrorism.[2] Legislation committing $40 billion in post–September 11 emergency spending was signed into law even before Congress and the Administration had determined specific spending priorities or their costs.[3] New spending is certainly needed at home and abroad to fight the war on terrorism, but Congress should first detail the objectives it wants to accomplish and then allocate the funds where and when they are needed, rather than set high but random spending amounts and look for ways to spend them.

Although the recession is reducing tax revenues, Congress is in danger of using the recession and terrorism as an excuse to increase wasteful spending. As Representative James Moran (D–VA) reportedly exclaimed, "It's an open grab bag, so let's grab."[4] Relief for beleaguered taxpayers is generally absent from this grab

2. Ronald D. Utt, Ph.D., "Lobbyists Continue to Use Tragedy to Raid American Taxpayers: An Update," Heritage Foundation *Backgrounder* No. 1502, November 13, 2001, at *www.heritage.org/library/backgrounder/bg1502.html.*
3. P.L. 107–38.
4. Craig Timberg, "VA Seeks $3 Billion in Disaster Assistance," *The Washington Post*, October 13, 2001, p. B1.

bag. Under the guise of stimulating the economy, for example, the 107th Congress has considered spending billions on:

- A massive farm bill that included millions of dollars in subsidies to *Fortune* 500 companies; multimillionaires like Ted Turner, Scottie Pippen, David Rockefeller; and even some Members of Congress.[5]
- Mass transit systems with few riders, a "magnetic levitation" train between Las Vegas and Los Angeles, and large subsidies for travel agencies and car rental companies.

FACT: Economic growth, not Congress, balanced the federal budget even as Congress failed to reduce the size of government.

The federal budget surplus resulted not from congressional reductions in spending, but from the extraction of more taxes from working people than the government needed.

- Between fiscal year 1993 and FY 2000, Congress and the President increased federal spending 27 percent, from $1,410 billion to $1,789 billion. The budget went from deficit to surplus during that time only because the booming economy had increased tax revenues 75 percent, from $1,154 billion to $2,025 billion.
- Had Congress and the President simply allowed spending to increase at the rate of inflation between 1993 and 2000, the budget surplus in 2000 would have been $109 billion higher—$1,033 per household—money that could have been used to reduce taxes and the national debt. Instead, they gave most federal programs large increases and, beyond the U.S. Department of Defense and the 1996 welfare reforms, did not eliminate or significantly reduce one major spending program. Congress resisted giving the extra tax dollars back to the taxpayers.

FACT: Runaway entitlement spending threatens to overwhelm any hope of fiscal discipline.

Just as families have mandatory expenditures, like mortgages and car payments made under contract, for which they can change the payments only by changing the contract, the federal govern-

---

5. See Environmental Working Group Web site at *www.ewg.org*.

ment has mandatory spending, such as paying interest on the national debt and funding Social Security, Medicare, farm subsidies, and loan guarantees that are considered contracts. Because mandatory spending programs are long-term commitments outside the annual appropriations process, their growth will continue unabated unless lawmakers take the politically difficult step of legally changing the contracts to restrict program eligibility or payment levels.

- In 1962, mandatory spending (excluding net interest payments) comprised 26 percent of the federal budget. Between 1962 and 2001, inflation-adjusted mandatory spending grew 16 times faster than discretionary spending, increasing its share of the budget to 54 percent.[6]
- The retirement of the 70 million baby boomers, beginning around 2011, combined with the increasing cost of health care programs, threatens to increase entitlement spending further to unsustainable levels.

All in all, the federal government's "credit card debt"—the total future liabilities it owes on programs like Social Security, Medicare, the national debt, federal pensions, and guaranteed loans—is approximately $21 trillion, or $750,000 for every man, woman, and child in America.[7]

FACT: The federal budget bulges with outdated, duplicative, and unnecessary programs that waste vital resources.

Instead of performing a small number of functions well, the federal government has taken on an increasing number of commitments that collectively restrict its ability to perform most of its functions efficiently. The result is an uncontrollable bureaucracy of overlapping and inefficient programs that survive because

6. Office of Management and Budget, *Budget of the United States Government, Fiscal Year 2002, Historical Tables,* Table 8.2. Figures for 2001 are estimates.
7. Congressional Budget Office, *The Budget and Economic Outlook: Fiscal Years 2002–2011,* January 2001, p. 91, shows a $5.5 trillion national debt liability. OMB estimates Social Security's liability to be $8.7 trillion; see *www.whitehouse.gov/omb/budget/fy2002/bud15.html.* Medicare has an estimated $2.6 trillion liability, according to Senator Phil Gramm (R–TX), AEI Conference Summary, August 1997, at *www.aei.org/cs/cs7917.htm.* The final $4.2 trillion comes from loan guarantees, federal employee pensions, and hazardous waste liability.

Congress lacks the time to examine each program and the will to take on those that are failing.

- For example, under the category of waste and abuse, Congress should take a close look at the Earned Income Tax Credit (EITC). Of all EITC claims, 25 percent—worth about $4.4 billion—have been found to be in "error."[8]

Under the category of duplication and bureaucracy:[9]

- The federal education bureaucracy operates 788 programs across 40 different agencies at an annual cost of nearly $100 billion—of which $30 billion never makes it out of this maze, being spent on administrative costs.
- 13 federal agencies operate 342 economic development programs with little or no central coordination, creating a bureaucracy so complex that many local communities have simply stopped applying for assistance.
- The U.S. Department of Agriculture (USDA) employs nearly 100,000 workers, about one for every four full-time farmers.

Among the misdirected programming:

- The federal government provides approximately $75 billion per year in corporate welfare payments. Many of these payments go to profitable *Fortune* 500 companies to fund projects that the companies themselves could afford to fund.[10]
- Since 1996, two-thirds of federal farm subsidies have gone to just 10 percent of subsidy recipients, most of which are highly profitable large farms and agribusinesses.[11]

FACT: Federal government spending crowds out the private sector.

By performing functions best left to the marketplace, the federal government undermines the private sector. For example:

---

8. Office of U.S. Representative Richard K. Armey (R–TX), at *http://armey.house.gov/results/results1.htm* (December 2001).
9. *Ibid.*
10. Stephen Slivinski, "The Corporate Welfare Budget: Bigger Than Ever," Cato Institute *Policy Analysis* No. 415, October 10, 2001.
11. Data compiled by Environmental Working Group, at *www.ewg.org*.

- Federal flood insurance dominates the market so strongly that few firms bother to compete.
- The federal guarantees behind the federal housing loan programs Fannie Mae and Freddie Mac make them more attractive to borrowers than other private lenders.
- Amtrak runs as a continuously unprofitable federal boondoggle while monopolizing train service in much of the country.[12]
- Other areas where the federal government crowds out the private sector include job training, weather forecasting, and business finance.

These federal programs are examples of spending that is so unnecessary the private sector would not need to replace federal involvement:

- The Rural Utilities Service brought electric and telephone service to rural America by the mid-1950s; even though it has achieved its goal, it continues to operate at an annual cost of $107 million.
- The Conservation Reserve Program pays farmers $1.3 billion per year *not* to farm 36 million acres of good cropland.
- While cable television includes substantial art and educational programming that does not receive any government funding, public television and artists still receive nearly $600 million annually.

FACT: The federal government usurps local control and imposes high costs on state and local governments.

As the federal government has grown, it has seized authority from state and local governments. Instead of allowing the level of government closer to the problems to address those problems with local solutions, Washington imposes a distant, unaccountable, one-size-fits-all policy.

For example, though highways and roads are properly the domain of local governments, the federal government imposes a

12. Ronald D. Utt, Ph.D., "New Amtrak Boondoggle May Outdo All Others," Heritage Foundation *Backgrounder* No. 1392, August 28, 2000, at *www.heritage.org/library/backgrounder/bg1392.html.*

federal gas tax, administratively shuffles the money around in Washington, and then sends the money back to the states with specific strings attached. Washington bureaucrats tell the states what roads and highways can be worked on, who can be hired to do the work, how much they can be paid, and how the road or highway should be financially managed after its completion.

The U.S. Department of Education collects billions of dollars, decides what type of education spending is needed for each area, and then sends the money—minus the federal government's administrative costs—to states and local school districts with specific instructions on what type of programs to offer each type of student. A far better approach would be to empower local governments, which best understand the needs of their own communities, to make decisions.

FACT: The budget process lacks any real safeguards to slow the growth of government.

Baseline Budgeting. Only in Washington can spending more money on a program be defined as cutting it. The federal budget operates on an accounting tactic known as "baseline budgeting," which assumes that all program policies and services will remain unchanged from one year to the next, and therefore automatically adjusts expenditures to reflect inflation and population growth.

Thus, under baseline budgeting, spending the same amount from one year to the next is considered a "cut," and raising program spending—often by as much as 6 percent per year—is considered a "freeze." With annual spending increases automatically built into the budget process, taming the growth of the federal budget becomes nearly impossible.

Spending Caps or Pay–Go Rules. Other budget reforms like discretionary spending caps and "pay-as-you go" (or pay–go) rules have been too watered down and poorly designed to work effectively. Discretionary spending caps are intended to limit spending increases, but lawmakers have begun budget deliberations by considering the caps less as a spending ceiling than as a floor, whereby spending less than the cap is not an option. Then, after generously piling on spending proposals, Congress has simply voted to exceed these caps.

Pay–go rules require that the costs of any tax reductions or entitlement expansions be balanced by raising other taxes or reducing other entitlements. Pay–go rules are based on the assumption that all tax reductions will reduce revenue permanently and therefore need to be "paid for" by pitting them against politically sensitive entitlements or another group of taxpayers. In reality, reducing certain taxes (like capital gains) historically has increased economic activity and reduced revenues by much less than the amount of the tax cut. While well-intentioned, the failed budget reforms of discretionary caps and pay–go rules make real reform more difficult by lulling Congress into a false sense of fiscal responsibility.

Interactive Spending Reforms Tool: Heritage's Budget Information Site provides Internet users a list of every dollar the federal government has spent in a year, from entitlements and discretionary spending to paying interest on the debt. The numbers are broken down by department and agency and should help citizens better understand where government spending can be cut. Access this interactive tool at *www.heritage.org/calculators*.

WHAT TO DO IN 2003

Maintain fiscal discipline during the war on terrorism and the recession by freezing non-defense discretionary spending.

Although war and recession are seen by Congress as justification to increase spending on all programs, including those unrelated to national needs, Members must maintain fiscal discipline. Every dollar in unnecessary spending increases taxes and deficits and diverts funds away from real needs in the war on terrorism.

Instead of spending first and asking questions later, Congress and the President should first set specific national security priorities and then find the most cost-efficient way to fund those priorities. Then Congress and the President should freeze FY 2003 non-defense discretionary spending at its current level. During World War II, President Roosevelt cut non-defense spending by 18 percent between 1943 and 1945. During the Korean War, President Truman reduced non-defense spending by 24 percent in 1951 alone.[13] Spending was reduced not because Congress saw no value in these programs, but because in a time of war the nation's priorities change and the federal budget must reflect those changes.

With defense spending rising by 11 percent annually, entitlement spending growing 8 percent each year, and revenues stagnating, any growth in non-defense discretionary spending would be fiscally irresponsible. If even war and recession are not a sufficient justification for Congress to make the difficult budget choices, then runaway spending will continue to be the norm.

Address the long-term cost of entitlements.

With Social Security spending of $430 billion in 2001 and economists predicting bankruptcy within a generation, Congress cannot afford to ignore Social Security's rapidly expanding costs.[14] The recent report of the Social Security Commission recommends specific reforms to guarantee the program's long-term solvency—such as creating private retirement accounts while maintaining current benefit levels for retirees.[15]

Entitlement programs like Medicare, Medicaid, and agriculture subsidies are also growing at unsustainable rates. The longer Congress waits to reform these programs, the more uncontrollable their costs will become and the more painful reform will be. These reforms should be part of an overall examination of the government's approach to areas like health care, income support, and agriculture.

Appoint a commission to compile a list of unneeded programs that requires an up-or-down vote in Congress to continue, and then use the savings to finance a middle-income tax cut.

Many of the most wasteful, outdated, and duplicative programs have survived because they are regional in nature, serving the

---

13. Office of Management and Budget, *Budget of the United States Government, Fiscal Year 2002, Historical Tables*.
14. For more information, see the chapter on Social Security reform.
15. *Strengthening Social Security and Creating Personal Wealth for All Americans*, Final Report of the President's Commission to Strengthen Social Security, Washington, D.C., December 21, 2001, at *www.commtostrengthensocsec.gov/reports*.

special interests of a few Members of Congress at the expense of the nation as a whole. These Members are loath to have their local programs singled out for elimination. Furthermore, eliminating just one local program is geographically redistributive, because all the spending cuts take place in one area while the corresponding savings, whether allocated to other spending, tax cuts, or deficit reduction, are generally spread across the nation.

This dilemma can be overcome by appointing an independent commission, similar to President Ronald Reagan's Grace Commission, to compile a list of all unneeded programs. Congress must then set rules limiting Members to voting up or down on the entire list of recommendations without amending it. Finally, all savings from eliminated programs should be returned to the taxpayers as part of a middle-income tax cut.

This approach would solve both problems. The commission's recommendations would add elements of fairness and legitimacy to the process by affecting all Members, not singling out any one, and would not allow amendments to spare one Member at the expense of another. And because all regions would be affected more or less equally, there would be much less geographic redistribution; local spending cuts would be balanced with local tax reductions. This approach was used successfully in the early 1990s to decide which military bases to close. There is no reason it cannot work again.

Devolve transportation, education, law enforcement, job training, and economic development spending to the states.

To help state and local governments tailor their resources to local needs and create true laboratories of democracy, Congress should begin devolving several programs to the states, which would have the option of further devolving programs to local governments.

Congress should permit states to collect and retain the 18.4 cent federal gas tax and to spend the proceeds on their own transportation priorities. The federal government should also begin devolving K–12 education, law enforcement, economic development, and job training spending to the states by converting many of the current programs into open-ended block grants, allowing states flexibility in spending to achieve the goals of these programs.

These reforms would follow the path of the successful 1996 welfare reform, which devolved most federal welfare spending to the states while evaluating state performance according to outcome-based standards. Communities failing to meet the standards would have to return to traditional federal control.

Implement safeguards to combat pro-spending federal budget bias.

Discretionary spending caps must be made more difficult to bypass, and pay–go rules should be reformed to recognize that tax reductions do not always statistically reduce tax revenues dollar for dollar. Over the long run, Congress must move toward the budgetary reforms implemented by state legislatures across the country—such as constitutional tax and expenditure limitations, a balanced budget amendment, and the line-item veto allowing the President to veto individual expenditures in spending bills. In the meantime, Congress must be careful not to settle for watered-down budget reforms that give the impression of fiscal restraint while allowing the budget to continue growing unabated.

—Brian M. Riedl is Grover M. Hermann Fellow in Federal Budgetary Affairs, and Christopher B. Summers is a Research Assistant, in the Thomas A. Roe Institute for Economic Policy Studies at The Heritage Foundation.

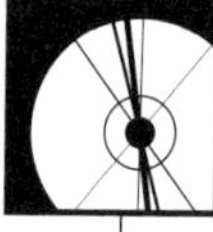

For a complete list and full-text versions of additional studies by Heritage on the federal budget process and budget reform, see the searchable *Issues 2002* companion CD–ROM.

EXPERTS

Heritage Foundation

Brian M. Riedl
Grover M. Hermann Fellow in Federal Budgetary Affairs
The Heritage Foundation
214 Massachusetts Avenue, NE
Washington, DC 20002
(202) 608-6201
fax: (202) 544-5421
brian.riedl@heritage.org

Lawrence Whitman
Director, Thomas A. Roe Institute for Economic Policy Studies
The Heritage Foundation

214 Massachusetts Avenue, NE
Washington, DC 20002
(202) 608-6215
fax: (202) 544-5421
lawrence.whitman@heritage.org

Ronald D. Utt, Ph.D.
Herbert and Joyce Morgan
Senior Research Fellow
The Heritage Foundation
214 Massachusetts Avenue, NE
Washington, DC 20002
(202) 608-6013
fax: (202) 544-5421
ron.utt@heritage.org

Christopher B. Summers
Research Assistant
Domestic Policy Studies
The Heritage Foundation
214 Massachusetts Avenue, NE
Washington, DC 20002
(202) 608-6238
fax: (202) 544-5421
christopher.summers
@heritage.org

Other Experts

John F. Cogan, Ph.D.
Senior Fellow, Hoover Institution
Stanford University
Stanford, CA 94305
(650) 723-2585
fax: (650) 723-1687
cogan@hoover.stanford.edu

Christopher Edwards
Director, Fiscal Policy Studies
Cato Institute
1000 Massachusetts Avenue, NW
Washington, DC 20001
(202) 842-0200
fax: 202-842-3490
cedwards@cato.org

Scott A. Hodge
Executive Director
Tax Foundation
1250 H Street NW, Suite 750
Washington, DC 20005
(202) 783-2760
fax: (202) 783-6868
shodge@taxfoundation.org

James C. Miller III, Ph.D.
Counselor
Citizens for a Sound Economy
1250 H Street NW, Suite 700
Washington DC 20005
(202) 783-3870
fax: (202) 783-4687
jmiller@cse.org

Stephen J. Moore
Senior Fellow
Institute for Policy Innovation
250 S. Stemmons Freeway
Suite 215
Lewisville, TX 75067
(972) 874-5139
smoore@ipi.org
and Senior Fellow
Cato Institute
1000 Massachusetts Avenue, NW
Washington, DC 20001
(202) 842-0200
fax: (202) 842-3490

Thomas A. Schatz
President
Citizens Against
Government Waste
1301 Connecticut Avenue, NW,
Suite 400
Washington, DC 20036
(202) 467-5300
fax: (202) 467-4253
tschatz@cagw.org

For continually updated and expanded information on major breaking developments on this issue over the campaign cycle, see *www.heritage.org/issues/budget.*

TAX REFORM

Making America More Prosperous and Competitive

Daniel J. Mitchell, Ph.D.

THE ISSUES

The pro-growth elements of President Bush's tax cut plan will be implemented in 2004, 2006, and 2010, but this strategy should be viewed only as the first step in effective tax reform. The total tax burden on Americans is—and will remain—at near-record levels; marginal tax rates are far too high, savings and investment are still subject to discriminatory taxation, and needless complexity in the Internal Revenue Code foments corruption and adds a hidden compliance tax on productive activity. The struggling economy needs policies that promote entrepreneurship and job creation, both of which result from innovation and risk-taking—but Uncle Sam's growing tax appetite threatens this vital arena of economic activity.

Amazingly, some politicians think that higher tax rates would help the economy. This would be akin to pouring gasoline on a fire. Higher tax rates discourage work, saving, investment, and entrepreneurship. Interest rates also would rise as investors demanded higher returns to offset the adverse effects of bigger tax burdens.

Such dangerous proposals should be summarily rejected. To maintain America's competitive advantage in the global economy, lawmakers instead should take steps to reduce the tax burden significantly and reform the voluminous tax code. Their efforts should be guided by the following principles:

5. **High tax rates have a particularly adverse effect on economic growth.** Taxes are, in effect, the price government imposes on productive behavior, and as every student of economics is taught, people buy less of a product when the price

goes up. But high tax rates are especially perverse: By increasing the price of productive activity, they lead people to work less, save less, invest less, produce less, and take fewer risks. Lower tax rates, by contrast, stimulate growth by reducing the tax on additional economic output. Additional output generates some additional revenue through job creation, increased income, and higher profits. This is both a good thing and a bad thing—good because it means tax cuts are "affordable" but bad because additional tax revenue makes it easier for politicians to expand government by funding nonessential and counterproductive domestic programs.

6. **Not all tax cuts are created equal.** Tax rebates and tax credits do not lower the price of productive behavior and therefore have little or no positive impact on economic performance. This also explains why government spending does not boost economic growth. For these reasons, market-oriented economists favor marginal tax rate reductions that lower the tax burden on each additional increment of work, saving, investment, and risk-taking. When the price of productive behavior falls, there will be more productive behavior. Thus, when reducing taxes, lower marginal tax rates generate the most "bang for the buck."

7. **Tax cuts should be permanent, not temporary.** Tax rate reductions that are permanent boost the economy's productive capacity by improving incentives to work, save, and invest. Temporary tax rate reductions, by contrast, have very little effect. Taxpayers may decide to shift the timing of income and expenses in response to an ephemeral tax cut, but they are not likely to increase their overall work effort, make new investments, or start new businesses. It also is unlikely that a temporary tax cut would attract capital from overseas or boost international competitiveness.

8. **The economy is most likely to benefit from a reduction in the highest tax rates.** It is always a good idea to reduce the tax rates that impose the most damage on economic performance. Policymakers therefore should seek to lower the top tax rate imposed on personal income, corporate income, and capital gains. Reductions in top tax rates will have the largest effect on small-business owners, entrepreneurs, investors,

and others who have the capacity to boost growth. This is a particularly smart choice when the economy is faltering.

9. **The tax code is confusing and unfair, but its problems would disappear under a simple system like the flat tax.** Ultimately, legislators should seek to replace the 17,000-page Internal Revenue Code with a simple and fair flat tax. A flat tax would impose one very low tax rate across the board. Hundreds of mind-numbing tax forms would be replaced by two simple, postcard-sized forms—one for households and one for businesses. A flat tax would eliminate all the preferences and penalties in the current code. No longer would there be additional layers of tax on income that is saved and invested. No longer could Congress lard the tax code with exemptions, deductions, credits, preferences, and other loopholes for special interests. If politicians thought electric cars and ethanol were critical activities, they would have to subsidize them in broad daylight, not create tax shelters that benefit the wealthy and powerful. Eliminating preferences is the best route to simplicity.

10. **Forgoing tax rate reductions in order to balance the budget or pay down the debt means less growth and bigger government.** A common objection to pro-growth tax policy is that it is more important for politicians to use revenues to balance the budget or pay down government debt. Such policies are, at best, a second-best option. Balanced budgets and debt reduction have minimal beneficial effects on economic performance. Reductions in punitive tax rates and fundamental tax reform, by contrast, would have substantial positive effects on economic growth and job creation. In any event, the fiscal austerity approach is politically unrealistic. As the past three years have demonstrated, surpluses encourage new spending.

11. **Legislators should dismiss class warfare politics.** Another objection to pro-growth tax policy is that "rich" people may benefit. Fortunately, this "us-versus-them" mentality does not seem to work as well in America as it does in Europe, probably because of our entrepreneurial culture and widespread economic opportunity. Nonetheless, growth advocates should explain that the role of tax policy is to collect necessary revenues (preferably, a modest amount) while imposing

the least possible amount of damage on the economy's performance. A vibrant, prosperous economy will create new jobs and enable people to climb the ladder of opportunity. This approach should appeal to honest liberals, since the so-called rich are less likely to put their money in the underground economy if the tax system does not impose an undue hardship on wealth creation. The Reagan tax cuts demonstrate that under low tax rates, the rich will pay their taxes. The richest 1 percent of taxpayers today, for instance, pay more than 36 percent of the income tax burden.

12. **International "tax harmonization" efforts threaten America's competitive advantage.** Politicians from high-tax nations like France get upset when jobs and capital shift to lower-tax economies like America's—a process they call "harmful tax competition" or "fiscal dumping." They are working through international bureaucracies like the United Nations, the European Union (EU), and the Organisation for Economic Co-operation and Development (OECD) to stop this process. In particular, they are seeking a form of tax harmonization known as "information exchange," which would allow high-tax governments to tax capital that escapes to America or other low-tax economies. Such schemes are greatly misguided. Tax competition is a liberalizing force in the world economy, a process that helps impose discipline on profligate politicians. America's comparatively low tax burden and appealing privacy laws attract trillions of investment dollars from overseas. Any effort to harmonize tax systems, either by adjusting tax rates upward or by giving high-tax nations the right to impose their oppressive tax rates on income earned in lower-tax countries, will harm America's competitive advantage.

THE FACTS

FACT: Despite the recent tax cuts, federal taxes still consume too much of the nation's economy.

Even with the Bush tax cut, federal taxes are expected to consume about one-fifth of the U.S. economy's output. This is a staggering tax burden, rivaled only by the record tax take during World War II, when America was fighting the combined might of the National Socialists in Germany and the warlords of Imperial Japan.

FACT: High tax rates are discouraging growth.

Periods of high tax rates, such as those that existed in the 1930s and 1970s, are associated with economic weakness in America. Periods of low-tax rates, by contrast, are associated with good economic times. The Kennedy tax cuts in the 1960s and the Reagan tax cuts in the 1980s, for instance, helped initiate strong economic expansions.[1] Rate reductions usually are the key to growth, but it also is important to reduce the tax bias against saving and investment. The capital gains tax cut in 1997, for instance, helped the economy prosper in the late 1990s. International evidence is also instructive. Places like Hong Kong and Switzerland, with their low tax burdens and flat tax systems, enjoy widespread prosperity. Overtaxed nations like France, by contrast, suffer from anemic growth and high unemployment.

FACT: Savings and investment are discouraged and penalized by excessive and discriminatory taxes.

It is unfair when the government taxes income more than one time, but it also is anti-growth. Every economic theory—even Marxism—agrees that capital formation is the key to long-run growth, higher wages, and rising living standards.[2] Yet because of the capital gains tax, the personal income tax, the corporate income tax, and the death tax, America's tax system subjects income that is saved to as many as four layers of tax. These multiple layers of tax should be abolished, either as part of fundamental tax reform or as part of tax cut packages.

FACT: Needless complexity in the tax code exacerbates the tax burden.

- Americans spend more than 5 billion hours every year trying to comply with over 1,000 forms, publications, and notices

1. See Joint Economic Committee, "The Mellon and Kennedy Tax Cuts: A Review and Analysis," June 18, 1982; see also Daniel J. Mitchell, "Time for Lower Income Tax Rates: The Historical Case for Supply-Side Economics," Heritage Foundation *Backgrounder* No. 1253, February 19, 1999, at *www.heritage.org/library/backgrounder/bg1253.html.*
2. Marxists, socialists, and fascists believe the government should decide where capital is invested. Fortunately, the collapse of the Soviet empire has discredited this approach.

Chart 1

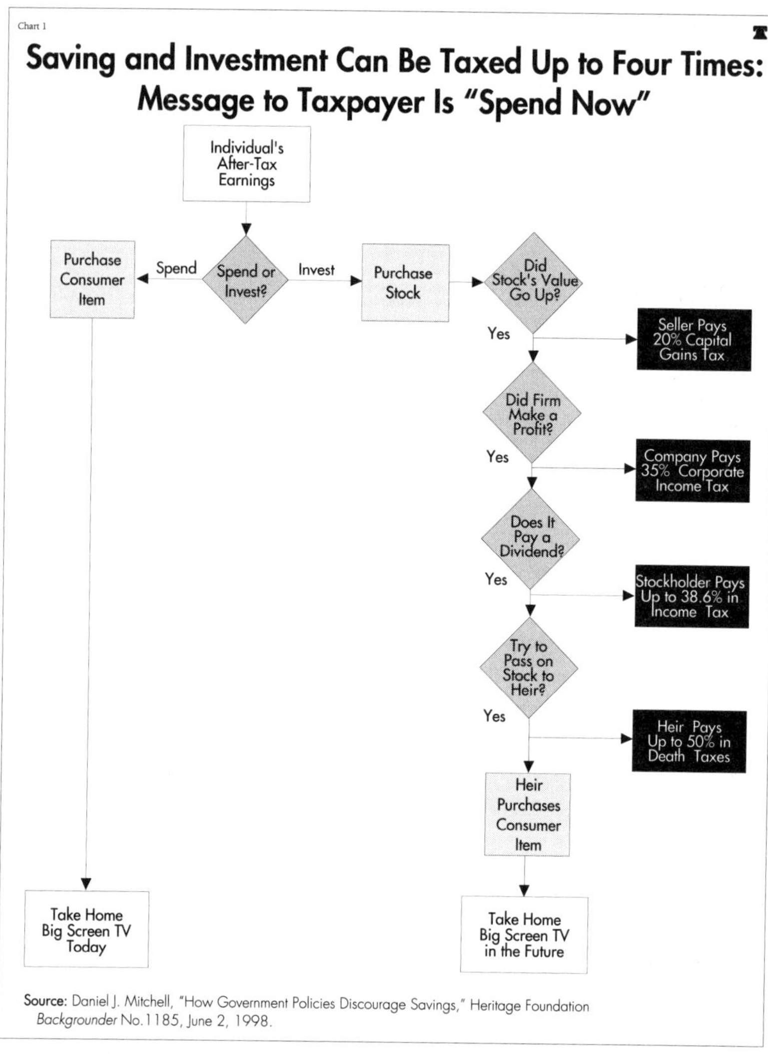

Source: Daniel J. Mitchell, "How Government Policies Discourage Savings," Heritage Foundation *Backgrounder* No.1185, June 2, 1998.

required by the income tax code.[3] This hidden tax is particularly harsh on businesses, which must divert some of their most talented employees to tax compliance. Some provisions, such as depreciation and the alternative minimum tax, are especially perverse since they force taxpayers to overstate their income.

- The tax code is so complex, in fact, that Internal Revenue Service (IRS) employees give correct answers to inquiries only

3. See *www.irs.gov/forms_pubs/forms.html* and *www.irs.gov/forms_pubs/pubs.html*.

about half the time, according to U.S. General Accounting Office (GAO) studies.[4] Even more amazing, a *Money* magazine study found that all 46 highly paid private-sector accountants and other tax experts surveyed were unable to fill in a hypothetical family's tax return without making thousands of dollars worth of mistakes.[5]

This system can be changed for the better. Under a flat tax, for example, the hundreds of individual tax forms and thousands of pages of indecipherable instructions would be replaced with two easy-to-understand, postcard-sized forms. Households and businesses would have more time for productive purposes, freed from engaging in a paper chase with an IRS bureaucracy so large that it exceeds the size of the combined navies of England, France, and Germany.

FACT: Tax reform, especially shifting to a flat tax, would boost growth.

A flat tax would spur an increase in work, saving, and investment. Hong Kong has a flat tax. It is no coincidence that over the past 50 years, Hong Kong has been the world's fastest-growing economy. Academic experts from such institutions as Harvard University, Stanford University, the National Bureau of Economic Research, and the World Bank have studied tax reform and have concluded unanimously that a flat tax would boost growth and increase family incomes.[6] The only debate is over how *much* growth and family incomes would increase under a flat tax.

FACT: The flat tax is simple and fair.

Every taxpayer would be treated the same under a flat tax. All households would receive a generous exemption based on family size and then pay a single low rate on income above that amount.

---

4. See, for instance, *www.gao.gov/new.items/d02144.pdf.*
5. Joan Caplin, "6 Mistakes Even the Tax Pros Make," *Money*, March 1998.
6. See, for example, Alan Auerbach, "Tax Reform, Capital Allocation, Efficiency, and Growth," in Henry J. Aaron and William G. Gale, eds., *Economic Effects of Fundamental Tax Reform* (Washington, D.C.: Brookings Institution Press, 1996); Michael J. Boskin, ed., *Frontiers of Tax Reform* (Stanford, Cal.: Hoover Institution Press, 1996); Dale Jorgenson, "The Economic Impact of Fundamental Tax Reform," in *Frontiers of Tax Reform Conference*, Hoover Institution, May 11, 1995; and Laurence J. Kotlikoff, "The Economic Impact of Replacing Federal Income Taxes with a Sales Tax," Cato Institute *Policy Analysis* No. 212, April 1993.

No longer could the rich and powerful get special deals by hiring lobbyists, lawyers, and accountants. If they made 10 times as much as their neighbors, they would pay 10 times as much in tax. The poor, meanwhile, would be shielded from the tax because of the generous exemption amount.

FACT: Special-interest groups are wrong about eliminating deductions.

Critics fret that a flat tax would lower charitable contributions and harm the housing market. This is not true. Fewer than 30 percent of taxpayers itemize, and those taxpayers tend to have higher incomes and therefore would benefit from other features of the flat tax. Moreover, research shows that both charity and home ownership are tied to disposable income, which would climb under a flat tax. Home ownership also is affected by interest rates, which would fall under a flat tax—by as much as 35 percent, according to a 1995 Kansas City Federal Reserve Bank study.[7]

FACT: International tax competition promotes good tax policy.

When Ronald Reagan slashed tax rates in the 1980s,[8] politicians in almost every other nation were forced to make similar reductions. This is not because they wanted to do the right thing. At the time, with the rare exception of leaders such as Margaret Thatcher in the United Kingdom, most nations were controlled by socialist politicians who believed in high tax rates and income redistribution, but they were forced to lower tax rates because of competition. They were losing jobs and capital to America. In the past 20 years, top personal and corporate income tax rates have fallen by about 20 percentage points.

FACT: International tax harmonization policies such as "information exchange" would harm America's economy.

The total tax burden in America may be near an all-time high (about 29 percent of GDP including state and local government), but we are in much better shape than Europe. The average tax burden in the 15 nations of the European Union is about 42 per-

7. John E. Golub, "How Would Tax Reform Affect Financial Markets?," *Federal Reserve Bank of Kansas City Economic Review*, Fourth Quarter, 1995.
8. President Reagan's across-the-board income tax rate reductions in the 1980s reduced the top individual rate from 70 percent to 28 percent and the top corporate tax rate from 46 percent to 34 percent.

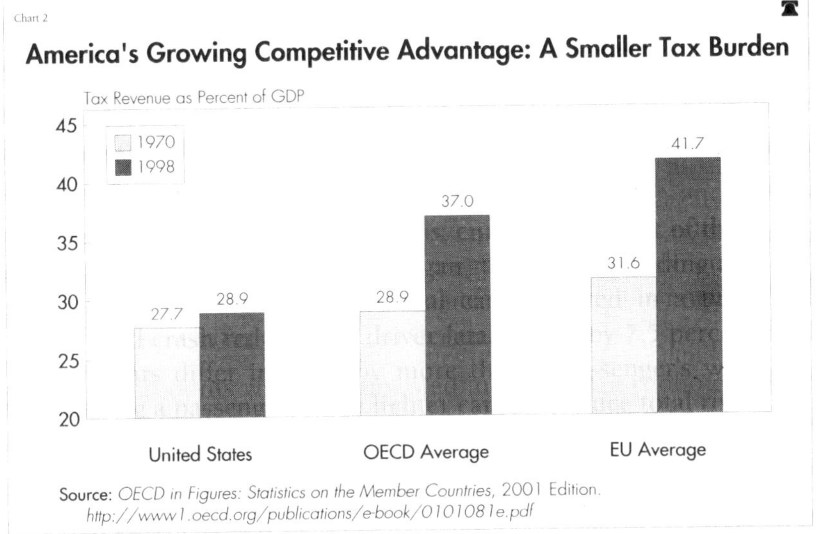

cent of GDP. This makes America much more competitive, which helps explain why our economy has been growing so much faster and our unemployment rate is so much lower. The United States also has attractive tax and privacy laws for foreign investors (indeed, international tax experts acknowledge that the United States is the world's largest tax haven). Any effort to hinder tax competition—especially information exchange policies that would make it easier for other governments to tax income earned in America—would harm America's competitive advantage and could drive hundreds of billions, and probably trillions, of dollars away from the U.S. economy.

Tax Calculator: The Heritage Tax Calculator shows the savings to taxpayers of the fully phased-in proposals by President Bush for marginal rates, the dual earner deduction for married couples, the doubling of the child tax credit to $1,000, and the deductibility of charitable contributions by taxpayers who use the standard deduction. By entering your income and a few other bits of information, you can quickly get an idea of how much money the President's tax cut plan will save you. Access the calculator at *www.heritage.org/calculators*.

WHAT TO DO IN 2003

Fundamental tax reform is the best way to improve the tax system and boost prosperity, but lawmakers do not have to make the shift in one fell swoop. It is possible to move to a flat tax by solving the tax code's myriad problems one at a time. This is called incremental tax reform, and it may be the most realistic way to implement pro-growth tax policy.

Accelerate the 2001 Bush tax cut and make it permanent.

The Bush tax cut enacted in June 2001 contained many supply-side initiatives, but the vast majority of these provisions do not take effect until 2004, 2006, and 2010. Even worse, they are automatically repealed in 2011. Needless to say, if pro-growth tax cuts do not take effect for several more years, the benefits will not be realized for several more years. Moreover, the possible benefits will be much smaller if workers, savers, investors, and entrepreneurs believe the tax cuts will disappear in 2011.

Simply stated, people will be much less likely to engage in productive activity if the vanishing tax cuts undermine the profitability of those actions. If that happens, taxpayers in the 25-percent tax bracket will be pushed to the 28-percent tax bracket, and the tax rate on investors, entrepreneurs, and small-business owners will jump from 35 percent to nearly 40 percent. This will discourage job creation and risk-taking by many of America's most productive citizens.

In addition, President Bush asked Congress to repeal the death tax, an unfair version of double taxation (the money was already taxed when it was first earned), not only to remove inequity in the code, but also to pursue sound economic policy. The economy suffers when families divert resources into tax shelters to avoid this punitive levy. By contrast, when small-business owners seek to maximize income rather than minimize tax, jobs are created and the economy grows. To reap the full benefits of the Bush tax cuts, the lower marginal income tax rates and death tax repeal should be implemented immediately and made permanent.

Reduce the top personal and corporate income tax rates.

The top personal income tax rate was only 28 percent when Ronald Reagan left office. It is now 38.6 percent and will fall to

35 percent—at least temporarily—because of the Bush tax rate reductions. But this is still too high. Returning to the 1988 level, at a minimum, should be a key goal. This lower rate will help spur faster growth by improving incentives to work, save, invest, and take risks. Small-business owners and entrepreneurs will have more reason to create jobs.

America's 35 percent corporate income tax rate imposes a heavy burden on business. When more than one-third of profits are taken by government (and then are taxed a second time since dividends are subject to the personal income tax), the incentive to invest and be productive is reduced. Equally important, a high corporate income tax rate makes American companies less competitive. Even high-tax nations like France and Sweden have lower corporate income tax rates than America—33.3 percent and 28 percent, respectively.

Lower the capital gains tax and ultimately abolish it.

The capital gains tax is a senseless form of double taxation that penalizes risk-taking and entrepreneurship. It drives capital to other nations and makes it difficult for small businesses to attract funds. If full repeal is not immediately possible, lawmakers should reduce the capital gains rate to 10 percent as an interim measure. Another interim strategy is to reduce or eliminate the tax on gains that are immediately reinvested. Such a step would be particularly helpful for investors in mutual funds.

Expand individual savings accounts.

Income that is saved and invested should not be taxed twice, but that is what happens today when people pay tax on their income, save a portion of what is left, and then pay another layer of tax on interest earnings. IRAs are a way to protect income from double taxation, and they should be substantially expanded. An unlimited back-ended (or Roth) IRA would be particularly desirable, since it would reduce paperwork and promote privacy. With a back-ended IRA, workers would pay tax on their income the year it is earned, but there would be no second layer of tax on that income if it is saved and invested. This would substantially boost incentives to save and invest and eliminate the need for taxpayers to tell the government about the level and composition of their financial assets.

Another strategy, albeit more limited in scope, would be to expand the number of tax-neutral IRA-like accounts, such as medical savings accounts (MSAs) and education savings accounts (ESAs). If enough of these accounts were created, a significant portion of savings would be protected from double taxation.

Shift to a territorial tax system so U.S. companies can compete more effectively overseas.

In recent years, companies such as Accenture, Ingersoll-Rand, Tyco, and Fruit-of-the-Loom have moved their headquarters out of the United States because the Internal Revenue Code requires U.S.-based companies to pay tax on worldwide income.[9]

To promote growth, competitiveness, and simplicity, lawmakers should stop taxing income earned by U.S. taxpayers in other nations. Overseas income already is subject to any applicable foreign taxes, and it is double taxation if the IRS also tries to tax this income. This double tax can be avoided by providing tax credits, but this is very complex and largely negates the purpose of taxing "worldwide" income in the first place. A territorial system would make America more competitive and greatly simplify the tax code.

Vigorously reject international tax harmonization schemes.

All of the previous initiatives will be for naught if America cannot reap the rewards of good tax policy. Tax reform and lower tax rates will help the U.S. economy by improving incentives and by luring more capital from overseas. If international bureaucracies like the United Nations, the EU, and the OECD succeed in crippling tax competition, however, the U.S. economy will lose its competitive advantage. Bloated welfare states should not be allowed to create a global tax cartel to protect their confiscatory tax systems.

---

9. See Robert Manor and Delroy Alexander, "Consulting Giant Accenture Leads Parade of Firms Moving on Paper to Bermuda," *Chicago Tribune*, July 21, 2001; De'Ann Weiner, "A Killing in the Caymans?" *Business Week*, May 11, 1998; Mike Godfrey, "Ingersoll-Rand Moves Corporate Base to Bermuda," December 20, 2001, at *www.tax-news.com/asp/story/story.asp?storyname=6778*; and Mike Godfrey, "Goldman Sachs Joins Bermuda-Bound US Insurers," November 28, 2001, at *www.tax-news.com/asp/story/story.asp?storyname=6456*.

Focus on the long-term goal of tax reform.

Pro-growth tax cuts inevitably bring us closer to a simple and fair system like the flat tax. Lower tax rates, depreciation reform, IRA expansion, capital gains relief, and other supply-side tax cuts are all ways of shifting to a system that taxes income only one time and at one low rate. When combined with other desirable reforms—such as repeal of the personal and corporate alternative minimum tax—these changes will make America's tax system much simpler. Most important of all, these tax cuts will make the United States more competitive and more prosperous. This may not be good news for the tax harmonization advocates at the OECD and EU who want to help prop up Europe's welfare states, but it is great news for American families.

—Daniel J. Mitchell, Ph.D., is McKenna Senior Fellow in Political Economy in the Thomas A. Roe Institute for Economic Policy Studies at The Heritage Foundation.

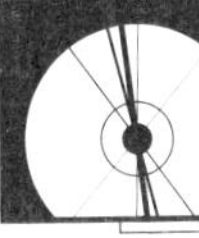

For a complete list and full-text versions of additional studies by Heritage on tax reform, see the searchable *Issues 2002* companion CD–ROM.

EXPERTS

Heritage Foundation

Daniel J. Mitchell, Ph.D.
McKenna Senior Fellow
in Political Economy
The Heritage Foundation
214 Massachusetts Avenue, NE
Washington, DC 20002
(202) 608-6224
fax: (202) 544-5421
dan.mitchell@heritage.org

William W. Beach
Director, Center for Data Analysis
John M. Olin Senior Fellow
in Economics
The Heritage Foundation
214 Massachusetts Avenue, NE
Washington, DC 20002
(202) 608-6206
fax: (202) 675-1772
bill.beach@heritage.org

Gerald P. O'Driscoll, Jr., Ph.D.
Director, Center for International
Trade and Economics
The Heritage Foundation
214 Massachusetts Avenue, NE
Washington, DC 20002
(202) 608-6185
fax: (202) 608-6129
jerry.odriscoll@heritage.org

Other Experts

Bruce R. Bartlett
Senior Fellow
National Center for Policy Analysis
439 Seneca Road
Great Falls, VA 22066-1113
(703) 421-7784
fax: (703) 421-7785
73440.3456@compuserve.com

Christopher Edwards
Director, Fiscal Policy Studies
Cato Institute
1000 Massachusetts Avenue, NW
Washington, DC 20001
(202) 842-0200
fax: (202) 842-3490
cedwards@cato.org

Stephen Entin
Executive Director and Chief Economist
Institute for Research on the Economics of Taxation
1730 K Street, NW, Suite 910
Washington, DC 20006
(202) 463-1400
fax: (202) 463-6199
sentin@iret.org

Kevin Hassett
Resident Scholar
American Enterprise Institute
1150 17th Street, NW
Washington, DC 20036
(202) 862-7157
fax: (202) 862-7177
khassett@aei.org

Scott A. Hodge
Executive Director
Tax Foundation
1250 H Street, NW, Suite 750
Washington, DC 20005
(202) 783-2760
fax: (202) 783-6868
shodge@taxfoundation.org

Lawrence Hunter
Chief Economist
Empower America
1701 Pennsylvania Avenue, NW
Suite 900
Washington, DC 20006
(202) 452-8200
fax: (202) 833-0388
hunterl@empower.org

Alvin Rabushka
Senior Fellow
Hoover Institution
Stanford University
Stanford, CA 94305
(650) 725-5674
fax: (650) 723-1687
rabushka@hoover.stanford.edu

Richard Rahn
President
NOVECON
333 North Fairfax Street
Alexandria, VA 22314
202-659-3200
fax: 202-659-3215
rwrahn@aol.com

Veronique de Rugy
Fiscal Policy Analyst
Cato Institute
1000 Massachusetts Avenue, NW
Washington, DC 20001
(202) 842-02001
fax: (202) 842-3490
vderugy@cato.org

For continually updated and expanded information on major breaking developments on this issue over the campaign cycle, see *www.heritage.org/issues/taxes.*

THE ECONOMY

Creating Job Opportunities with Economic Growth

William W. Beach

THE ISSUES

In the 2002 election, candidates will face voters who are more concerned about job creation, unemployment, and economic growth than they have been for over a decade. Indeed, public opinion polls repeatedly show that, next to the war on terrorism, Americans are most worried about the economy and job security. And their concerns increase as the unemployment rate rises.

Some candidates for Congress may try to manipulate these concerns by distorting the effects that sound tax, budget, and regulatory policies have on economic growth. They also may try to promise more federal spending on fine-sounding but ineffective government programs. Such rhetoric, however, increasingly falls on deaf ears. Most Americans understand that the best "job creation program" is faster economic growth, not government spending. Business expansion is key to increasing opportunities for workers. Most Americans prefer the independence afforded by their own paychecks to dependence on government unemployment and welfare checks.

It is vitally important that candidates understand and can explain clearly which government policies would foster economic growth and job creation and which ones, however well-intentioned, do nothing to improve the incentives Americans have to work, save, and invest—the real catalysts for economic growth. The lessons of the past two decades show that:

1. **The recession and rise in unemployment are products of flawed fiscal and monetary policies compounded by unexpected shocks to the economy.** Ask a middle-class voter what caused the recession, and you would probably get a perfectly

sensible response—record high taxes, the increasing regulatory cost of doing business, high interest rates in 2000 and early 2001, wildly fluctuating energy prices, and the September 11 terrorist attacks. If they were to add economic slowdowns in America's major trading partners, they would have a fairly clear picture of why the U.S. economy began its slide in March 2001 and fell deeper into economic contraction after the attacks. Interestingly, most of this list can be directly attributed to policy failures that continue to hinder economic recovery and long-term growth.

2. **High taxes and burdensome regulations choke off business expansion and America's prospects for growth.** Anyone who has run a business knows how important it is to have workers and capital available for expansion, and how much time and money is consumed complying with government regulation. The ability to save income or borrow at low interest rates for future expansion often makes the difference between success or failure. High taxes and costly regulations drive up the interest rates lenders charge on capital for business expansion and choke off some investments and job opportunities; only investments that pay higher interest rates or the "required rate of return" are pursued. Similarly, Americans think twice about working more hours if higher taxes will eat up most of their additional earnings.

3. **Reducing taxes will help the economy to recover more rapidly.** Congress can improve prospects for a stronger economic recovery by making permanent and accelerating to 2002 the President's planned tax relief for workers scheduled for 2004 and 2006. Tax relief for working women also should be expanded by eliminating any marriage penalties in the tax code, and every effort should be made to reduce the tax burden on self-employed workers.

4. **Repealing provisions in the code that penalize capital formation and wealth creation also would foster economic growth.** Congress can help improve the health of the economy by repealing parts of the tax code that make investing in new jobs or products more expensive and difficult. For example, repealing the current depreciation rules that increase the cost of buying new equipment would encourage businesses to switch more rapidly from making products that people no

longer want to ones that they do want. And repealing the capital gains tax would encourage investors to switch their funds more readily to businesses that produce more of what consumers want. Right now, some investors hesitate to do so because of the taxes that the government imposes on selling one stock to buy another.

5. **Making federal regulators more accountable for their actions will foster stronger economic growth.** Requiring independent third-party reviews of regulations would permit greater public scrutiny of the federal regulatory process to help keep overly burdensome regulations from ever being implemented. The major health, safety, and environmental statutes adopted by Congress 30 years ago also should be updated, based on principles of sound science and on prioritizing risks, increasing flexibility and compliance assistance, and minimizing the paperwork burden. Congress should hold agencies accountable as well to ensure that their regulatory decisions really do enhance people's lives.

6. **Every dollar the government spends—whether prudently or foolishly—is a dollar that is taken out of the private sector.** Government spending does not improve the pace of real economic activity. Rather, Congress's willingness to maintain fiscal discipline benefits the ability of entrepreneurs to create jobs and expand business activity. Congress already has approved a substantial amount of new spending since the emergence of budget surpluses two years ago, and more will be enacted in the future. Some of this spending will fund a long-overdue restoration of national defense and intelligence capabilities. But some of it will be used for misguided pork-barrel projects that have nothing to do with national security or the recession. In neither case will the new spending boost national income to help the economy.

THE FACTS

FACT: History shows that recessions are caused by policy mistakes and external shocks to the economy.

Since 1999, federal policies have significantly weakened the U.S. economy in three ways, effectively tying a huge anchor around its legs and dragging millions of workers into unemployment.

- The federal tax burden climbed to a record high 20.4 percent of the gross domestic product (GDP) in 2000, draining resources away from the private sector.
- The cost of federal regulations rose to 8 percent of GDP, or $4,722 per worker, in 2000.[1]
- The Federal Reserve raised interest rates in 1999 and 2000 and kept them too high for too long.

Four external shocks further weakened the economy and finally tripped it into recession in 2001. The following shocks combined with the problems created by poor policies to form a perfect economic storm that ended the longest economic expansion in U.S. history.

- Investment spending slumped in 2000 after having increased significantly before that year.
- Oil-producing countries increased the price of oil significantly, further taxing consumers and squeezing business profits.
- The Asian financial crisis and slow economic growth of America's major trading partners substantially reduced the demand for manufactured goods.
- The September 11 terrorist attacks dealt a severe blow to consumer confidence.

FACT: Government has never taxed and spent its way to prosperity.

Higher government spending has a dismal track record when it comes to promoting economic growth.

- From 1930 to 1936, federal spending rose from 3.4 percent to 10.5 percent of GDP, while the unemployment rate doubled from 8.4 percent to 16.9 percent.[2]

---

1. W. Mark Crain and Thomas D. Hopkins, "The Impact of Regulatory Costs on Small Firms," U.S. Small Business Administration, Office of Advocacy, 2001.
2. Richard K. Vedder and Lowell E. Gallaway, *Out of Work: Unemployment and Government in Twentieth-Century America* (New York: Holmes & Meier, 1993), p. 77, and U.S. Office of Management and Budget, *Budget of the United States Government, Fiscal Year 2002, Historical Tables*, p. 23.

- In the 1960s and 1970s, many countries, especially in Europe, relied on government spending and targeted tax breaks to improve their economies. Instead of boosting growth, they saw their economies stagnate.[3] In more recent times, Japan's economy has been mired in 10 years of stagnation in spite of—and perhaps because of—repeated doses of government spending.[4]
- In 1993, President Clinton and Congress raised taxes; a year later, the unemployment rate had declined 0.8 percent—from 6.9 percent to 6.1 percent—and the interest rate on 10-year Treasury bonds had risen from 5.9 percent to 7.1 percent. Rapid growth in spending accompanied this increase in taxes: Between 1990 and 1994, spending grew at an average annual rate of 3.3 percent. It took a new Congress in 1995 to reduce the rate of growth in federal spending to an annual average rate of 2.4 percent between 1995 and 1999, which supported significant economic growth and increases in new jobs in the late 1990s.
- Supporters of increasing spending as way to end the recession point to the New Deal programs of the 1930s to suggest that "pump priming" spending programs will boost economic activity. The historical record belies this view. By 1937, the United States lagged behind nearly all other Western economies in annual economic growth rates, at –7.0 percent. In 1940, on the eve of World War II and in the midst of America's re-armament, the unemployment rate stood at 10 percent, with 10,650,000 people looking for work.[5]

FACT: Tax relief and tax reform have never caused a recession.

The historical record is equally clear on this point.

- President John F. Kennedy's tax cuts helped trigger a record economic expansion. Between 1965 and 1969, inflation-adjusted economic growth averaged more than 5 percent.

---

3. Daniel J. Mitchell, Ph.D., "Essential Elements for a Pro-Growth Stimulus Package," Heritage Foundation *Executive Memorandum* No. 793, November 27, 2001, at *www.heritage.org/library/execmemo/em793.html*.
4. *Ibid.*
5. John A. Garraty, "The New Deal, National Socialism and the Great Depression," *American Historical Review*, Vol. 78 (October 1973), p. 944, and Otis L. Graham, Jr., ed., *The New Deal: The Critical Issues* (Boston: Little, Brown, 1971), p. 88.

President Ronald Reagan's tax cuts ushered in a seven-year boom with yearly economic growth averaging more than 4 percent between 1984 and 1990.

- The 1997 tax relief bill increased the rate of economic growth from 2.7 percent in 1996 to an average of 4.3 percent per year between 1998 and 2000, even though the tax burden on the economy grew to record levels.

Critics of tax relief argue that lower federal revenues produce deficits, which in turn increase interest rates. They routinely ignore the relationship between tax cuts, stronger economic growth, and healthier federal revenues. On interest rates, the historical record is inconsistent. Although interest rates increased after the Kennedy tax cuts (in large part because America entered an unpopular and divisive war), they fell after the Reagan tax cuts and after the 1997 tax relief bills were enacted. Real interest rates are determined by global capital markets, in which trillions of dollars change hands every day. Even a $100 billion shift in the federal government's fiscal balance is unlikely to have much effect compared with such factors as worldwide demand for credit, tax policy, risk, and economic growth.[6]

FACT: The current labor market is weak, but unemployment is still less than it was after other recessions.

According to the National Association of Business Economists, most economists expect the unemployment rate to average 5.9 percent in 2002.[7] A recent forecast from DRI–WEFA, a widely respected econometric consulting firm, predicts that unemployment will continue rising through the third quarter of 2002, begin falling by the end of 2002, and continue declining through 2003.[8] Most economists forecast unemployment rates well below those reached after the 1990–1991 recession (7.8 percent) and the 1981–1982 recession (10.8 percent).

---

6. For more information on the relationship between deficits and interest rates, see Brian M. Riedl, "What Really Is Turning Budget Surpluses into Deficits, Heritage Foundation *Backgrounder* No. 1515, January 30, 2002, at *www.heritage.org/library/backgrounder/bg1515.html*.

7. "Business Economists See Mild Recession with Modest Turnaround Early Next Year," Bureau of National Affairs, *BNA Daily Report for Executives*, November 15, 2001, p. A43.

8. DRI–WEFA, *U.S. Economic Outlook* (Lexington, Mass.: DRI–WEFA, 2001).

Over the past year, the national unemployment rate has risen 1.8 percentage points—from a 30-year low of 3.9 percent in October 2000 to 5.8 percent in December 2001, just about the average during the 1990s and well below the 7.3 percent average of the 1980s.

- While media and public attention focus on the loss of 1 million-plus net jobs in manufacturing and 712,000 jobs in the business services, transportation, and hotel industries in 2001, these losses have been offset by significant job gains in 2001 in health services (304,000), social services (134,000), and educational services (112,000).[9]

FACT: The dynamic U.S. economy is continuously creating and eliminating jobs.

Economic freedom, which underpins the U.S. economy, permits workers and entrepreneurs to find better ways to meet the needs of consumers. In the process, some jobs will be lost while many new ones are created. If this were not the case, workers in Detroit's automobile factories might still be producing buggy whips and celluloid collars. New technologies, products, and services displace old ones; more efficient firms replace the less efficient.

Even when unemployment rates are low, job creation and job elimination can account for changes totaling more than 15 percent of employment in a three-month period.[10] This "creative destruction" is a source of economic strength when the economy is growing but can present a real hardship for some workers when the economy slows.

Critics of the market complain when low-paying, labor-intensive jobs (like making shoes) leave the United States to take advantage of lower average wages in other countries. But when this happens, American workers usually find new jobs that pay more money: Of the displaced workers who lost full-time jobs during and shortly after the 1990–1991 recession, more than half (53 percent) found jobs within two years that paid the same or more

---

9. U.S. Department of Labor, Bureau of Labor Statistics, "The Employment Situation: December 2001," January 4, 2002, Table B-1.
10. R. Jason Faberman, "Job Creation and Destruction Within Washington and Baltimore," *Monthly Labor Review*, U.S. Department of Labor, Bureau of Labor Statistics, September 2001.

than the job they had lost.[11] Over 27 percent were earning 20 percent more than they earned in their previous jobs.

FACT: Employers face a persistent skills gap in job candidates despite the fact that more people are looking for work during the economic slowdown.

There simply are not enough skilled workers to fill all of the skilled jobs available in the U.S. market. Nearly 80 percent of manufacturers continue to experience a moderate to serious shortage of qualified candidates for even entry-level production jobs.[12] The top deficiency cited is a lack of basic employability skills (such as attendance, timeliness, and work ethic).[13]

The need to improve the quality of primary and secondary education is paramount to improving employability skills and economic growth. The Bureau of Labor Statistics projects that almost 70 percent of all job opportunities over the next eight years will require a high school diploma and work-related training.[14] Almost 21 percent will require at least a four-year college degree, and just 9 percent will require an associate degree or postsecondary vocational training.

FACT: In 1998, Congress consolidated over 60 of 163 federal job-training programs into state block grants with tough new performance requirements.

This was a good first step, but two large programs still remain under federal control—the Job Corps and Trade Adjustment Assistance. A recent study of the Job Corps program shows that it fails to help Hispanic youth and 18- to 19-year-olds.[15]

---

11. U.S. Department of Labor, Bureau of Labor Statistics, "Worker Displacement During the Early 1990s," September 14, 1994. Many people are worried about the effect of the North American Free Trade Agreement on U.S. employment, but their concerns are unwarranted. NAFTA has added many times more jobs to the U.S. economy than have moved to Mexico or Canada as a result of greater free trade. For more details, see the chapter on trade policy.

12. National Association of Manufacturers, "The Skills Gap 2001," October 2001.

13. *Ibid.*

14. U.S. Department of Labor, Bureau of Labor Statistics, "BLS Releases 2000–2010 Employment Projections," December 3, 2001.

15. Mathematica Policy Research, Inc., "National Job Corps Study: The Impacts of Job Corps on Participants' Employment and Related Outcomes," June 2001.

FACT: Long-term economic growth depends on economic freedom, innovation, productivity, and labor force growth.

It may surprise some to learn that the bedrock foundation of economic growth consists of institutions, not labor or capital. Countries that adhere to the rule of law and equality before the law, protect property rights, and encourage free internal and external trade consistently outperform those that reject these institutions and values.[16] When countries (including the United States) diminish the force of these fundamental economic freedoms, long-term growth subsides.

The United States has experienced significant periods of entrepreneurship and technological innovation when the institutional and policy climate was right for economic growth. For example, although the microcomputer and software industry traces its roots back to the 1920s, it was not until the 1980s—with massive tax reductions and regulatory reform—that it began to grow and the economic benefits of desktop computing and robotics began to flow.

It is just as important that people have freedom to move across borders as it is for capital to move around the globe. High net immigration will be an important part of employment growth, and therefore economic growth, over the next 10 years. From 2000 to 2010, Hispanics and Asians will account for almost 51 percent, or 8.5 million, of America's 16.9 million net new jobs.[17]

---

16. For a discussion of how economic institutions and values support economic growth, see William W. Beach and Gerald P. O'Driscoll, Jr., "The Role of Property Rights in Economic Growth: An Introduction to the *2002 Index*," in Gerald P. O'Driscoll, Jr., Kim R. Holmes, and Mary Anastasia O'Grady, *2002 Index of Economic Freedom* (Washington, D.C.: The Heritage Foundation and Dow Jones & Company, Inc., 2002).
17. Bureau of Labor Statistics, "BLS Releases 2000–2010 Employment Projections."

WHAT TO DO IN 2003

Candidates for Congress should call for immediate reform of the government's policies and activities that restrict capital formation, business expansion, and economic growth. The federal government should:

Maintain spending discipline.

Spending more for a long-overdue restoration of national defense and intelligence capabilities, of course, is a proper function of government to protect the nation's interests. But while some government spending may be necessary and desirable, it does not stimulate an economy by itself.

"Government spending" by definition means that the political process, not markets and economic forces, is deciding where to allocate capital. Political factors and bureaucratic inefficiencies cause money to be spent inefficiently. Some tax dollars will go to misguided domestic spending programs intended to boost economic activity, but spending programs cannot lift growth rates even to the level that is required to keep up with population growth and replace worn-out equipment. Japan's economy, for example, has suffered through three recessions in just 10 years; policymakers tried massive spending programs and negative interest rates to spur household spending, but the economy continued to perform at rates below what was needed for the growing population and aging factories and equipment. Controlling the size of government is the best way to ensure more growth.

Reform the tax code and provide additional tax relief.

Providing more tax relief would be good long-run tax policy; but it also is good economic policy. Getting more of government out of the way of entrepreneurs and workers would unleash their talents, abilities, and financial resources. Candidates should call for the following reforms.

- **Accelerate** the pro-growth elements of the Bush tax cut so they take place right away rather than in 2004, 2006, and 2010.
- **Reduce** the capital gains tax rate, a form of double taxation that penalizes risk-taking and entrepreneurship. A large reduction in this tax would stimulate new invest-

ment and more productive use of capital. The reduction should be made permanent, since a temporary rate cut would have its largest effect on the timing of stock sales, when the real focus should be on boosting new investment.

- **Repeal** provisions in the tax code that penalize capital formation and wealth creation, such as the depreciation rules that increase the cost of buying equipment and the federal death taxes. The latter would lead to an unlocking of land and assets for investment, which under current law are tied up in complex and expensive estate plans and tax avoidance schemes.

Increase job opportunities by expanding trade and giving the President trade promotion authority (TPA).

The President needs the ability to negotiate free trade agreements that will build prosperity. Past trade agreements have benefited America greatly. One in three U.S. acres under cultivation, for example, is planted for export, and 25 percent of gross farm income is derived from exports. But of the 131 trade and investment agreements in force around the world, the United States is party to only three—putting American workers and consumers at a disadvantage. New trade agreements must be forged to spur additional exports, which makes the granting of trade promotion authority by Congress especially urgent.

Except for the past seven years, every President since Gerald Ford has had TPA (formerly called fast-track negotiating authority). This authority enables the Administration to negotiate agreements that will be considered in a straight up-or-down vote by Congress.[18] The House has approved it; but as of January 2002, the Senate had not. Countries have been hesitant to negotiate with the United States and open their markets further to U.S. goods and services for fear that their agreements will get bogged down in Congress with countless amendments.

Support business innovation and investment.

As odd as it seems for any country to tax savings when trying to achieve higher levels of economic growth and prosperity,

18. For further discussion on the importance of trade to consumers and U.S. workers, see the chapter on trade policy.

that is exactly what the United States does. In fact, the U.S. government taxes the money that makes up savings when it is earned, again when it produces interest, and yet again when it is passed on to an heir. The multiple taxation of savings reduces the amount of capital that is available for investment.

Economic analysis shows that when the tax rate on capital is reduced, investment grows and the economy expands. For example, the Kennedy tax rate reductions led to a 6.1 percent increase in investment between 1962 and 1969. This rate of investment growth overshadowed the paltry 3 percent growth in the last years of the Eisenhower Administration (when tax rates were as high as 90 percent of income) and the 2.3 percent growth rate during the 1969 to 1976 period.[19]

The ability of small businesses to raise funds and have access to the capital markets is key to innovation and economic growth. In 1999, a Securities and Exchange Commission (SEC) regulation significantly reduced the amount of capital small businesses could raise from a public stock offering in a misplaced effort to reduce the number of offerings from companies that appeared to have little or no business future.[20] Within a few months, the small capital markets stalled, hurting small-business owners and the millions of Americans who worked for them. The SEC should review this 1999 rulemaking and be required to account to Congress for its full impact on efficiency, competition, and capital formation.

Telecommunication regulation undermines investment and discourages advancements in broadband technology, thereby limiting such things as the availability of high-speed Internet service to consumers and small businesses. Congress should eliminate outdated regulatory barriers in this sector and, to level the broadband playing field, allow Baby Bell companies to offer broadband services in the same way cable and satellite companies do. This policy would catalyze broadband deployment by the Bells, which are somewhat reluctant to roll out new services under the regulatory uncertainty concerning the treatment of broadband investments.

---

19. Report, *Taxes and Long-Term Economic Growth*, Joint Economic Committee, U.S. Congress, February 1997, p. 3.

20. Amending SEC Rule 504.

Increase accountability in federal rulemaking.

The federal regulatory system should be open, transparent, and accountable. Congress should use its constitutional authority to ensure that federal agencies give the public better information about their regulatory goals, strategies, rules, and outcomes. Federal agencies also should be held accountable for their regulatory decisions and for ensuring that those decisions do in fact enhance social and economic well-being. Independent third-party reviews of regulations would open the process to greater public scrutiny.

Improve federal education and job training programs.

More can be done to ensure that federally funded job training programs are as effective as possible. Washington should finish what it began in 1998 in reforming the federal job training programs by allowing states with Job Corps centers to opt out of the federal program if they have a better way to help at-risk youth. Moreover, Trade Adjustment Assistance should have to meet the same rigorous performance requirements that state programs must now satisfy.

To increase competition to improve education for tomorrow's workers, Congress should consider school choice options. Allowing states to attach federal funding to poor students (as is done with Pell Grants); encouraging pilot school choice plans in cities like Washington, D.C.; and allowing federal funds to follow students from failing schools to a school of choice are all key steps to consider. The federal government should continue its grant program for charter schools and expand existing education savings accounts for higher education to include savings for K–12 expenses, lifting the limit on the amount that can be saved in these accounts and offering taxpayers a tax credit for opening one.

Congress should monitor the effectiveness of federal education programs to assure that they teach children and meet their goals. The U.S. Department of Education should build a research and evaluation component into each federal program and contract more often with independent researchers to study or audit them. For example, a recent study by the Manpower Demonstration Research Corp. found that the Career Academy program did not improve standardized math and reading achievement test scores and produced only slight reductions in dropout rates and modest increases in other measures of school engagement.[21]

—William W. Beach is Director of the Center for Data Analysis and John M. Olin Senior Fellow in Economics at The Heritage Foundation.

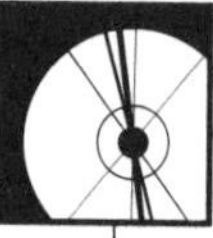

For a complete list and full-text versions of additional studies by Heritage on how economic growth affects job opportunities, see the searchable *Issues 2002* companion CD–ROM.

EXPERTS

Heritage Foundation

William W. Beach
Director, Center for Data Analysis
John M. Olin Senior Fellow in Economics
The Heritage Foundation
214 Massachusetts Avenue, NE
Washington, DC 20002
(202) 608-6806
fax: (202) 675-1772
bill.beach@heritage.org

Lawrence H. Whitman
Director, Thomas A. Roe Institute for Economic Policy Studies
The Heritage Foundation
214 Massachusetts Avenue, NE
Washington, DC 20002
(202) 608-6215
fax: (202) 544-5421
lawrence.whitman@heritage.org

Daniel J. Mitchell
McKenna Senior Fellow in Political Economy
Thomas A. Roe Institute for Economic Policy Studies
The Heritage Foundation
214 Massachusetts Avenue, NE
Washington, DC 20002
(202) 608-6224
fax: (202) 544-5421
dan.mitchell@heritage.org

Ralph A. Rector
Research Fellow
Center for Data Analysis
The Heritage Foundation
214 Massachusetts Avenue, NE
Washington, DC 20002
(202) 608-6115
fax: (202) 675-1772
ralph.rector@heritage.org

Other Experts

Robert J. Barro
Robert C. Waggoner Professor of Economics
Department of Economics
Littauer Center, Room 218
Harvard University
Cambridge, MA 02138
(617) 495-3203
fax: (617) 496-8629
rbarro@harvard.edu

21. Manpower Demonstration Research Corp., "Career Academies: Impacts on Students' Engagement and Performance in High School," March 2000.

Bruce R. Bartlett
Senior Fellow
National Center for
Policy Analysis
439 Seneca Road
Great Falls, VA 22066-1113
(703) 421-7784
fax: (703) 421-7785
73440.3456@compuserve.com

Lawrence Kudlow
CEO, Kudlow & Company
Financial Editor,
National Review Online
Kudlow & Company, LLC
One Dag Hammarskjold Plaza
885 Second Avenue at 48th Street,
26th Floor
New York, NY 10017
(212) 644-8610
fax: (212) 588-1636
svarga@kudlow.com

William Niskanen
Chairman
Cato Institute
1000 Massachusetts Avenue, NW
Washington, DC 20001
(202) 842-0200
fax: (202) 842-3490
wniskan@cato.org

Bryan S. Wesbury
Vice President and
Chief Economist
Griffin, Kubik, Stephens &
Thompson, Inc.
300 Sears Tower
233 South Wacker Drive
Chicago, IL 60606
(312) 441-2500
fax: (312) 441-2665
bwesbury@sprynet.com

For continually updated and expanded information on major breaking developments on this issue over the campaign cycle, see www.heritage.org/issues/economy.

Regulation

Reining in the Federal Bureaucracy

Erin M. Hymel and Lawrence H. Whitman

THE ISSUES

Although Congress has considered several proposals since 1994 to improve the federal regulatory system, there has been a relentless rise in the volume and cost of regulations. The regulatory process remains slow, sloppy, and secretive. Congress must improve the way unelected federal bureaucrats implement the programs and policies funded by the American taxpayer, because regulatory decisions affect every American, and sometimes in perverse ways.

1. **The federal regulatory bureaucracy is huge and growing.** In 2000, the Code of Federal Regulations was printed on almost 75,000 pages. The federal regulatory bureaucracy includes at least 54 agencies that spent approximately $20.29 billion in fiscal year 2002 on their regulatory programs. This amount is far too costly for a country fighting a war on terrorism and battling back from a recession.

2. **The federal regulatory system should be open, transparent, and accountable.** As the Competitive Enterprise Institute notes, "Congress, our body of elected representatives, shirks its duty to make the tough calls and delegates too much of its lawmaking power to nonelected agencies, and then fails to require that they guarantee net benefits."[1] Regulatory agencies should be required to articulate their goals, strategies, and outcomes and be held accountable for decisions that do not achieve their intended objectives. The enforcement process should be transparent and non-discriminatory, and should include an appeals process.

---

1. Clyde Wayne Crews, Jr., "Ten Thousand Commandments: An Annual Policymaker's Snapshot of the Federal Regulatory State—2001 Edition," Competitive Enterprise Institute, July 2001.

Today, there is no effective way to tell how much a new regulation will cost. New regulations are not attached to direct spending or taxation, and policymakers are able to transfer these hidden costs to businesses, consumers, and taxpayers, effectively lowering productivity and slowing economic growth. The lack of transparency provides little or no incentive for agencies to prioritize their decisions based on how much each regulation will benefit society and allows the federal government to expand its regulatory reach to activities that are more appropriately state and local responsibilities, such as hazardous waste cleanup.

3. **The costs of the current regulatory system are counted not just in dollars, but in lives.** A 1996 Harvard University study found that roughly 60,000 deaths occur each year because billions of dollars are squandered on programs to eliminate negligible or nonexistent risks rather than spent on programs that protect the public from more serious hazards—such as innoculations and programs to reduce the loss of life and property from natural disasters.[2] The federal government needs risk-based regulatory priorities based on sound science to help policymakers make smarter decisions that save more lives.

More deregulation, not new regulation, is needed for economic vitality. The deregulatory successes of the late 1970s and early 1980s in the airline, railway, and interstate trucking industries show how well this approach works. Deregulation should be broadened in such industries as electricity and telecommunications. The rise of the Internet, electronic commerce, and other technologies has revolutionized the economy; but further growth is hampered by outdated regulatory approaches that cost jobs, lower wages, and increase prices. Washington appears eager to impose new taxes and regulations as quickly as new technologies develop. In the telecommunications industry alone, according to the Cato Institute, the "regulatory regime and the litigation that goes along with it have severe consequences: the market works

2. Tammy O. Tengs and John D. Graham, "The Opportunity Costs of Haphazard Social Investments in Life-Saving," in Robert W. Hahn, ed., *Risks, Costs and Lives Saved* (New York: Oxford University Press, 1996).

less efficiently; the uncertainty...deters investment; the regulatory system is used to impede and delay competition."[3]

The Bush Administration has made regulatory reform a priority. As regulatory experts have noted:

> The restoration of OIRA [Office of Information and Regulatory Affairs] to its historic oversight role of providing meaningful supervision of agency rule-making also is evident in the current Bush Administration actions. Sixteen rules have already been returned to the agencies during its first ten months in office (as compared to only thirteen rules returned by the Clinton Administration in its entire eight years).[4]

Members of Congress should also get serious about regulatory reform before America's competitive advantage is lost forever in a sea of red tape.

THE FACTS

FACT: The federal regulatory system has mushroomed over the past decade.

- In 2000, according to the federal Regulatory Information Service Center's October 2000 *Unified Agenda of Federal Regulations*, the federal agencies, departments, and commissions issued 4,699 rules. Of these, 158 were "major rules"—defined as costing the economy more than $100 million annually. Thus, these major rules cost a minimum of $15.8 billion in 2000 alone, an increase of 15.3 percent since 1999.[5]
- In 2000, the massive Code of Federal Regulations (CFR), an annual listing of all executive agency regulations in effect that is published in the *Federal Register*, required 74,258 pages—

---

3. Cato Institute, *Cato Handbook for Congress: Policy Recommendations for the 107th Congress*, 2001, p. 457.
4. Ernest Gellhorn, Wendy L. Gramm, and Susan E. Dudley, "President Expands Oversight of Federal Agency Rulemaking," Washington Legal Foundation *Legal Backgrounder*, Vol. 16, No. 51 (November 16, 2001).
5. Crews, "Ten Thousand Commandments."

the most since the Carter Administration. The number of pages had grown 4.3 percent over the total in 1999.[6]

- The Code of Federal Regulations extends 19 running feet.[7]
- From 1991 to 2000, the number of pages in the CFR increased by 28.1 percent.[8]

FACT: The cost of regulation to the economy may exceed $800 billion, or nearly $8,000 each year for every American household.

The FY 2002 federal budget called for spending $20.29 billion on 54 regulatory departments and agencies that employ 130,759 federal workers.[9] This is even more spending than was projected in FY 2001 budget. According to the Center for the Study of American Business, this spending (in current dollars) "is the highest level of spending ever projected for the administrative budgets of the 54 regulatory agencies."[10]

The Small Business Administration recently estimated that the economic costs of the regulatory state exceed $800 billion. This figure is larger than the discretionary federal budget and translates into an average annual cost of nearly $8,000 per household.[11]

It is not easy to estimate the costs of federal regulation. Unlike federal spending, regulatory costs are not accounted for in the budget process. Though agencies are supposed to calculate the costs and benefits of regulations they promulgate,[12] their calculations often grossly underestimate the cost or substantially overestimate the benefits of regulation.[13]

---

6. *Ibid.*
7. National Federation of Independent Business, *NFIB National Small Business Poll*, Vol. I, No. 5 (2001).
8. *Ibid.*
9. Information provided by Melinda Warren, Director, Weidenbaum Center Forum, Washington University, St. Louis, Missouri, February 12, 2002.
10. Melinda Warren, "Federal Regulatory Spending Reaches a New Height: An Analysis of the Budget of the U.S. Government for the Year 2001," Center for the Study of American Business *Regulatory Budget Report* No. 23, June 2000.
11. John D. Graham, Ph.D., Administrator, Office of Information and Regulatory Affairs, Office of Management and Budget, speech to Weidenbaum Center Forum, "Executive Regulatory Review: Surveying the Record, Making it Work," National Press Club, Washington, D.C., December 17, 2001.

- Regulatory costs in 2000 ran $788 billion—7.9 percent of the gross domestic product. This figure exceeded Canada's total gross national product of $581 billion in 1998 and more than doubled Mexico's 1998 total gross national product of $368 billion.[14]
- The Competitive Enterprise Intstitute reports that the Environmental Protection Agency is "a prominent regulator" that spends "more than any other agency to enforce regulations." It cites projections by the Center for the Study of American Business that the EPA was expected to spend $4.8 billion to enforce regulations during FY 2001—24 percent of the total expected to be spent by all the regulatory agencies.[15]

FACT: Small businesses—the engine of economic growth in America—are especially burdened by regulation.[16]

Small and medium-size businesses create two out of every three new jobs. More than 90 percent of all businesses employ fewer than 100 workers, and more than 80 percent employ fewer than 20. Less than 1 percent of all firms employ 500 or more people.[17]

Regulation imposes its heaviest burden on small and medium-sized businesses because it is harder for these firms to spread the overhead costs of paperwork, attorney and accountant fees, and staff time that are needed to negotiate the federal regulatory

12. Executive Order 12866, "Regulatory Planning and Review," issued September 30, 1993, directs federal agencies to conduct economic analyses of proposed or existing regulations to inform decision-makers of the impact of a range of alternative regulatory approaches being considered.
13. See Robert W. Hahn, "Regulatory Reform: Assessing the Government's Numbers," AEI–Brookings Joint Center for Regulatory Studies *Working Paper* No. 99–6, July 1999, p. 5.
14. U.S. Department of Commerce, Bureau of the Census, *Statistical Abstract of the United States 2000*, Table No. 1364, Gross National Product, by Country: 1998, p. 831; U.S. Small Business Administration, Office of the Chief Counsel for Advocacy, *The Changing Burden of Regulation, Paperwork, and Tax Compliance on Small Business: A Report to Congress*, October 1995, Table 3, p. 28, as cited in Crews, "Ten Thousand Commandments."
15. Crews, "Ten Thousand Commandments."
16. In broad terms, a small business is defined as any business that does not dominate its field of business. In manufacturing, small businesses are usually defined as businesses that employ fewer than 500 persons. In the services industry, small businesses are usually defined as businesses that generate less than $5 million in gross annual receipts.
17. U.S. Department of Commerce, Bureau of the Census, "County Business Patterns, 1993," Table 1b.

maze. Small-business owners face regulatory requirements from the federal, state, and local governments.

- Small-business owners most frequently identify the federal government as the major source of their regulatory problems, and they cite the sheer volume of regulations as the most significant problem.[18]
- According to the Small Business Administration, the average annual cost of regulation, paperwork, and tax compliance for firms with fewer than 500 employees is about $5,000 per employee. For firms with more than 500 employees, the cost is about $3,400 per employee.[19]
- Costs for businesses with fewer than 50 employees run seven to 10 times higher than costs for firms with 50 to 100 employees.[20]

FACT: New regulations often threaten emerging industries and new technology.

The rise of new markets and advanced technologies has been met with new forms of regulation that particularly threaten emerging industries and innovative technological developments. For example:

- **Questionable antitrust regulation.** In addition to a Department of Justice assault on the Microsoft Corporation, federal regulators have increased their antitrust enforcement efforts against other high-technology industries, frequently using the merger review process to coerce concessions from industry. A Heartland Institute study finds that in 1996 alone, regulatory merger delays in restructuring industries resulted in costs of more than $12 billion.[21]
- **Delays in access to new technology.** Ensuring high-quality access to the Internet and broadband communications net-

---

18. National Federation of Independent Business, *NFIB National Small Business Poll.*
19. Small Business Administration, *The Changing Burden of Regulation, Paperwork and Tax Compliance on Small Business*," pp. 4–5.
20. *Ibid.*
21. Robert B. Ekelund, Jr., and Mark Thornton, "The Cost of Merger Delay in Restructuring Industries," Heartland Institute *Policy Study* No. 90, June 23, 1999, p. 1.

works and technologies has been a key policy concern. Many companies could offer broadband services and faster Internet access to customers if federal regulation did not hinder the expansion of such services. For instance, government rules have required local telephone companies to provide facilities to competitors at low rates, reducing the incentive to invest in new or expanded capabilities.

FACT: Federal regulations significantly dampen productivity and job creation.

When a business devotes resources to complying with regulatory mandates, it uses those resources less efficiently and is operating in a less productive and more costly manner. This drag on productivity denies workers a higher standard of living.

A study by Richard Vedder of Ohio University demonstrated the high cost on the economy that regulations impose by dramatically reducing productivity.[22] He estimated that federal regulations lowered economic output each year by $1.5 trillion (in 1999 dollars)—roughly the entire economic output of the Mid-Atlantic region (Delaware, the District of Columbia, Maryland, New Jersey, New York, and Pennsylvania).

FACT: Twenty years of deregulation produced lasting benefits.

Considerable evidence suggests that such reform would increase productivity, lower prices, eliminate shortages, and stimulate innovation and consumer choice—ultimately enhancing economic growth.

A May 1999 review of economic deregulation initiatives in the United States by the Organisation for Economic Co-operation and Development (OECD) concluded that:

> the removal of most restrictions on pricing, entry and exit in network industries led directly to increased productivity and lower costs.... More vigorous competition stimulated industry restructuring and innovation and benefited consumers through better service and lower prices.... An extraordinary

22. Richard K. Vedder, "Federal Regulation's Impact on the Productivity Slowdown: A Trillion-Dollar Drag," Center for the Study of American Business *Policy Study* No. 131, July 1996, p. 16.

> surge in innovation and faster introduction of new technologies, services, and business practices multiplied benefits for consumers and produced new high growth industries.... These effects allowed the US economy to adapt more quickly to changes in technology and to external shocks, improved the trade-offs between inflation, growth, and unemployment, and boosted the US lead in productivity.[23]

Robert Crandall of the Brookings Institution and Jerry Ellig, then of the Center for Market Processes at George Mason University, studied five major "network" industries—natural gas, telecommunications, airlines, trucking, and railroads—and found the following benefits of deregulation:[24]

- **Prices fall.** The authors found that within the first two years of deregulation, prices fell by 4 percent to 15 percent, and even more for certain groups of customers. Within 10 years of deregulation, they found prices to be at least 25 percent lower and sometimes almost as much as 50 percent lower.
- **Service quality improves.** Crandall and Ellig found that deregulation combined with customer choice aligned service quality with customers' desires. Airline safety, reliability of gas service, and the reliability of telecommunications networks did not decline, and in some cases improved, by these factors.
- **A rising tide really does lift all boats.** As the authors observed,

  > Regulatory reform is not a zero sum game; it has generated genuine gains for consumers and society as a whole. It is possible to find narrowly defined groups of customers in special circumstances who paid somewhat higher prices after deregulation, but the gains

---

23. Organisation for Economic Co-operation and Development, *The OECD Review of Regulatory Reform in the United States*, May 1999, p. 17.
24. Robert Crandall and Jerry Ellig, *Economic Deregulation and Customer Choice: Lessons for the Electric Industry*, Center for Market Processes, Fairfax, Virginia, 1997, pp. 3–5.

to the vast majority of consumers far outweighed the effects on these small groups.

- **More freedom equals more benefits.** Crandall and Ellig also found that rates fell faster in parts of the market where greater customer choice was allowed by regulators. They noted that "Choice for all customers for all competitive services will provide the most benefits."

The Crandall–Ellig study shows that the benefits of deregulation are not limited to one industry. As they observe, "Given the history of natural gas, telecommunications, airline, railroad, and trucking regulation, is it reasonable to expect that customer choice in electricity could generate consumer benefits? The experience of all these industries suggests that the answer is a resounding 'Yes.'"[25] Unfortunately, the federal government forgot this lesson. It has re-regulated previously deregulated industries or rushed to regulate emerging industries.

FACT: Sound science is critical.

Using sound science that puts risks in perspective is critical to ensuring that resources are allocated effectively. Yet the government frequently has used poor-quality science to estimate the magnitude of health risks; it also has regulated purely hypothetical health risks that likely pose no danger at all.

A September 2001 U.S. Department of Agriculture report explains why sound science is important: "Science-based risk assessments can help set priorities for further risk reductions. Economic analysis of the benefits and costs of risk reduction can enable the maximum net benefit to society while minimizing the regulatory burden on the private sector."[26]

Sound science is particularly important in creating effective health regulations. University of California researchers Bruce Ames and Lois Swirsky Gold have done extensive studies of the causes of cancers. From their findings, it is clear that regulating pollution for the purpose of reducing cancer, for example, would have minimal effect. Specifically:[27]

---

25. *Ibid.*, p. 7.
26. U.S. Department of Agriculture, *Food and Agricultural Policy: Taking Stock for the New Century*, September 2001.

- Pollution accounts for less than 1 percent of human cancer. The factors with the biggest impact on reducing cancer rates include reduction of smoking, increased consumption of fruits and vegetables, control of infections, reduced exposure to the sun, and increased physical activity.
- Regulatory resources are allocated disproportionately to address fears about chemicals as pollutants. Even assuming that EPA worst-case risk estimates for synthetic pollutants are true, the proportion of cancer cases that the EPA could prevent by regulating these pollutants would be negligible.[28]

Thus, according to Ames and Gold, risk assessment is key:

> Society must distinguish between significant and trivial cancer risks. Regulating trivial risks or exposure to substances erroneously inferred to cause cancer at low doses can harm health by diverting resources from programs that could be effective in protecting public health. Moreover, wealth creates health; poor people have a shorter life expectancy than wealthy people. When government policy results in wasting money and resources on trivial problems, it reduces society's wealth and hence harms health.[29]

FACT: Well-intentioned regulations can kill, and wrong-minded regulations prevent the optimal use of resources.

Regulatory reform should ensure that the nation's regulatory resources are used to save *more*, not fewer, lives. The above-mentioned 1996 Harvard University study examined more than 500 life-saving interventions and concluded that more than 60,000 people die each year because the regulatory system wastes billions of dollars on efforts to eliminate negligible or nonexistent risks while failing to protect people from more serious risks.[30]

---

27. Bruce N. Ames and Lois Swirsky Gold, "The Causes and Prevention of Cancer: Gaining Perspectives on Management of Risk," in Hahn, ed., *Risks, Costs and Lives Saved.*
28. *Ibid.*
29. *Ibid.*, p. 6.
30. Tengs and Graham, "The Opportunity Costs of Haphazard Social Investments."

Federal fuel economy laws originally passed in 1975 as a response to the Arab oil embargo, for example, led to the manufacture of smaller, more fuel-efficient, but less safe cars.[31]

- A 1989 Harvard–Brookings Institution study revealed that reducing a car's weight by 500 pounds increases fatalities by 2,200 to 3,900 per year.[32]
- A 2000 study by Leonard Evans, current President of the Science Serving Society in Michigan, "found that adding a passenger to one of two identical cars involved in a two-car frontal crash reduces the driver fatality risk by 7.5 percent. If the cars differ in mass by more than a passenger's weight, adding a passenger to the lighter car will reduce total risk."[33]
- The Department of Transportation found that passenger car standards caused an additional 2,000 deaths and 20,000 serious injuries per year.[34]
- Weight and size reductions resulting from CAFE standards have been linked with 46,000 deaths as well as thousands of injuries through 1998.[35]
- According to Jerry Ralph Curry, former head of the National Highway Traffic Safety Administration, "Since CAFE (Corporate Average Fuel Economy) legislation took effect, more people have been killed because of it than died in Vietnam."[36]

---

31. Kenneth Cole, "Federal Rules Fuel the Size Gap between Trucks and Cars," *The Detroit News*, March 29, 1998.
32. Competitive Enterprise Institute, "Automobile Fuel Economy Standards," *Issue Brief*, March 1, 1999.
33. See Leonard Evans, D.Phil., "Causal Influence of Car Mass and Size on Driver Fatality Risk," *American Journal of Public Health*, Vol. 91, No. 7 (2001). The author cites three studies from 1971–1974, including a study presented at an international conference in Washington, D.C., hosted by the National Highway Traffic Safety Administration. See Charli E. Coon, J.D., "Why the Government's CAFE Standards for Fuel Efficiency Should Be Repealed, Not Increased," Heritage Foundation *Backgrounder* No. 1458, July 11, 2001, at *www.heritage.org/library/backgrounder/bg1458.html*.
34. Competitive Enterprise Institute, "Automobile Fuel Economy Standards."
35. Coon, "Why the Government's CAFE Standards for Fuel Efficiency Should Be Repealed, Not Increased."
36. Cole, "Federal Rules Fuel the Size Gap between Trucks and Cars."

WHAT TO DO IN 2003

Candidates for Congress should illustrate how the federal regulatory system hurts Americans and offer alternatives that would improve the regulatory decisionmaking process.

Require the federal regulatory system to be more open, transparent, and accountable to the public.

Regulatory agencies should impose regulations that provide optimal benefits at minimal costs, and should be held accountable for their decisions. Agencies should be required to provide solid information about the process they use to make regulatory decisions, and Congress must hold them accountable for their decisions and reclaim its responsibility for regulating by approving rulemakings before they take effect. Regulatory programs that fail to achieve their intended objectives should be eliminated.

Establish a regulatory budget and lead by example.

The White House and Congress should work together to establish a federal regulatory budget that places a ceiling on the total estimated cost imposed by federal regulations each year. Such a regulatory budget would follow the model of the federal government's spending budget. For every government department and agency, the regulatory budget would list clearly each federal regulation and a realistic estimate of the costs imposed on the economy by it. The information on regulatory costs and benefits provided by such a budget would help policymakers clarify which regulations are worthwhile and set regulatory priorities to minimize the economic burden on Americans. When the budget ceiling was reached, an agency wishing to add a new regulation would have to repeal or modify an existing regulation that imposed the same or greater costs.

Reframe the debate on social (environmental, public health, and safety) policies to focus regulators on making smarter decisions that maximize benefits and minimize burdens.

Federal agencies increasingly impose ineffective and costly regulations that do little to improve public health and safety. The belief that increased regulation saves lives is naïve. Well-intentioned regulations can kill or have other harmful consequences. Social regulations must be based on sound science and rigorous cost-benefit analyses to be effective.

Identify industries that should be deregulated.

Federal involvement in electricity, communications, transportation, and agriculture has been counterproductive and costly. Congress should liberate these industries from any outdated and detrimental barriers to competition, including licensing laws and tariffs, price controls, or other regulations that discourage efficiencies and lessen consumer choice. The deregulatory successes of the late 1970s and early 1980s in the airline, railway, and interstate trucking industries prove that deregulation benefits the country. Regulators must resist the bureaucratic temptation to intervene whenever a new industry or technology emerges.

Take advantage of independent analyses of problematic rules.

Several organizations provide analyses of the effects of federal regulations and identify rules that are harmful to Americans, businesses, and the economy. Such groups include the AEI–Brookings Joint Center for Regulatory Studies, the Mercatus Center at George Mason University, the Center for Regulatory Studies and Improvement at Carnegie Mellon University, and the Center for the Study of American Business at Washington University. Policy analysis is also available from organizations like the Cato Institute and The Heritage Foundation, which offers econometric analyses of proposals by its experts in the Center for Data Analysis.

Support the Administration in reestablishing a centralized review mechanism, including review of general guidance documents, within the Office of Management and Budget's Office of Information and Regulatory Affairs (OIRA).

Congress should support the President's efforts to rescind regulatory executive orders and replace them with deregulatory orders. Agencies and OMB should also disclose as much information as possible to Congress and the public, as early as possible in the regulatory development process, through the Internet and other means to obtain public comment and risk assessments and to revise the proposed rules accordingly. Independent regulatory agencies like the EPA, moreover, should be subject to the same rulemaking principles that apply to all other agencies.

—Erin M. Hymel is a Research Assistant in, and Lawrence H. Whitman is Director of, the Thomas A. Roe Institute for Economic Policy Studies at The Heritage Foundation. James L. Gattuso, Research Fellow in Regulatory Policy at The Heritage Foundation, also contributed to this chapter.

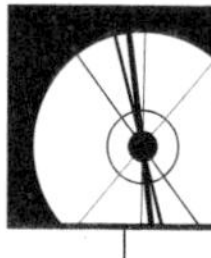

For a complete list and full-text versions of additional studies by Heritage on regulatory reform, see the searchable *Issues 2002* companion CD–ROM.

EXPERTS

Heritage Foundation

James L. Gattuso
Research Fellow in Regulatory Policy
The Heritage Foundation
214 Massachusetts Avenue, NE
Washington, DC 20002
(202) 608-6244
fax: (202) 544-4521
james.gattuso@heritage.org

Erin M. Hymel
Research Assistant, Thomas A. Roe Institute for Economic Policy Studies
The Heritage Foundation
214 Massachusetts Avenue, NE
Washington, DC 20002
(202) 608-6212
fax: (202) 544-5421
erin.hymel@heritage.org

Lawrence H. Whitman
Director, Thomas A. Roe Institute for Economic Policy Studies
The Heritage Foundation
214 Massachusetts Avenue, NE
Washington, DC 20002
(202) 608-6215
fax: (202) 544-5421
lawrence.whitman@heritage.org

Charli E. Coon, J.D.
Senior Policy Analyst for Energy and the Environment
Thomas A. Roe Institute for Economic Policy Studies
The Heritage Foundation
214 Massachusetts Avenue, NE
Washington, DC 20002
(202) 608-6139
fax: (202) 544-4521
charli.coon@heritage.org

Becky Norton Dunlop
Vice President, External Relations
The Heritage Foundation
214 Massachusetts Avenue, NE
Washington, DC 20002
(202) 608-6041
fax (202) 675-1753
bndunlop@heritage.org

Todd Gaziano
Senior Fellow in Legal Studies and Director, Center for Legal and Judicial Studies

The Heritage Foundation
214 Massachusetts Avenue, NE
Washington, DC 20002
(202) 608-6182
fax: (202) 547-0641
todd.gaziano@heritage.org

Robert E. Moffit, Ph.D.
Director, Domestic Policy Studies
The Heritage Foundation
214 Massachusetts Avenue, NE
Washington, DC 20002
(202) 608-6210
fax: (202) 544-5421
robert.moffit@heritage.org

Virginia Thomas
Director, Executive Branch Relations
The Heritage Foundation
214 Massachusetts Avenue, NE
Washington, DC 20002
(202) 608-6240
fax: (202) 608-6068
ginni.thomas@heritage.org

Other Experts

Kameran Bailey
Associate Director, Regulatory Studies Program
Mercatus Center
George Mason University
3401 North Fairfax Drive
Suite 450
Arlington, VA 22201-4433
(703) 993-4929
fax: (703) 993-4935
kbailey@gmu.edu

Richard Belzer, Ph.D.
President, Regulatory Checkbook
819 7th Street, NW, Suite 305
Washington, DC 20001
(202) 898-2050
fax: (202) 478-1626
belzer@regulatorycheckbook.org

Wayne T. Brough, Ph.D.
Chief Economist
Citizens for a Sound Economy
1250 H Street, NW, Suite 700
Washington, DC 20005
(202) 783-3870
fax: (202) 783-4687
wbrough@cse.org

James Burnley
Director
Citizens for a Sound Economy
1250 H Street, NW, Suite 700
Washington, DC 20005
(202) 783-3870
fax: (202) 783-4687
cse@cse.org

Robert Crandall, Ph.D.
Senior Fellow
Brookings Institution
1775 Massachusetts Avenue, NW
Washington, DC 20005
(202) 797-6291
fax: (202) 797-6181
rcrandall@brook.edu

Clyde Wayne Crews, Jr.
Director of Technology Policy
Cato Institute
1000 Massachusetts Avenue, NW
Washington, DC 20001
(202) 842-0200
fax: (202) 842-3490
wcrews@cato.org

Susan E. Dudley
Senior Research Fellow,
Regulatory Studies Program
Mercatus Center
George Mason University
3401 North Fairfax Drive
Suite 450
Arlington, VA 22201-4433
(703) 993-4930
fax: (703) 993-4935
sdudley@gmu.edu

Susan Eckerly
Director, Federal Government Relations
National Federation of Independent Business
1201 F Street, NW, Suite 200
Washington, DC 20004
(202) 554-9000

fax: (202) 554-0496
susan.eckerly@nfib.org

Wendy Lee Gramm, Ph.D.
Director, Regulatory Studies Program
Mercatus Center
George Mason University
3401 North Fairfax Drive Suite 450
Arlington, VA 22201-4433
(703) 993-4930
fax: (703) 993-4935

C. Boyden Gray
Chairman
Citizens for a Sound Economy
1250 H Street, NW, Suite 700
Washington, DC 20005
(202) 783-3870
fax: (202) 783-4687
cse@cse.org

Robert W. Hahn, Ph.D.
Director and Resident Scholar
AEI–Brookings Joint Center for Regulatory Studies
1150 17th Street, NW
Washington, DC 20036
(202) 862-5909
fax: (202) 862-7169
rhahn@aei.org

Thomas D. Hopkins, Ph.D.
Dean, College of Business
Rochester Institute of Technology
107 Lomb Memorial Drive
Rochester, NY 14623
(716) 475-7042
fax: (716) 475-7055
TDHBBU@rit.edu

Sam Kazman
General Counsel
Competitive Enterprise Institute
1001 Connecticut Avenue, NW, Suite 1250
Washington, DC 20036
(202) 331-1010
fax: (202) 331-0640
info@cei.org

Robert Litan, Ph.D.
Director and Vice President of Economic Studies
Brookings Institution
Co-Director, AEI–Brookings Joint Center for Regulatory Studies
1775 Massachusetts Avenue, NW
Washington, DC 20005
(202) 797-6120
fax: (202) 797-6181
rlitan@brook.edu

Randall Lutter, Ph.D.
Fellow, AEI–Brookings Joint Center for Regulatory Studies
1150 17th Street, NW
Washington, DC 20036
(202) 862-5875
fax: (202) 862-7169
rlutter@aei.org

James C. Miller III
Counselor
Citizens for a Sound Economy
1250 H Street, NW, Suite 700
Washington, DC 20005
(202) 783-3870
fax: (202) 783-4687
jmiller@cse.org

Adrian T. Moore
Executive Director
Reason Public Policy Institute
3415 South Sepulveda Boulevard
Suite 400
Los Angeles, CA 90034
(310) 391-2245
fax: (310) 391-4395
adrianm@ppi.org

William Niskanen, Ph.D.
Chairman
Cato Institute
1000 Massachusetts Avenue, NW
Washington, DC 20001
(202) 842-0200
fax: (202) 842-3490
wniskan@cato.org

Fred L. Smith, Jr.
President
Competitive Enterprise Institute
1001 Connecticut Avenue, NW,
Suite 1250
Washington, DC 20036
(202) 331-1010
fax: (202) 331-0640
info@cei.org

Adam D. Thierer
Director of Telecommunications Studies
Cato Institute
1000 Massachusetts Avenue, NW
Washington, DC 20001
(202) 789-5211
fax: (202) 842-3490
athierer@cato.org

For continually updated and expanded information on major breaking developments on this issue over the campaign cycle, see *www.heritage.org/issues/regulation*.

ENERGY

Achieving Independence, Ensuring Security

Charli E. Coon, J.D.

THE ISSUES

Not since the oil embargoes of the 1970s has the United States faced such challenges in trying to meet its energy needs. The U.S. Department of Energy's Energy Information Administration (EIA) predicts that, if production continues to grow at a rate comparable to that of the past decade, the growth in demand over the next 20 years will increasingly outpace production.[1] Limited access to known resources, regulatory constraints, and uncertainty in the industry that inhibits investment, as well as the failure of past federal efforts to coordinate the nation's energy, environment, and trade policies, have contributed to the growing gap between supply and demand. In the long run, this imbalance threatens not only the economy and Americans' standard of living, but also national security.

Washington can begin to solve America's energy problems by making energy policy a national priority and implementing a long-term energy plan that balances supply and demand, ensures reliable and affordable supplies of energy for the future, and provides responsible stewardship of the nation's resources. Conservative candidates should promote a comprehensive plan that addresses the following core issues:

1. **Insufficient and unreliable energy supplies are a threat to national security.** Dependable supplies of energy are essential for the nation's economy and the needs of its military forces in times of peace, but especially when they engage in military

---

1. National Energy Policy Development Group, *Report of the National Energy Policy Development Group*, May 2001, p. viii; cited hereafter as National Energy Policy Report.

action. The U.S. Department of Defense accounts for about 80 percent of the federal government's energy use, of which nearly 75 percent is for jet fuel. It is essential that Washington pursue a diverse supply of oil and more independence from imported oil to meet the nation's security needs.

2. **Americans can have both clean air and reliable, affordable energy.** Some fear that increasing America's energy use will have negative effects on air quality, but history shows otherwise. Over the past 30 years, the levels of six key air pollutants fell by 29 percent while the nation's gross domestic product (GDP) increased almost 160 percent, energy consumption increased 45 percent, and vehicle miles traveled increased 143 percent.[2]

3. **Federal energy policies have dramatic effects on the economy.** The availability of energy at reasonable prices is key to economic growth and stability. Over the past decade, restrictive energy policies have eroded surplus supplies, compounding intermittent energy shortages and causing volatility in energy prices. Such instability of supplies, uncertainty of cost, and erratic spikes in prices will continue unless Washington adopts a long-term plan to encourage domestic energy development. An analysis of the Administration's plan,[3] which encourages development and fuel diversity, suggests that it would have dramatic effects if implemented. By 2025, GDP would be $540 billion higher, and there would be over 1.5 million more job opportunities; in addition, investment would increase by $65 billion each year from 2005 to 2025 with no significant changes in inflation or interest rates. By 2030, lower energy prices and higher economic growth would increase disposable family income by over $1,800.[4]

---

2. U.S. Environmental Protection Agency, *National Air Quality 2000 Status and Trends*, at *www.epa.gov/oar/aqtrndoo/*.
3. Heritage Foundation analysis; see CDA Project Team, *Econometric and Policy Evaluation of the National Energy Plan: A Report of the Center for Data Analysis of The Heritage Foundation*, August 2001, p. 88, at *www.heritage.org/shorts/PDF/20010803energyfull.pdf*; for a shorter version of this report, see "Summary of the Center for Data Analysis Evaluation of the President's National Energy Plan," August 3, 2001, at *www.heritage.org/shorts/20010803energy.html*.
4. *Ibid.*

4. **America needs a comprehensive energy plan that lessens U.S. dependence on foreign oil and promotes fuel diversity.** Federal policy should not favor one fuel source over another. Coal, natural gas, nuclear power, oil, and renewable energy sources should all be included in the mix of fuel sources. A new and comprehensive policy, which encourages the development of these resources, should allow the marketplace to determine the winners and losers.

5. **Enhancing energy conservation will require investments in technology.** The use of innovative and modern technologies will increase energy efficiency, reduce demand, and improve the quality of the environment. The United States already is the world's leader in technological advancements, but businesses can be discouraged from investing in new technology if the regulatory environment is too restrictive. The current New Source Review program, intended to assure that air quality does not decline, provides an example of how regulation can be counterproductive; it discourages plants from making improvements that would improve efficiency to avoid its expensive requirements.

6. **The nation's energy infrastructure is outdated.** America's aging infrastructure has failed to keep pace with changing energy requirements. Since 1980, 50 percent of U.S. refineries have closed.[5] No major refineries have been built in the past 25 years.[6] Infrastructure must be modernized to ensure the dependable and safe delivery of energy supplies to industry and consumers. Pipelines and transmission lines must be enhanced and upgraded. And refineries that are operating at capacity must be expanded to ensure stable fuel supplies.

7. **International pressure on the United States to ratify an environmental treaty—despite its adverse consequences for industry and consumers—is growing.** The Kyoto Protocol of the United Nations Framework Convention on Climate Change calls for industrial countries, such as the United States, Canada, Japan, and members of the European Union (EU), to greatly reduce their overall emissions of so-called

---

5. U.S. Department of Energy, Energy Information Administration, *Annual Energy Review 2000*, Table 5.9, at *www.eia.doe.gov/emeu/aer/txt/tab0509.htm*. The 2000 figure is preliminary.
6. National Energy Policy Report, p. 7-13.

greenhouse gases by 2012. The Clinton Administration committed the United States to an even higher reduction, and agreed that developing countries—including China, India, and Brazil—should be excluded from the targets. This agreement, with its unachievable standards that would harm the U.S. economy and significantly raise the cost of living, is patently unfair.[7]

THE FACTS

FACT: Growth in U.S. energy consumption outpaces domestic production.

- Americans consume 19.5 million barrels of oil per day, with demand growing an average of 1.5 percent annually through 2020.[8]
- Domestic crude oil production averages about 5.8 million barrels per day—40 percent less than the nation's refineries produced in 1970.[9] The shortfall is made up with imports.
- Between 1991 and 2000, Americans used 17 percent more energy than they did in the previous decade; but during that period, domestic energy production rose only 2.3 percent.[10]
- The U.S. Department of Energy projects that energy consumption will increase by about 32 percent by 2020,[11] creating a shortfall between energy supply and demand. Estimates indicate that during this time, U.S. consumption of oil will increase by 33 percent and that consumption of natural gas will increase by over 50 percent.[12]

---

7. Charli E. Coon, J.D., "Why President Bush Is Right to Abandon the Kyoto Protocol," Heritage Foundation *Backgrounder* No. 1437, May 11, 2001, at *www.heritage.org/library/backgrounder/bg1437.html.*
8. U.S. Department of Energy, Energy Information Administration, *Annual Energy Outlook 2002 with Projections to 2020*, Table A1, at *www.eia.doe.gov/oiaf/aio/results.html#tables.*
9. U.S. Department of Energy, Energy Information Administration, *Annual Energy Review, Crude Oil Production and Oil Well Productivity, 1954–2000*, Table 5.2, at *www.eia.doe.gov/emeu/aer/txt/tab0502.htm.*
10. National Energy Policy Report, p. 1-1.
11. Energy Information Administration, *Annual Energy Outlook 2002*, Table A1.
12. National Energy Policy Report, p. x.

FACT: Imports of oil and natural gas are expected to increase significantly to meet America's growing energy demands.

The daily shortfall in domestic supplies—about 13.7 million barrels of oil—must be made up by importing foreign oil. Increasing domestic production, diversity of oil supplies, and trade and investment with exporting nations would mitigate disruptions in supplies from the Middle East with dramatic consequences for America's military forces, as well as industries and consumers.

- Between 1973 and 2000, U.S. dependence on foreign oil rose from 35 percent to more than 52 percent of consumption. Imports of oil are projected to increase to over 60 percent, much of it coming from the Persian Gulf region, by the year 2030.[13]
- Between 1973 and 2000, the import share of natural gas consumption climbed from less than 5 percent to more than 15 percent, and it continues to rise.[14]
- Though about half of America's imports comes from the Western Hemisphere, one-fifth comes from Persian Gulf states, which include Iraq and Saudi Arabia. Oil production in the Caspian Basin, offshore West Africa, and Mexico is expected to increase over current production levels.[15]

FACT: The nation's growing military obligations require affordable and reliable energy resources.

- The Department of Defense accounts for about 80 percent of the federal government's energy consumption, with three-quarters of that spent on jet fuel. The requirements of expanding the global war on terrorism could increase these needs significantly.
- Each soldier's needs now require eight times more oil than during World War II.[16]

---

13. CDA Project Team, *Econometric and Policy Evaluation of the National Energy Plan*, p. 49; see also National Energy Policy Report, p. 8-4.
14. National Energy Policy Report, p. 2-9.
15. Energy Information Administration, *Annual Energy Outlook 2002*, Overview.
16. Natalie M. Henry, "Oil: Attacks Heighten Call for Reduced Dependence on Foreign Oil," *Greenwire*, September 17, 2001.

FACT: Untapped domestic energy resources should be explored in order to lessen America's dependence on imports and vulnerability to disruptions in supply.

Federal law prohibits exploration in the eastern Gulf of Mexico and on the outer continental shelves and severely restricts access to resources in the Rocky Mountains. Difficulties in acquiring permits to drill wells on government land and overly restrictive leases also limit natural gas production. Such regulatory controls make the United States more vulnerable to disruptions in supply at a time when its energy needs demand greater development of domestic resources.[17]

- Studies estimate that there is a mean undiscovered recoverable resource of 46 billion barrels of oil and 268 trillion cubic feet of natural gas—2.5 times the offshore reserve found to date—lying in the U.S. outer continental shelf. Yet a federal moratorium prohibits exploration in these potentially vast reserves until 2012.[18]
- America's technically recoverable onshore oil resource base is 110 billion barrels—five times its proven reserves, onshore and offshore, of 21 billion barrels. Gas resources include as much as 1,074 trillion cubic feet in the lower 48 states and an additional 261 trillion cubic feet in Alaska—more than a 33-year potential supply.[19] It is also estimated that 75 billion barrels of oil and 362 trillion cubic feet of natural gas underlie U.S. coastal areas.[20]
- The prospects for major new discoveries of natural gas are most promising on public land in the Rocky Mountain sedimentary basins, as well as offshore in the Gulf of Mexico

---

17. Testimony of Naresh Kumar, Ph.D., Vice Chairman, Committee on Resource Evaluation, American Association of Petroleum Geologists, before the Subcommittee on Energy and Mineral Resources, Committee on Resources, U.S. House of Representatives, 107th Cong., 1st Sess., March 22, 2001, p. 6, at *http://resourcescommittee.house.gov/107cong/energy/2001mar22/2001_0322agenda.htm.*
18. *Ibid.*, p. 7.
19. *Ibid.*, p. 6.
20. Testimony of Carolita Kallaur, Associate Director, Offshore Minerals Management, Minerals Management Service, Department of the Interior, before the Subcommittee on Energy and Mineral Resources, Committee on Resources, U.S. House of Representatives, 107th Cong., 1st Sess., March 22, 2001, p. 6, at *http://resourcescommittee.house.gov/107/cong/energy2001mar22/2001_0322.*

(particularly the eastern Gulf) and on the Atlantic and Pacific outer continental shelves. Total estimated gas resources in these areas amount to 213 trillion cubic feet, or a nine-year supply at current rates of consumption.[21]

FACT: Drilling in the Arctic National Wildlife Refuge (ANWR) will increase America's energy independence while not threatening that preserve.

ANWR, a reserve in the Arctic Circle in northeast Alaska, consists of 19 million acres, about the size of South Carolina. Studies by the U.S. Geological Survey estimate that drilling in just one remote 2,000-acre area of ANWR could yield up to 16 billion barrels of oil—an amount roughly equal to 30 years of oil imports from Saudi Arabia. The 2,000-acre site (called Section 1002), a flat, treeless tundra with harsh winters, is no bigger than Dulles Airport near Washington, D.C. Temperatures with the wind chill can go as low as minus 110 degrees, and darkness envelops the area for 56 continuous days. Summers are no better, with puddles of water breeding swarms of mosquitoes everywhere.[22] Drilling there poses no threat to that environment.

FACT: The government's corporate average fuel economy (CAFE) standards raise safety risks and have perverse effects.

The federal CAFE standards set an average miles-per-gallon minimum for U.S.-made automobiles sold in the United States. While CAFE standards do not mandate that manufacturers make small cars, producing smaller, lightweight vehicles that can perform satisfactorily using low-power, fuel-efficient engines is the most efficient and affordable way for automakers to meet these requirements. However, the CAFE standards are having unintended consequences.

- Between 1975 and 1999 (following implementation of the CAFE standards), at least 46,000 people died in car crashes who would have survived if they had been traveling in bigger, heavier cars, according to government and insurance industry statistics.[23]

21. Testimony of Naresh Kumar, p. 6.
22. Jonah Goldberg, "Ugh, Wilderness," *National Review*, August 6, 2001, p. 28.

- Sales of "light trucks," which include SUVs, vans, and pickup trucks, have risen steadily and now make up nearly 47 percent of the light vehicle market—more than twice their market share in 1983.[24] Many people choose to drive vehicles such as SUVs, even though they are often less fuel-efficient than lightweight cars, because of their special features and added utility, such as seating capacity, power for hauling and towing, safety, and durability.[25]
- The CAFE standards perversely encourage automakers to promote SUVs, which are in the mid- to high-end mileage range of the truck category,[26] rather than full-size cars that are in the high-mileage end of the car category,[27] in order to be in compliance with their annual assessments under the CAFE rule.

FACT: America needs new electricity generation and transmission capacity to meet growing demands.

Electricity is a secondary source of energy, generated through the consumption of primary sources like coal. In fact, coal and nuclear energy account for over 70 percent of U.S. electricity generation. A sound national energy policy must address the use of these resources to meet the projected demand for electricity.

- Estimates indicate that demand for electricity will rise by 45 percent over the next 20 years.[28] Even with efficiency gains of as much as 20 percent by 2020 under the President's energy plan, the nation will need to build over 1,300 power plants to meet this increased demand.[29]

---

23. James R. Healey, "Death by the Gallon: Push for Better Mileage Raises Death Tolls," *USA TODAY*, Special Reprint Edition of article from *Money* magazine, July 2, 1999; based on previously unpublished fatality statistics from the National Highway Traffic Safety Administration and the Insurance Institute for Highway Safety.
24. U.S. Environmental Protection Agency, *Light-Duty Automotive Technology and Fuel Economy Trends, 1975 Through 2001*, EPA420–R–01–008, September, 2001, at *www.epa.gov/otagq/fetrends.htm.*
25. Coalition for Vehicle Choice, at *www.vehiclechoice.org/truck/index.html.*
26. United States Environmental Protection Agency, *Light-Duty Automotive Technology and Fuel Economy Trends 1975 Through 2001*, EPA420-R-01-008, September 2001, p. 16.
27. *Ibid.*
28. National Energy Policy Report, p. x.

- Since 1989, while electricity sales to consumers have increased by 2.1 percent annually, transmission capacity has increased by only 0.8 percent annually, impeding the movement of electricity to consumers.[30] Investment in new transmission capacity is needed to remove these bottlenecks and enhance the flow of electricity both within and between regions.

FACT: As U.S. energy consumption and GDP have increased, the nation's air quality has improved.

Advanced technologies, enhanced energy efficiency, and environmental regulation based on sound science all contribute to declining air pollution. Data show that it is possible to promote economic growth and protect the environment at the same time: Between 1970 and 1999, U.S. energy consumption increased by about 42 percent and the gross national product increased by 147 percent, while key air emissions decreased by 31 percent.[31]

FACT: Market competition, not government regulation, encourages improvements in energy efficiency.

Since 1970, as the economy has shifted toward greater use of more efficient technologies, U.S. energy use intensity (the amount of energy it takes to produce a dollar of GDP) has declined by 30 percent.[32] If the intensity of U.S. energy use had remained constant since 1972, consumption would have been about 74 percent higher in 1999 than it in fact was.[33]

Energy Calculator: Use this calculator to estimate how many fewer power plants will need to be built in a particular state if the Bush energy plan is adopted. The calculator also estimates the number of households that can be powered because of energy savings from the plan. Access the calculator at *www.heritage.org/calculators*.

29. CDA Project Team, *Econometric and Policy Evaluation of the National Energy Plan*, p. 100; see also National Energy Policy Report, p. 1-6, Figure 1-2.
30. National Energy Policy Report, p. 1-5.
31. *Ibid.*, p. 3-3, Figure 3-1; based on data from the U.S. Department of Energy and the Environmental Protection Agency.
32. National Energy Policy Report, p. 8-1.
33. *Ibid.*, p. xi, Figure 4.

WHAT TO DO IN 2003

Reduce America's reliance on oil imports from the Middle East.

Periodic efforts by the Organization of Petroleum Exporting Countries (OPEC) to maintain oil prices above levels dictated by market forces have increased price volatility and prices paid by consumers. Concentration of world oil production in any one region of the world can contribute to market instability.

Federal policy and congressional action in the short term should encourage greater diversity of oil production and transportation within and among geographic regions. Technological advances should be promoted to enable the United States to diversify oil supplies through deep-water offshore exploration and development in the Atlantic Basin, from offshore Canada to the Caribbean, Brazil, and West Africa. Strengthening international relations in these regions as well as with Mexico, Venezuela, and the Caspian Sea area would lessen the impact of supply disruptions from the Middle East on the United States and world economies.

Congress should allow greater access to federal land for energy exploration and development and expand offshore drilling. It should pass the necessary legislation to open up Section 1002 in the Arctic National Wildlife Refuge (ANWR) to exploration and development. This 2,000-acre segment is estimated to have the equivalent of 30 years of oil imports from Saudi Arabia.

Promote fuel diversity.

A primary goal for Congress should be to increase domestic supply from a diverse mix of fuel sources—such as coal, natural gas, nuclear, and renewable energy. Over-reliance on any one source leaves consumers vulnerable to price spikes and supply disruptions. The United States has enough coal to last another 250 years.[34] Building coal-powered electric plants using clean coal technologies and making greater use of nuclear power should be encouraged. Advanced technologies make oil and natural gas exploration and production more efficient and environmentally sound. And innovative technologies combined with lower costs enable non-hydroelectric renewable

---

34. *Ibid.*, p. xiii.

resources, such as wind and solar power, to gain greater market share.

Expand the nation's energy infrastructure.

A dependable system to deliver energy to industry and consumers is vital. Existing transmission constraints limit the flow of power and cause consumers to pay higher prices for electricity, and insufficient domestic pipeline capacity has caused peak-load problems in moving oil and petroleum products from one region of the country to another. Improvement and expansion of the nation's electricity grid and pipeline systems are needed to increase reliability, lower prices, and meet increased demand. This involves better maintenance of the existing system and expansion, adding capacity where needed, and expediting the permitting process.

The Clean Air Act allows states, under specified circumstances, to implement their own clean fuel programs. As the number of fuel types, known as "boutique fuels," that they require grows, greater stress is placed on the distribution system, and the flexibility of supply is decreased. The fear is that occasional and isolated supply problems could become broader and more frequent, causing more supply disruptions and price spikes. President Bush has directed the EPA to review this problem.[35] One solution may be to reduce the total number of such fuels required.

Prohibit back-door implementation of unratified environmental treaties that would harm the U.S. economy.

The Kyoto Protocol to the United Nations Framework Convention on Climate Change sets targets for industrial countries, such as the United States, Japan, Canada, and members of the European Union, to reduce their overall emissions of so-called greenhouse gases, including carbon dioxide, by at least 5 percent below their 1990 levels between 2008 and 2012. As of December 11, 2001, only one "developed" country—Romania—has ratified the agreement.

The Clinton Administration committed the United States to a 7 percent reduction level and agreed that developing countries

---

35. *Ibid.*, p. 7-14; see also *Inside EPA.com*, "EPA Recommends Changes to Reformulated Gasoline Program," October 24, 2001.

such as China, India, and Brazil, which are typically large emitters, should be excluded from these targets. The Protocol limits are unachievable, unfair, and economically harmful to the United States.

- The Senate expressed unanimous disapproval of the terms of this treaty in Senate Resolution 98 (the Byrd–Hagel Resolution) in July 1997, stating that the treaty's measures "could result in serious harm to the United States economy." The 106th Congress also approved the Knollenberg Amendment, which prevents government agencies from proposing or issuing rules or regulations that advance the provisions of the Protocol.[36]

- If the Protocol were to be implemented, it is estimated that U.S. productivity would fall by $100 billion to over $400 billion in 2010, prices for gasoline would increase from about 30 percent to 50 percent, and increases in prices for electricity would climb 50 percent to 80 percent; Americans would see reductions in wage growth of 5 percent to 10 percent, and living standards would fall by 15 percent.[37]

- Despite President Bush's announcement in March 2001 that he would not sign any agreement that would "harm our economy and hurt our workers,"[38] some in Washington support drastic Kyoto-like emissions reductions. The House and Senate Appropriations Committees should remove from any department's budget request—and reject any amendments to appropriations bills that include—provisions that seek to implement the terms of the Kyoto Protocol without Senate ratification of the treaty. The House and Senate should also reject legislative attempts to regulate carbon dioxide under the Clean Air Act.

---

36. Appropriations for the Department of Veterans Affairs and Housing and Urban Development, and for Sundry Independent Agencies, Boards, Commissions, Corporations, and Offices for Fiscal Years 1999 (P.L. 105–276), 2000 (P.L. 106–74), and 2001 (P.L. 106–377).

37. Margo Thorning, Ph.D., "A U.S. Perspective on the Economic Impact of Climate Change Policy," American Council for Capital Formation, Center for Policy Research, *Special Report*, December 2000.

38. "Bush Firm Over Kyoto Stance," *CNN.com*, March 29, 2001.

Oppose multi-pollutant legislation that would undermine economic and energy security.

Some in Congress want to impose stringent emissions reductions on power plants in an unreasonably short period of time,[39] but this approach would drive up electricity prices, compromise the reliability of electricity supply, and undermine America's economic strength. Over the past three decades, air quality has improved as GDP and energy consumption have increased. The Clean Air Act of 1970 and its amendments already limit air emissions pursuant to ongoing, scheduled reductions. Congress should not enact legislation that would "add on" to this act's requirements without first reforming existing programs—such as New Source Review, which discourages improvements that would enhance energy efficiency and air quality—and eliminating programs and regulations that impede energy supply.

—Charli E. Coon, J.D., is Senior Policy Analyst for Energy and the Environment in the Thomas A. Roe Institute for Economic Policy Studies at The Heritage Foundation.

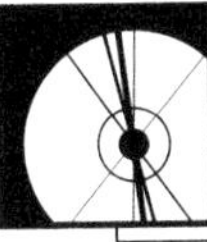

For a complete list and full-text versions of additional studies by Heritage on energy issues, see the searchable *Issues 2002* companion CD–ROM.

EXPERTS

Heritage Foundation

Charli E. Coon, J.D.
Senior Policy Analyst,
Energy and the Environment
The Heritage Foundation
214 Massachusetts Avenue, NE
Washington, DC 20002
(202) 546-6139
fax: (202) 544-5421
charli.coon@heritage.org

Lawrence Whitman
Director, Thomas A. Roe Institute
for Economic Policy Studies
The Heritage Foundation
214 Massachusetts Avenue, NE
Washington, DC 20002
(202) 546-6215
fax: (202) 544-5421
lawrence.whitman@heritage.org

William W. Beach
Director, Center for Data Analysis

39. See, for example, S. 556, introduced by Senator James Jeffords (I–VT), March 15, 2001, at *www.thomas.loc.gov*.

John M. Olin Senior Fellow in Economics
The Heritage Foundation
214 Massachusetts Avenue, NE
Washington, DC 20002
(202) 608-6806
fax: (202) 675-1772
bill.beach@heritage.org

Rea S. Hederman, Jr.
Manager of Operations, Center for Data Analysis
The Heritage Foundation
214 Massachusetts Avenue, NE
Washington, DC 20002
(202) 546-6296
fax: (202) 675-1772
rea.hederman@heritage.org

Becky Norton Dunlop
Vice President for External Relations
The Heritage Foundation
214 Massachusetts Avenue, NE
Washington, DC 20002
(202) 546-6041
fax: (202) 675-1753
bndunlop@heritage.org

Brett D. Schaefer
Jay Kingham Fellow in International Regulatory Affairs
Center for International Trade and Economics
The Heritage Foundation
214 Massachusetts Avenue, NE
Washington, DC 20002
(202) 546-6123
fax: (202) 675-6129
brett.schaefer@heritage.org

Other Experts

Terry L. Anderson, Ph.D.
Executive Director
Political Economy Research Center
502 South 19th Avenue, Suite 211
Bozeman, MT 59718
(406) 587-9591
fax: (406) 586-7555
tla@perc.org

Kenneth Green, Ph.D.
Director, Environmental Studies, and Deputy Director
Reason Public Policy Institute
3415 South Sepulveda Boulevard, Suite 400
Los Angeles, CA 90034
(310) 391-2245
fax: (310) 391-4395
keng@reason.org

David Ridenour
Vice President
National Center for Public Policy Research
777 North Capitol Street, NE, Suite 803
Washington, DC 20002
(202) 371-1400
fax: (202) 408-7773
dridenour@nationalcenter.org

S. Fred Singer, Ph.D.
President
Science and Environmental Policy Project
4084 University Drive
Suite 206–A
Fairfax, VA 22030
(703) 527-8282
fax: (703) 352-7535
singer@sepp.org

Fred Smith, Jr.
President
Competitive Enterprise Institute
1001 Connecticut Avenue, NW
Suite 1250
Washington, DC 20036
(202) 331-1010
fax: (202) 331-0640
fsmith@cei.org

Jerry Taylor
Director,
Natural Resource Studies
Cato Institute
1000 Massachusetts Avenue, NW
Washington, DC 20001
(202) 789-5240
fax: (202) 842-3490
jtaylor@cato.org

Margo Thorning, Ph.D.
Senior Vice President and
Chief Economist
American Council for
Capital Formation
1750 K Street, NW, Suite 400
Washington, DC 20036
(202) 293-5811
fax: (202) 785-8165
mthorning@aol.com

For continually updated and expanded information on major breaking developments on this issue over the campaign cycle, see *www.heritage.org/issues/energy.*

SOCIAL SECURITY

Improving Retirement Income

David C. John

THE ISSUES

Despite increased public awareness of Social Security's problems, there is still a danger that campaigns will grandstand the issue, obscure facts, and distort the potential effects of various reform plans. Candidates should not be allowed to rely on fine-sounding but empty phrases to avoid addressing the real issues where critical decisions must be made. As Social Security reform is debated in this election cycle, it will be important to highlight the following issues:

1. **The low rate of return on Social Security is a problem as critical as the financial status of the trust fund.** Social Security has been a good deal for older workers, but the children and grandchildren of today's retirees will pay high taxes for fairly low benefits. Many younger workers, especially African–American males, will actually receive less in retirement benefits than they have paid in taxes. Raising taxes or cutting benefits may be proposed as quick fixes for the Social Security system, but both approaches would only make the program an even worse deal for these workers than it is now.

2. **The only effective way to make Social Security a better deal is to allow workers to invest a portion of their retirement taxes in personal retirement accounts.** Investing part of their taxes would allow workers to get more for their money. Any financial planner would say that retirement planning needs three elements—insurance against emergencies, an annuity that provides a stable income, and savings for retirement goals. Today's Social Security system provides insurance and a low annuity, but it does not include savings. Personal retirement accounts would both provide a better annuity and enable workers to build a retirement nest egg.

3. **Social Security reform must not reduce the benefits of current retirees and should provide an adequate minimum retirement income.** America's promise to those who have already retired must be honored. In addition, true reform of the system would allow Americans of all income levels to build a nest egg for the future. It should also guarantee an adequate minimum retirement income for all workers. Finally, it should provide today's workers with the option of participating in a Social Security system that incorporates personal retirement accounts or remaining within the existing system and accepting whatever benefits are available at the time that they retire.

4. **Social Security personal retirement accounts can be implemented with relatively low administrative costs and would raise retirement income.** Studies of personal retirement accounts show that they would allow younger workers to earn over twice the rate of return that they would receive from the existing system. The administrative costs that would be charged on these accounts could be as low as $3.50 to $6.75 a year.[1]

5. **The longer Washington waits to act, the harder and more expensive it will be to make Social Security a better deal for workers.** Every year of delay means a decrease in the Social Security surplus that could be used to fix the system. According to U.S. Comptroller General David Walker, the cost of keeping Social Security solvent in its present form will more than double by 2034.[2]

6. **International experience shows the value of a comprehensive system that allows workers to build a retirement nest egg through Social Security.** More than 20 countries—including Great Britain, Switzerland, and Sweden—already have social security programs that allow their workers to build wealth for their retirement. These programs combine a lifetime annuity with an insurance element and the ability to

---

1. State Street Corporation, "Administrative Challenges Confronting Social Security Reform," Boston, March 22, 1999.

2. David M. Walker, Comptroller General of the United States, "Social Security: What the President's Proposal Does and Does Not Do," testimony before the Committee on Finance, U.S. Senate, 106th Cong., 1st Sess., February 9, 1999.

invest. Workers in those countries not only have trillions of dollars in real assets, but also enjoy much more flexibility in planning for retirement. American workers would be better off with a more comprehensive Social Security system that included personal retirement accounts, which could stimulate savings and bring a greater return on pension investments.

THE FACTS

FACT: The current Social Security system is a very poor investment.

When one compares the amount of retirement taxes typical workers pay throughout their careers with the amount of retirement benefits they will receive, Social Security proves to be an extremely poor investment. Workers could accumulate far more for retirement if they were allowed to invest at least a portion of that money for themselves.

An average-income, 30-year-old two-earner couple earns only the equivalent of about 1.23 percent (after inflation) on their Social Security retirement taxes.[3] The same couple could earn a 5 percent rate of return by investing their taxes in a conservative portfolio of 50 percent super-safe U.S. Treasury bonds and 50 percent stock index funds. This is four times higher than the rate of return they currently receive; they could expect to have $975,000 by the time they retired—$525,000 more than the benefits they would receive from Social Security.

FACT: African–Americans have extremely poor rates of return, and many African–American males will receive less in benefits than they paid in Social Security payroll taxes.

Due to generally lower life expectancies, African–Americans experience particularly poor rates of return from Social Security. In fact, a single, low-income African–American male born after 1959 is likely to lose money in the current Social Security system. For example, a single African–American male in his mid-20s who earns about $13,000 a year would receive only about 88 cents in retirement benefits for every dollar that he pays in taxes. This

3. William W. Beach and Gareth G. Davis, "Social Security's Rate of Return," Heritage Foundation *Center for Data Analysis Report* No. CDA98–01, January 15, 1998, at *www.heritage.org/library/cda/cda98-01.html*.

equals a lifetime loss of about $13,400. African–American females typically live longer than their male counterparts, yet even they have a rate of return lower than that of the general population.

FACT: Today's Social Security taxes crowd out other savings.

The average American family now spends as much for Social Security taxes as they do for housing and nearly three times more than they do for annual health care expenses.[4] Because of rising payroll taxes for retirement, more poor and middle-income workers do not have the after-tax funds that would allow other savings. In 1972, the average worker (together with his or her employer) paid 8.1 percent of the first $9,000 of wages in Social Security retirement taxes. By 2002, this had increased to 10.6 percent of the first $84,900 of income.[5]

FACT: Social Security is the only retirement plan that many Americans now have.

Currently, about 8.2 million Americans over the age of 65 receive all of their retirement income from Social Security.[6] The program provides 90 percent or more of retirement income to almost 13.2 million people. In the future, nearly 30 million workers will retire with no other income than Social Security. Moreover, this problem is not restricted to low-income workers. A recent study showed that 20 percent of the workers in every income group (except the very highest) either had no net worth or owed more than they owned.[7]

---

4. U.S. Department of Labor, Bureau of Labor Statistics, *Consumer Expenditures in 1995*, June 1997, Table A. This report estimates average family income before taxes to be $36,918. Heritage Foundation analysts added $2,289 to reflect the additional compensation that the average worker would receive if the employer's share of Social Security was converted to wages.
5. Taxable threshold levels for 1972 and 2002. For 2002 information, see *www.ssa.gov/cola/cola2002.htm*. For earlier years, see *www.ssa.gov/history/reports/k2b.html*. To determine the tax rate for retirement and survivors insurance, subtract the amount designated for disability coverage (which is in parentheses next to the overall OASDI tax rate) from the aggregate figure.
6. Social Security Administration, *Fast Facts and Figures About Social Security*, June 2001.
7. Hal Varian, "For Too Many, Social Security Is Main Retirement Plan," *The New York Times*, December 20, 2001, p. C2.

FACT: Social Security is not a comprehensive retirement system and does not allow workers to build wealth.

Today's Social Security provides workers with both a retirement annuity and some insurance coverage. The annuity is in the form of a monthly retirement check for life, while the insurance aspect pays monthly benefits if a worker who dies has young children or a spouse who does not have retirement income. However, today's program does not allow workers to build wealth that could be used for important family goals during their working years. Workers cannot use Social Security to create a nest egg that could help to put a grandchild through college, purchase a retirement home, help start a family business, or increase their own retirement income.

FACT: Social Security is running out of money.

The ratio of workers (who pay into the system) to retirees (who receive benefits from the system) is rapidly declining. In 1950, 16 workers supported each Social Security recipient. Today, there are barely three workers per recipient, and by 2030, the ratio will fall to two workers per beneficiary.[8] The fact that life expectancy is increasing means that the burden on younger workers will be even greater. In 1935, the average 65-year-old was expected to live about 12.6 more years. Today, people who reach age 65 are expected to live more than 17 additional years. By 2040, they will be expected to live at least 19 more years.[9] As a result, Social Security will begin to run cash flow deficits by 2016, and all of its trust fund IOUs will be exhausted by 2038.[10] At that point, the program will be able to pay only about 75 percent of the benefits that it has promised.

FACT: There is no trust fund.

Some people incorrectly think that Social Security has an actual account in their name that contains cash or investments. In reality, the Social Security trust fund contains only IOUs. As an aging population grows, these IOUs can be redeemed only by imposing

8. Social Security Administration, 2001 *Annual Report of the Board of Trustees of the Federal Old-Age and Survivors Insurance and Disability Insurance Trust Funds* (Washington, D.C.: U.S. Government Printing Office, 2001).
9. Peter G. Peterson, *Gray Dawn* (New York: Random House, 1999).
10. Social Security Administration, 2001 *Annual Report of the Board of Trustees of the Federal Old-Age and Survivors Insurance and Disability Insurance Trust Funds.*

higher taxes on future workers.[11] The annual surpluses that many thought were being used to build up a reserve for baby boomer retirees have been spent on other government programs or used to reduce the federal debt. The Clinton Administration admitted the true nature of the trust fund, stating in its proposed budget for fiscal year 2000 that

> These [trust fund] balances are available to finance future benefit payments and other trust fund expenditures—but only in a bookkeeping sense. *These funds are not set up to be pension funds, like the funds of private pension plans. They do not consist of real economic assets that can be drawn down in the future to fund benefits.* Instead, they are claims on the Treasury, that, when redeemed, will have to be financed by raising taxes, borrowing from the public, or reducing benefits or other expenditures. *The existence of large trust fund balances, therefore, does not, by itself, make it easier for the government to pay benefits.*[12]

FACT: Workers would get higher benefits with personal retirement accounts.

Two federal studies show that workers would receive higher retirement benefits under a reformed system of Social Security that includes personal retirement accounts than they would under other types of reform. Contrary to the scare tactics of opponents who claim that personal retirement accounts are "risky," both the Congressional Research Service and the President's Commission to Strengthen Social Security have found that personal retirement accounts increase workers' retirement security.[13]

---

11. The formal name of the trust fund is the Old-Age, Survivors, and Disability Insurance (OASDI) trust fund. It contains two independent sub-trust funds: the Old-Age and Survivors Insurance (OASI) trust fund, which pays for retirement and survivors benefits, and the Disability Insurance (DI) trust fund, which pays for disability benefits. There is also a Health Insurance (HI) trust fund that pays for part of Medicare.
12. Office of Management and Budget, *Budget of the United States Government, Fiscal Year 2000, Analytical Perspectives*, p. 337 (emphasis added).

FACT: Neither government investment of money in the trust fund nor raising the income cap on payroll taxes would fix Social Security.

Experience at the state and local levels with public employee pension funds demonstrates that politicians and their appointees often are tempted to steer a government-controlled pot of money toward special interests, political allies, or corporate contributors.[14] Federal Reserve Board Chairman Alan Greenspan has testified that such investment strategies "would arguably put at risk the efficiency of our capital markets and thus, our economy."[15] This was one of the reasons that the U.S. Senate voted 99–0 against allowing the government to invest a portion of the Social Security trust funds in the stock market.[16]

Eliminating the cap on wages subject to Social Security payroll taxes will not solve the problem. Based on the Social Security Administration's own projections, eliminating the cap on wages would generate only enough revenue to delay the date of the system's insolvency by a few years. Moreover, by 2035, the program would have enough revenue on hand to pay only 87 cents on every promised dollar in benefits.[17]

---

13. Congressional Research Service, "Social Security: The Relationship of Taxes and Benefits for Past, Present, and Future Retirees," June 22, 2001. See also *Strengthening Social Security and Creating Personal Wealth for All Americans*, Final Report of the President's Commission to Strengthen Social Security, Washington, D.C., December 21, 2001, at *www.commtostrengthensocsec.gov/reports*.
14. For additional information, see Daniel J. Mitchell, "Why Government-Controlled Investment Would Undermine Retirement Security," Heritage Foundation *Backgrounder* No. 1248, February 5, 1999, at *www.heritage.org/library/backgrounder/bg1248.html*.
15. Alan Greenspan, testimony before the Committee on the Budget, U.S. Senate, 106th Congress, 1st Sess., January 29, 1999.
16. The Ashcroft amendment to S. Con. Res. 20, the concurrent resolution on the budget for FY 2000, was approved on March 24, 1999. Although it only expressed the opinion of the Senate and did not carry the force of law, not one Senator spoke in opposition.
17. D. Mark Wilson, "Removing Social Security's Tax Cap on Wages Would Do More Harm Than Good," Heritage Foundation *Center for Data Analysis Report* No. CDA01-07, October 17, 2001, at *www.heritage.org/library/cda/cda01-07.html*.

FACT: Many other countries have established some form of personal retirement account as part of their social security systems.

Over 20 countries throughout the world already allow workers to build assets through their social security systems. Ranging from Great Britain, Switzerland, and Sweden to Chile, Mexico, Kazakhstan, and Australia, these countries have begun to take effective action to address the problems of their social security systems. Even China has recently announced plans to establish personal retirement accounts. But the United States has yet to take any action.

Social Security Calculator: Simply enter your age and gender to calculate what an American worker of your same age and gender could expect to receive from Social Security. Access the calculator at *www.heritage.org/calculators.*

WHAT TO DO IN 2003

Create Social Security Part B, comprised of personal retirement accounts that workers would own and could use to build nest eggs for retirement.

The new Congress should move quickly to establish Social Security Part B, comprised of personal retirement accounts that would be funded with a portion of the taxes that workers now pay. If the money that goes into these accounts comes from any other source, the accounts will do nothing to improve an individual's Social Security rate of return. On the other hand, if Social Security Part B is funded from a portion of Social Security taxes that workers now pay, it will make the program a much better deal for most Americans, since its returns are anticipated to be higher than those of the conventional Social Security system.

Once the Part B accounts are created, the existing Social Security system would be designated as Social Security Part A. Workers would have the choice of either participating in Part B or remaining exclusively in Social Security Part A. Both parts would be funded by the same payroll taxes that a worker pays today, not by new taxes. Most of the payroll taxes would go into Part A, and the rest would go to fund a Part B account. Whereas today's benefits are paid entirely through Part A, future retirees' retirement benefits could be paid through a combination of Part A and Part B. This system could comfortably provide at least the same monthly Social Security retirement benefits that workers are currently promised, and most likely would provide more. Given the personal retirement accounts' anticipated returns, Congress could easily mandate that the sum of a worker's Part A and Part B benefits must equal or exceed what is promised under current law.

Part B accounts would be invested in a mixed portfolio of low-risk assets such as stock index funds and super-safe government bonds. This type of investment would allow workers to earn higher rates of return without requiring them to choose specific stocks or to guess which sectors of the economy are going to do best. It is possible to implement this type of investment with very low administrative costs.

Improve the information that workers receive about Social Security.

Congress should make the Social Security statement that the Social Security Administration sends to every taxpayer over the age of 25 more accurate and informative. The statement should be improved by adding accurate information about Social Security's financial crisis and the real nature of Social Security's trust funds—information without which American workers cannot plan adequately for retirement. In addition, the statement should include a chart that plots implicit rates of return by birth year. This chart would illustrate that the rate of return from Social Security has decreased both steadily and dramatically. Workers would see that, unless the current system is reformed, their rate of return on the taxes they have paid into the system will be lower than the rate that their parents and grandparents received.[18] More important, they would see that their children and grandchildren will receive even less from Social Security in the future.[19]

18. Workers can calculate this number for themselves by using The Heritage Foundation's Social Security Calculator, located at *www.heritage.org/socialsecurity*.

Grant existing retirees a written guarantee of their benefits.

Any real reform plan must guarantee in law that seniors will receive every cent that they have been promised, including an accurate annual cost-of-living increase. As a first step toward saving Social Security for future generations, Congress should pass a law giving every retired American a contract that provides a legal guarantee of his or her Social Security retirement benefits. This guarantee should be a legally binding property right to their Social Security retirement benefits. An explicit property right would change the nature of the relationship between the federal government and Social Security recipients to that of a contract that could not be broken or altered without the consent of both parties. Such a guarantee would give seniors peace of mind without making meaningful reform of the system more difficult or expensive.[20]

—David C. John is a Research Fellow at The Heritage Foundation.

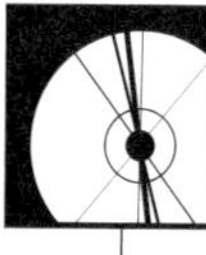

For a complete list and full-text versions of additional studies by Heritage on Social Security reform, see the searchable *Issues 2002* companion CD–ROM.

19. Legislation now before Congress would require that the statements include this information. Representatives Jim DeMint (R–SC) and John Sununu (R–NH), respectively, have introduced H.R. 634 and H.R. 930. In the Senate, Senators John McCain (R–AZ) and Rick Santorum (R–PA), respectively, have introduced S. 354 and S. 563.
20. Legislation now before Congress would establish such a property right. Senator Tim Hutchinson (R–AR) and Representative Walter Jones (R–NC), for example, have introduced the Social Security Benefits Guarantee Act (S. 806 and H.R. 832); Senator Santorum and Representative DeMint have introduced S. 1558 and H.R. 3135, which contain similar language.

EXPERTS

Heritage Foundation

David C. John
Research Fellow
The Heritage Foundation
214 Massachusetts Avenue, NE
Washington, DC 20002
(202) 608-6229
fax: (202) 544-5421
david.john@heritage.org

Stuart M. Butler, Ph.D.
Vice President, Domestic and Economic Policy Studies
The Heritage Foundation
214 Massachusetts Avenue, NE
Washington, DC 20002
(202) 608-6202
fax: (202) 544-5421
stuart.butler@heritage.org

William W. Beach
Director, Center for Data Analysis
John M. Olin Senior Fellow in Economics
The Heritage Foundation
214 Massachusetts Avenue, NE
Washington, DC 20002
(202) 608-6206
fax: (202) 544-5421
bill.beach@heritage.org

Robert E. Moffit, Ph.D.
Director, Domestic Policy Studies
The Heritage Foundation
214 Massachusetts Avenue, NE
Washington, DC 20002
(202) 608-6210
fax: (202) 544-5421
robert.moffit@heritage.org

Daniel J. Mitchell, Ph.D.
McKenna Senior Fellow in Political Economy
The Heritage Foundation
214 Massachusetts Avenue, NE
Washington DC 20002
(202) 608-6224
fax: (202) 544-5421
dan.mitchell@heritage.org

Other Experts

Theodore Abram
Executive Director
American Institute for Full Employment
P.O. Box 1329
Klamath Falls, OR 97601
(541) 273-6731
fax: (541) 885-7454
teda@jeld-wen.com

Louis Enoff
Enoff Associates Limited
103 Streaker Road
Sykesville, MD 21784
(410) 549-0455
fax: (410) 549-0460
Louenoff@erols.com

Stephen Entin
Executive Director
Institute for Research on the Economics of Taxation
1300 19th Street, NW, Suite 240
Washington, DC 20036
(202) 463-1400
fax: (202) 463-6199
iret_entin@ibm.net

Charles W. Jarvis
Chairman and Chief Executive
United Seniors Association
3900 Jermantown Road, Suite 450
Fairfax, VA 22030
(703) 359-6500
fax: (703) 359-6510
usa@unitedseniors.org

Thomas R. Saving
Director
Private Enterprise Research Center
Texas A&M University
3028 Academic Building W, 4231 TAMU
College Station, TX 77843-4231
(979) 845-7559
fax: (979) 845-6636
t-saving@tamu.edu

Sylvester J. Schieber, Ph.D.
Vice President and Director
Research and Information Center
Watson Wyatt & Company
6707 Democracy Boulevard
Suite 800
Bethesda, MD 20817
(301) 581-4600
fax: (301) 581-4752
syl_schieber@watsonwyatt.com

Bruce Schobel
New York Life Insurance Company
51 Madison Avenue, Suite 602
New York, NY 10010
(212) 576-6807
fax: (212) 576-7316
bdschobel@aol.com

C. Eugene Steuerle
Senior Fellow
Urban Institute
2100 M Street, NW
Washington, DC 20037
(202) 833-7200
fax: (202) 429-0687
esteuerl@ui.urban.org

Michael Tanner
Director of Health and Welfare Studies
Cato Institute
1000 Massachusetts Avenue, NW
Washington, DC 20001
(202) 842-0200
fax: (202) 842-3490
mtanner@cato.org

For continually updated and expanded information on major breaking developments on this issue over the campaign cycle, see *www.heritage.org/issues/socialsecurity.*

HEALTH CARE

Achieving Health Coverage for All Americans

Robert E. Moffit, Ph.D., and Nina Owcharenko

THE ISSUES

The outcome of the ongoing debate about health care will have a critical impact on millions of Americans. The opposing sides of the debate represent two conflicting philosophies. On one side are those who envision a system in which government officials make all of the key decisions for American families, including which services should be covered and their prices. On the other side are those who believe that individuals are best suited to make health care decisions for their families and who therefore promote a reformed system that incorporates patient choice and free-market competition.

Conservative candidates should make the case for patient choice and individual responsibility. They should promote policies that advance personal ownership and control over health plans and benefits and work to restore the traditional doctor–patient relationship. The urgency of the debate is highlighted by several key issues.

1. **Individuals and families are losing control over their key health care decisions.** The current legal and regulatory structure of employment-based insurance plans and public programs gives little or no choice to most Americans regarding the benefits they receive or their access to medical procedures. Instead, employers, insurers, and government officials are making these critical health care decisions for most families. Though many Americans are frustrated with the decisions that such third parties make for them, they cannot fire government bureaucrats or dump work-based insurance plans that are not meeting their needs. They are, practically speaking, powerless.

2. **The federal tax code discourages the individual purchase of health care coverage.** Americans today can receive unlimited tax relief for the purchase of health insurance if—and only if—they are covered by a plan through their workplace. Individuals who want or need to purchase their own insurance plans must use after-tax dollars, and this can increase the cost of coverage by as much as 40 percent.[1] Thus, for example, a restaurant worker with two children and working for the minimum wage gets no help to buy health insurance for her family, while the CEO of a *Fortune* 500 company gets thousands of dollars toward his coverage.

3. **Government mandates are pricing many families out of the market for health care insurance.** Government officials in the states often dictate the design of insurance plans through mandated benefits, including legal requirements for individuals and families to pay for alcohol and substance abuse coverage, chiropractic coverage, and even psychologists and the services of social workers, whether they want such services or not. Officials also impose often burdensome regulations on insurance plans. The result: The cost of health insurance has risen, pricing many families out of coverage. Individuals and families should be able to choose a plan that meets their unique medical and financial needs—needs that they, not politicians or regulators, can best identify.

4. **Faced with huge financial problems, Medicare and Medicaid are reducing the quality of care.** With the impending retirement of the baby-boom generation and with more and more lower-income families enrolled in public programs, neither Medicare nor Medicaid will be able to sustain skyrocketing costs and dependency. While structural reform is what is really needed, quick fixes have been proposed, such as cutting reimbursements to doctors and hospitals or limiting the availability of medical treatment and technology. The quality of care will suffer under such cost-containment measures.

---

1. Greg Scandlen, "Health Care Tax Credit Benefits," *The Washington Times*, December 13, 2001, p. A18.

THE FACTS

FACT: The federal tax code keeps most Americans from owning their health insurance policies.

Current tax policy allows individuals an unlimited tax exclusion on the cost of their coverage but only if they are covered through their employer. There is no corresponding tax break for coverage obtained outside the workplace. Individuals who want or need to purchase coverage on their own must do so with after-tax dollars. Current tax policy is unfair and makes choice unaffordable.

FACT: The employer-based health care system does not meet the needs of today's highly mobile workforce.

The current employer-sponsored health care system is a vestige of the past. While this 60-year-old system has continued to dominate, America's workforce has changed rapidly. Today, the average 32-year-old has changed jobs nine times.[2] Each job change has meant changing insurers and, often, changing doctors. This system prevents true portability and continuity of coverage.

FACT: Many Americans have been forced into health care plans that violate their privacy and values.

Many people have moral and religious objections to certain medical procedures but find their contributions paying for them within a health care plan that was not of their choosing. Many employees are also concerned with the access that employers and insurers have to their sensitive medical information. A person's medical history, including a genetic predisposition for cancer or treatment for mental illness, could be vulnerable to unauthorized disclosure.

FACT: Most of the uninsured are in working families.

It is estimated that over 80 percent of America's uninsured—currently 39 million and expected to increase—are working or living in households with someone who has a full-time job.[3] Many peo-

---

2. The Honorable Elaine L. Chao, U.S. Secretary of Labor, "Making America Work: Meeting the Challenges of the 21st Century Workforce," June 20, 2001, at *www.dol.gov/_sec/media/speeches/main.htm*.
3. Bowen Garrett, Len. M. Nichols, and Emily K. Greenman, "Workers Without Health Insurance: Who Are They and How Can Policy Reach Them?" Urban Institute, *Community Voices*, August 2001, p. 2, at *www.communityvoices.org/PDF/Workers-Without-Insurance.pdf*.

ple are uninsured because they chose not to participate in their employer's coverage or because their employer does not offer coverage.[4] Small businesses, in particular, often find group coverage too costly to provide for their employees.

FACT: Workers and their families bear the brunt of increased health care costs.

As the price of health care increases, families will bear the brunt of added expenses or suffer from decreased services. With premium increases in 2002 expected to be as high as 16 percent, many employers have already begun to make changes.[5] Within the past five years, 93 percent of *Fortune* 500 companies have reduced the number of plan options they offer to their employees.[6] Even further changes are expected in the near future, including the imposition of greater cost-sharing requirements and reductions in benefits and services. In a recent William M. Mercer survey, an estimated 17 percent of employers said they will raise deductibles, co-payments, or out-of-pocket maximums for employees.[7]

FACT: The combination of excessive state mandates for benefits and over-regulation limits affordable coverage options for families.

Nationwide, an estimated 1,403 state mandates require insurers to cover (and patients to pay for) a wide variety of specific conditions, services, or procedures—including such items as acupuncture, infertility treatments, and alternative therapies.[8] A study conducted for the Health Insurance Association of America con-

---

4. *Ibid*, p. 7.
5. "Double-Digit Health Care Cost Increases Expected to Continue in 2002," press release, Hewitt Associates, October 2001, at *www.hewitt.com/hewitt/resource/newsroom/pressrel/2001/10-29-01.htm*. Other surveys have reported similar figures. See, for example, "Health Care Costs 2002—A Watson Wyatt Worldwide Survey," at *www.wastonwyatt.com/us/research/reports.asp*.
6. Milt Freudenheim, "Fewer Choices for Workers on Benefits," *The New York Times*, November 9, 2001, p. C1.
7. "Accelerating Health Benefit Cost in 2000 Has Employers Bracing for Double-Digit Rise in 2001," news release on a William M. Mercer Survey, at *www.wmmercer.com/usa/english/resource/resource_news_topic_121200.htm*.
8. See Susan S. Laudicina *et al.*, *State Legislative Health Care and Insurance Issues: 2000 Survey of Plans* (Washington, D.C.: Blue Cross and Blue Shield Association, December 2000). Maryland leads the nation with 50 such benefit mandates, followed by California with 42.

cludes that as many as one in four uninsured Americans are without coverage because of the costs of these mandates.[9]

Congress has also pursued an aggressive regulatory approach to health care policy. In 1996, Congress enacted the Health Insurance Portability and Accountability Act[10] with the intent of improving access to the private market. In fact, the law and its regulatory provisions increased the overall cost of coverage for individuals and families.[11]

In response to growing patient frustration due to cost-cutting in employer-sponsored HMOs, many Members of Congress support the so-called patients' bill of rights legislation. However, rather than giving patients greater choice regarding their health care plans, this legislation would open up new avenues for litigation against health plans and greatly expand the reach and scope of federal regulation over virtually every major aspect of private health plan operations.[12] The Congressional Budget Office has calculated that the new mandates would raise premiums by up to 4.2 percent and cost $22 billion when fully implemented.[13] Using estimates from the Lewin Group, a major econometrics firm that models health policy changes, as many as 1.2 million individuals could lose their health care coverage.[14]

---

9. Gail A. Jensen and Michael Morrisey, *Mandated Benefit Laws and Employer Sponsored Health Insurance* (Washington, D.C.: Health Insurance Association of America, January 1999), p. i.
10. Public Law 104–191, at *http://thomas.loc.gov*.
11. "Making a Federal Case Out of Health Care: Five Years of HIPAA," A Cato Institute Health Policy Studies Conference, July 31, 2001, at *www.cato.org/events/hipaa/index.html*.
12. See John S. Hoff, "The Patients' Bill of Rights: A Prescription for Massive Federal Health Regulation," Heritage Foundation *Backgrounder* No. 1350, February 29, 2000, at *www.heritage.org/library/backgrounder/bg1350/html*.
13. "Letter to the Honorable Don Nickles Regarding the Estimated Ultimate Effect of S. 283 on Premiums for Employer-Sponsored Health Insurance," Congressional Budget Office Cost Estimate, April 2001, at *www.cbo.gov*.
14. The Lewin Group estimates that every 1 percent increase in premium results in an additional 300,000 uninsured Americans. See "Health Plan Liability: What You Need to Know," American Association of Health Plans, March 2001, p. 5. Other surveys conclude that as many as 15.4 million Americans could lose their health care coverage. See Hoff, "The Patients' Bill of Rights: A Prescription for Massive Health Regulation," p. 2.

FACT: The individual health insurance market can offer affordable coverage options, and even a modest tax credit would encourage uninsured families to purchase coverage.

A 2002 health insurance analysis, which sampled a large number of products sold in the individual market, found that more than two-thirds of all plans purchased included modest deductibles and "comprehensive" coverage, with average premiums at $159 per person per month for individuals and $110 per person per month for families.[15] In addition, recent research by Professor Mark Pauly and his colleagues at the University of Pennsylvania shows that even with a modest tax credit of $1,000, as many as 85 percent of the uninsured would buy coverage in the individual market.[16]

FACT: Exploding Medicaid costs are forcing states to ration care.

For fiscal year 2001, 37 states reported spending that exceeded their Medicaid budgets.[17] To regain control of this ballooning state and federal health care program, states are recommending reducing benefits, cutting enrollment, and limiting reimbursements, which will result in a reduction in the quality of care and services.[18] Last year, 42 states had already proposed legislative measures to contain the costs of Medicaid.[19] This program is spiraling out of control, and congressional efforts to expand its eligible population are both shortsighted and ill-advised.

---

15. Vip Patel, "Health Care Coverage for Uninsured Americans," testimony before Committee on Ways and Means, U.S. House of Representatives, February 13, 2002. "Comprehensive" defined as a health insurance plan with benefits including inpatient services, outpatient services, lab and test services, and in most policies, prescription drugs.
16. A policy with a $1,000 deductible and a 20 percent co-insurance and a $2,000 limit on out-of-pocket spending. See Mark Pauly, Bradley Herring, David Song, "Tax Credits, the Distribution of Subsidized Health Insurance Premiums, and the Uninsured," National Bureau of Economic Research, September 2001, at *www/papers.nber.org/papers/w8457*.
17. Vernon Smith, Ph.D., and Eileen Ellis, *Medicaid Budgets Under Stress: Survey Findings for State Fiscal Year 2000, 2001, and 2002*, Kaiser Commission on Medicaid and the Uninsured, October 2001.
18. Robert Gavin, "States Look to Ration Health Care," *The Wall Street Journal*, November 14, 2001, B8.
19. National Association of State Budget Officers, *The Fiscal Survey of States*, June 2001, at *www.nasbo.org/Publications/PDFs/FSJUN2001.pdf*.

FACT: Medicare is a bureaucratic nightmare.

Based on the principles of central planning and price regulation, Medicare is governed by well over 111,000 pages of rules, regulations, guidelines, and related paperwork, and that red tape is growing. The Medicare bureaucracy and its contractors control virtually every aspect of the financing and delivery of medical care to approximately 40 million beneficiaries. The result is a complex, cumbersome, and sluggish system that shortchanges patient care. A recent survey of physicians conducted by the American Medical Association found that more than one-third of responding doctors spend an hour completing Medicare paperwork for every four hours of patient care.[20] Another recent study found that for every hour of care delivered to a Medicare patient in an American hospital, hospital officials spend roughly a half hour, and sometimes even an hour, complying with Medicare paperwork. [21] It is estimated that Medicare's bureaucratic procedures have resulted in delays ranging from 15 months to over five years in bringing new medical technologies to Medicare patients.[22]

FACT: The coming retirement of the baby boomers will bankrupt Medicare.

It is projected that overall Medicare spending will more than double from an estimated $238 billion in 2001 to $503 billion in 2011.[23] At that time, the first big wave of the huge baby-boom generation will start retiring, resulting in a sharp increase in demand for medical services, including highly advanced medical technology, while the cohort paying for those services grows relatively smaller. The number of Americans aged 65 years and older

---

20. Statement of Richard F. Corlin, M.D., President-Elect, American Medical Association, on "Medicare Reform: Bringing Regulatory Relief to Beneficiaries," hearing before the Subcommittee on Health, Committee on Ways and Means, U.S. House of Representatives, 107th Cong. 1st sess., March 15, 2001, p. 12.
21. *Patients or Paperwork? The Regulatory Burden Facing America's Hospitals*, a report by PricewatershouseCoopers for the American Hospital Association (Washington, D.C.: American Hospital Association, 2001), p. 2.
22. Advanced Medical Technology Association, "Medicare Overview; Improving Patient Access to Innovative Medical Technology," briefing paper, 2000. Congress has attempted to improve patient access to medical technology with enactment of the Benefits Improvement and Protection Act of 2000.
23. Congressional Budget Office, *The Budget and Economic Outlook: An Update*, August 2001, p. 12.

will increase from roughly 36 million today to 69 million in 2030—an increase of 90 percent. During that same period, the number of working-age Americans will increase by only 15 percent.[24] These new and unfavorable 21st century demographics will impose unprecedented pressures on a program that has remained structurally unchanged since the 1960s.

WHAT TO DO IN 2003

Congress should implement market-based reforms that encourage individual ownership, portability, and personal responsibility by taking the following steps.

Reform tax policies regarding health insurance.

Replace the existing system of tax breaks for health insurance and health care, such as the tax-exempt status of health benefits through the workplace, with a national system of refundable tax credits. The system would ensure that every American family receives a generous tax credit that can be used to offset the cost of coverage of their choice, whether it is a managed care-style plan or a medical savings account. This would make individuals and families the key decision-makers in the health care system and would transform the distorted health insurance market into a real market in which costs are determined by supply and demand, just as they are for every other service, good, or commodity in the American economy.[25]

If comprehensive reform is not achieved, Congress and the Administration should at least design a refundable tax credit that would help low-income, uninsured individuals and families to purchase private coverage.

A refundable, "advanceable" tax credit would provide direct assistance to individuals and families to obtain private health

---

24. Dan L. Crippen, Director, Congressional Budget Office, "Social Security: The Challenges of an Aging Population," testimony before the Special Committee on Aging, U.S. Senate, 107th Cong., 1st Sess., December 10, 2001, p. 3.
25. The Heritage Foundation has developed such a universal tax credit proposal. For an updated version of the Heritage approach, see Stuart M. Butler, "Reforming the Tax Treatment of Health Care to Achieve Universal Coverage," in Jack A. Meyer and Elliott K. Wicks, eds., *Covering America: Real Remedies for The Uninsured* (Washington, D.C.: Economic and Social Research Institute, 2001), pp. 21–42.

care coverage. Low-income families, many of whom are on limited budgets and/or do not have a tax liability, would be able to receive this health credit "up front" from the U.S Treasury for the exclusive purpose of assisting them in purchasing private health care coverage. An individual would assign this credit directly to an insurance plan of choice. This would give a convenience store cashier, whose employer does not offer coverage, real-dollar assistance to purchase insurance on his own. This health credit could be further supplemented by employer contributions or special assistance from the states. Such an approach to meet the needs of uninsured Americans has received support from the House, the Senate, and President Bush.[26] A refundable tax credit system could also help unemployed workers maintain health care coverage and could easily be administered through the unemployment compensation system.

Give equal support to associations, organizations, and employers to sponsor health care coverage.

Current federal and state laws, which favor group coverage through the place of work, should permit large organizations with a national membership to sponsor health care coverage. Organizations such as religious institutions, fraternal and service organizations, trade and professional associations, and even university alumni associations would also be able to offer health care coverage to their members without facing excessive tax or regulatory penalty. Employees who have serious ethical, moral, or religious conflicts with their employer's coverage of certain treatments or procedures would be able to choose coverage that is more compatible with their personal convictions and values. If a person thinks that an association plan would better meet his personal health needs, he should be able to take advantage of it. Legislation in this area has already been considered by the House of Representatives.[27]

---

26. Proposals in the 107th Congress include S. 590, introduced by Senator Jim Jeffords (I–VT); H.R. 1331/S. 683, introduced in the House by Representatives Richard Armey (R–TX) and William Lipinski (D–IL) and in the Senate by Senators Richard Santorum (R–PA) and Robert Torricelli (D–NJ); and H.R. 2250, introduced by Representative John Cooksey (R–LA). For further information, see *http://thomas.loc.gov*.

Encourage states to roll back excessive mandates and regulations on health plans and replace them with requirements for basic categories of benefits.

Instead of micromanaging what health plans cover with excessive mandates and increasingly detailed regulations, government officials should simply ensure that all health plans meet basic consumer protection and fiscal solvency rules. Requirements for benefits would be limited to basic categories, such as catastrophic protection, hospitalization, and physician services. This would get government officials out of the business of trying to dictate specific benefits and medical procedures, which has only increased costs and failed to meet the unique needs of individuals and families. For example, a person who is battling chronic depression would be free to choose a plan with more generous mental health services rather than being tied to a plan that focuses on pediatric benefits or sports medicine. A model for such categorical coverage already exists in the Federal Employees Health Benefits Program (FEHBP), which provides flexible health coverage to federal workers, retirees, and their families—including Members of Congress.

Allow employers to convert defined benefit plans into defined contribution plans for their employees more easily.

Employers should have the flexibility to offer their employees a financial contribution, in lieu of traditional group coverage, to assist them in purchasing health care coverage on their own. Such a system of employer contributions now exists in 401(k) plans, but current law does not recognize this type of assistance for health insurance. This should be changed. A gas station owner who cannot afford a conventional, heavily mandated, and regulated group policy for his employees would then be able to offer them a monthly pre-tax contribution to help them buy health coverage, and allow both to receive tax-preferred benefits.[28]

---

27. H.R. 1774, introduced by Representative Ernest Fletcher (R–KY), was included in a comprehensive managed care reform proposal (H.R. 2315) that included both patients' bill of rights provisions and access provisions. See *http://thomas.loc.gov*.

28. For a comprehensive approach to promoting defined contribution, see H.R. 2658, introduced by Representative Jim DeMint (R–SC). See *http://thomas.loc.gov*.

Permit flexible saving account (FSA) rollovers.

Currently, FSA accounts allow employees to set aside a portion of their pre-tax salary for medical expenses, but these accounts are limited by a "use-it-or-lose-it" rule. If an employee does not use the money in this fund by the end of the year, it reverts to the employer. Ending this outdated rollover prohibition would encourage individuals to be more prudent users of health care services, eliminating an end-of-the-year rush to spend. Instead of wasting the remaining amount in his account on a third pair of driving glasses, an employee could save this money for unexpected medical expenses the following year. Legislation to end these restrictions has been introduced in the 107th Congress.[29]

Remove regulatory restrictions on medical savings accounts (MSAs).

Medical savings accounts were created to enable individuals and families to set aside funds to pay doctors and other health care providers and keep the remainder of these savings without a tax penalty. Most MSA plans combine a high-deductible insurance plan with a tax-free savings account for uncovered health care expenditures. The flexibility and efficiency of this system was undermined by the 1996 Health Insurance Portability and Accountability Act, which imposed numerous restrictions and limitations on the use of MSA funds. For example, the bill restricted availability by employer size and the number of policies sold. It also limited joint employer-employee contributions and imposed restrictive caps on contributions. Americans should have more control over their health care expenditures and greater freedom to choose the type of coverage that best fits their needs. For example, younger workers, who have little disposable income and are typically in good health, may find a high-deductible/low-monthly-premium MSA plan more affordable than a "Cadillac " policy with high monthly payments. In 2001 and 2002, President George W. Bush proposed removing the current regulatory restrictions,[30] and there is strong congressional interest in following suit.[31]

29. In the 107th Congress, Representative Ed Royce (R–CA) introduced H.R. 167, a bill providing for a rollover of flexible spending accounts. See *http://thomas.loc.gov*.

Encourage states to restructure their Medicaid and SCHIP programs to incorporate private health coverage.

By using the new HIFA (Health Insurance Flexibility Accountability) waiver launched by the Centers for Medicare and Medicaid Services (CMS), states will be able to provide assistance for private health insurance to some of their Medicaid, SCHIP (State Children's Health Insurance Program), and uninsured populations.[32] For example, a state could add additional premium subsidies to the federal tax credits provided for the uninsured. This would allow low-income families who might otherwise be limited to minimum-level Medicaid benefits to have access to private insurance and higher quality health care services.

Provide welfare-to-work families with financial assistance to purchase private health care coverage.

In lieu of expanding eligibility for Medicaid or SCHIP programs, states could provide individuals who are entering the workforce with financial assistance (similar to refundable tax credits or premium subsidies) that would enable them to purchase private health care coverage from a variety of sources. For example, as a single mother works to make the transition from welfare to the workforce, a premium subsidy for health insurance would free her from reliance on the poorly performing and financially troubled Medicaid program, and allow her and her family to obtain superior private health care coverage as enjoyed by her coworkers.

---

30. Executive Office of the President, The White House, "The President's Proposal for Health Security in the World's Best Health Care System," February 10, 2002, at *www.whitehouse.gov/infocus/medicare/health-care/health-accts.html.*

31. See, for example, H.R. 1524, introduced by Representative Williams Thomas (R–CA). This bill was included in a comprehensive access package passed by the House. Senator Charles Grassley (R–IA) introduced similar legislation (S. 1067). For further information, see *http://thomas.loc.gov.*

32. "HHS to Give States New Options for Expanding Health Coverage," press release, Centers for Medicare and Medicaid Services, August 4, 2001, *www.hhs.gov/news/press/2001pres/20010804.html.*

Reform Medicare to incorporate patient choice and market competition, as the Federal Employees Health Benefits Program does.

Congress and the Administration must get serious about reforming Medicare, which is weighed down by old bureaucratic structures created in the 1960s and tangled in red tape and paperwork. A reformed system should follow the 1999 majority recommendations of the National Bipartisan Commission on the Future of Medicare and should be based on the model provided by the Federal Employees Health Benefits Program, the patient-driven system that provides coverage for approximately 9 million federal workers and retirees—including Members of Congress—and their families. In sharp contrast with Medicare, the FEHBP has far fewer regulatory burdens and provides solid catastrophic coverage to its recipients through numerous competitive private plans which cover between 80 percent and 90 percent of the costs of prescription drugs, making it unnecessary for them to purchase supplemental health insurance coverage.

—Robert E. Moffit, Ph.D., is Director of Domestic Policy Studies and Nina Owcharenko is Policy Analyst for Health Care at The Heritage Foundation.

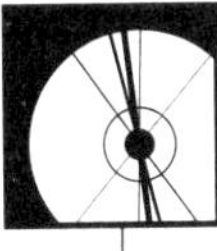

For a complete list and full-text versions of additional studies by Heritage on health care reform, see the searchable *Issues 2002* companion CD–ROM.

EXPERTS

Heritage Foundation

Nina Owcharenko
Health Care Policy Analyst
The Heritage Foundation
214 Massachusetts Avenue, NE
Washington, DC 20002
(202) 608-6221
fax: (202) 544-5421
nina.owcharenko@heritage.org

Robert E. Moffit, Ph.D.
Director of Domestic Policy Studies
The Heritage Foundation
214 Massachusetts Avenue, NE
Washington, DC 20002
(202) 608-6210
fax: (202) 544-5421
robert.moffit@heritage.org

Stuart M. Butler, Ph.D.
Vice President, Domestic and Economic Policy Studies
The Heritage Foundation
214 Massachusetts Avenue, NE
Washington, DC 20002
(202) 608-6200
fax: (202) 544-5421
stuart.butler@heritage.org

Other Experts

Joseph R. Antos
Resident Scholar
American Enterprise Institute
1150 17th Street, NW
Washington, DC 20036
(202) 862-5800
fax: (202) 862-7177
janotos@aei.org

John Goodman, Ph.D.
President
National Center for Policy Analysis
12655 North Central Expressway, Suite 720
Dallas, TX 75243
(972) 386-6272
fax: (972) 386-0924

Edmund F. Haislmaier
President
Strategic Policy Management
777 North Capitol Street, NE, Suite 803
Washington DC 20002
(202) 408-0620
fax: (202) 408-0621
ed@haislmaier.com

Robert B. Helms, Ph.D.
Resident Scholar
Director, Health Policy Studies
American Enterprise Institute
1150 17th Street, NW
Washington, DC 20036
(202) 862-5800
fax: (202) 862-7177
rhelms@aei.org

Daniel H. Johnson, Jr., M.D.
Former President, American Medical Association
Clearview Medical Imaging
3100 Clearview Parkway
Metairie, LA 70006
(504) 885 4223
fax: (504) 887 6620
stormyj@aol.com

Sandra Mahkorn, M.D., M.P.H., M.S.
3050 South Superior
Milwaukee, WI 53207
(414) 482-0225
fax: (414) 482-9896
smahkorn@prodigy.net

Greg Scandlen
Senior Fellow in Health Policy
National Center for Policy Analysis
7688 McKaig Road
Frederick, MD 21701
(301) 898-1700
fax: (301) 898-4646
GMScan@aol.com

Michael Tanner
Director of Health and Welfare Studies
Cato Institute
1000 Massachusetts Avenue, NW
Washington, DC 20001
(202) 842-0200
fax: (202) 842-3490
mtanner@cato.org

Grace-Marie Turner
President
Galen Institute
P.O. Box 19080
Alexandria, VA 22320-0080
(703) 299-8900
fax: (703) 299-0721
gracemarie@galen.org

Gail Wilensky, Ph.D.
Senior Fellow
Project Hope
7500 Old Georgetown Road
Suite 600
Bethesda, MD 20814
(301) 656-7401
fax: (301) 654-0629
gwilensky@projecthope.org

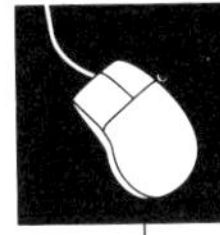

For continually updated and expanded information on major breaking developments on this issue over the campaign cycle, see *www.heritage.org/issues/healthcare*.

WELFARE REFORM

Requiring Work and Rebuilding Marriage

Robert Rector

THE ISSUES

Even with the historic reform of welfare in 1996, the welfare system is expensive and growing. In the more than 30 years since President Lyndon Johnson launched the War on Poverty, the nation has spent $8.29 billion (in constant 2000 dollars) on means-tested assistance: food, housing, medical care, and social services for poor and low-income Americans. Welfare spending dwarfs many other government expenditures. In recent years, for example, the nation has spent $1.45 on means-tested welfare for every $1.00 spent on national defense.

Despite such prolific spending, throughout most of the period since the beginning of the War on Poverty, most social problems have grown worse, not better. More needs to be done to strengthen the reforms of the past five years.

1. **In 1996, Congress successfully reformed part of the welfare system to build self-sufficiency.** The conventional welfare system rewarded non-work and non-marriage. By promoting dependence and illegitimacy, it increased poverty, crime, and a host of social ills. In 1996, Congress partially changed the direction that welfare assistance takes by replacing the failed Aid to Families with Dependent Children (AFDC) with a new program, Temporary Assistance to Needy Families (TANF). Under TANF, many recipients are required to work or engage in constructive activities that lead to self-sufficiency as a condition of getting aid. The result: Child poverty and dependence have plummeted, and employment among single mothers has skyrocketed.

2. **Welfare reform remains incomplete.** Despite this success, even the work-related aspects of welfare reform are incomplete. Half of the 2 million adults in TANF are idle on the rolls, merely collecting welfare and not engaging in work or other constructive activities. Moreover, there are no meaningful work requirements in closely related programs, such as food stamps and public housing.

3. **Welfare continues to subsidize illegitimacy and penalize marriage.** Today, one child in three is born out of wedlock. Not surprisingly, the welfare system for families is overwhelmingly a subsidy system for single parents. Some 75 percent of the aid to children in programs such as public housing, food stamps, TANF, and the Earned Income Tax Credit (EITC) goes to single-parent homes. Last year, the nation spent $150 billion in means-tested aid to single-parent families. Overall, the government spends $1,000 subsidizing single parents for every $1 it spends trying to reduce illegitimacy and increase marriage.

4. **The erosion of marriage is the predominant cause of child poverty and welfare dependence and a major factor in America's crime problem.** The absence of marriage and fathers in the home has a strong negative impact on almost all aspects of child development. Children from single-parent families are three times more likely to engage in criminal activity. Congress, in recognizing these facts, established in the 1996 welfare reform act two basic national goals: to reduce illegitimacy and to restore marriage. Since then, the states have received nearly $100 billion in federal TANF dollars. Despite the existence of many promising experimental pro-marriage programs (mainly in the private sector), state welfare bureaucracies have failed to implement any significant pro-marriage agenda. As a consequence, the nation continues to run a welfare system that actively penalizes rather than promotes marriage, with devastating social consequences.

THE FACTS

FACT: The federal welfare system is enormous and growing.

The federal government runs over 70 major means-tested aid programs to assist poor and low-income people.[1] These programs provide cash, food, housing, medical care, and social services.

- The total cost of means-tested aid, including both federal and state aid, in fiscal year (FY) 2000 was $434 billion,[2] or about $5,600 for each taxpaying household in the nation.
- As a nation, we spend 10 times as much on welfare today, after adjusting for inflation, as was spent when the War on Poverty began. We spend twice as much as when Ronald Reagan was first elected President.

FACT: There is little material poverty in the United States as the public generally understands the term.

Advocates of the welfare state often urge large expansions of welfare spending to combat widespread poverty in America. Allegedly widespread poverty is a legitimate concern; however, to the average American, saying someone is poor implies that he is malnourished, poorly clothed, and living in dilapidated, overcrowded housing. In reality, there is little material poverty in the United States as the public generally understands that term.[3]

- Today, the typical American defined as poor today by the government not only has a refrigerator, a stove, and a clothes washer, but also has a car, air conditioning in his home, a microwave, a color TV, a VCR, and a stereo. His home is in good repair and is not over-crowded. He is able to obtain medical care. By his own report, his family is not hungry, and

---

1. Means-tested programs are designed explicitly to assist poor and low-income Americans; they restrict eligibility for benefits to those with non-welfare income below a certain level. Thus, food stamps, TANF benefits, and Medicaid are means-tested and constitute welfare, but Social Security and Medicare benefits are not. Slightly over half of all means-tested aid is medical care.
2. Robert Rector, "The Size and Scope of Means-Tested Welfare Spending," testimony before the Committee on the Budget, U.S. House of Representatives, 107th Cong., 1st Sess., August 1, 2001.
3. For a detailed explanation, see Robert E. Rector, Kirk Johnson, Ph.D., and Sarah E. Youssef, "The Extent of Material Hardship and Poverty in the United States," *Review of Social Economy*, September 1999, pp. 351–387.

in the past year, he had sufficient funds to meet his essential needs.

While this individual's life is not opulent, it is equally far from the popular images of poverty conveyed by politicians, the press, and activists.

FACT: Rather than being materially poor, America's "poor" suffer from the effects of behavioral poverty, which has been heavily subsidized by the welfare state.

The term "behavioral poverty" refers to a breakdown in the values and conduct that lead to the formation of healthy families, stable personalities, and self-sufficiency. Behavioral poverty incorporates a cluster of severe social pathologies, including eroded work ethic and dependency, lack of educational aspiration and achievement, inability or unwillingness to control one's children, increased single parenthood and illegitimacy, criminal activity, and drug and alcohol abuse. Although material poverty may be rare in the United States, behavioral poverty, which is closely linked to underclass culture, is abundant. The core dilemma of the traditional welfare state is that prolific spending intended to alleviate material poverty has led to a dramatic increase in behavioral poverty.

FACT: The traditional welfare state rewarded non-work and non-marriage.

The anti-marriage and anti-work effects of welfare are simple and profound. The system created during the War on Poverty may best be conceptualized as one that offered each single mother with two children a "paycheck" of combined benefits worth an average of between $8,500 and $15,000, depending on the state.[4] The mother had a contract with the government: She would continue to receive her "paycheck" as long as she fulfilled two conditions: She must not work, and she must not marry an employed male.

Thus, the conventional liberal welfare system provided heavy incentives for individuals to work less or to leave the labor force entirely and to rely on the taxpayers for support. Even worse, it made marriage economically irrational for most low-income par-

---

4. This sum equals the value of welfare benefits from different programs for the average mother on AFDC.

ents; it converted the low-income working husband from a necessary breadwinner into a net financial handicap and transformed marriage from a legal institution designed to protect and nurture children into an institution that financially penalized nearly all low-income parents who entered into it.

FACT: Conventional welfare erodes the work ethic and rewards dependence.

For a large number of poor Americans, the existence of generous welfare programs has made not working a reasonable alternative to long-term employment. A number of studies have demonstrated the effects of welfare in eroding the work ethic. Most notable is the Seattle–Denver Income Maintenance Experiment (SIME–DIME), a federally funded, tightly controlled scientific evaluation of the effect of welfare on work.[5]

- The SIME–DIME study found that each $1.00 of extra welfare given to low-income persons reduced labor and earnings by an average of $0.80.[6] Thus, it showed that while conventional welfare was relatively ineffective in increasing income, it was very effective in reducing work effort. The result was long-term dependence under the traditional welfare system in which millions of single mothers remained on the rolls for a decade or longer.[7]

FACT: Welfare dependence and eroded work ethic harm children and society.

Welfare dependence, in turn, is harmful to children's development. Research shows that children on welfare do poorly when compared with children from poor families that are not on welfare. Children from welfare-dependent families tend to have lower levels of cognitive development and are more likely to drop out of school. Welfare dependence has serious long-term negative

---

5. See SRI International, *Final Report of the Seattle–Denver Income Maintenance Experiment, Vol. 1: Design and Results* (Washington, D.C.: SRI International, May 1983).
6. Gregory B. Christiansen and Walter E. Williams, "Welfare Family Cohesiveness and Out of Wedlock Births," in Joseph Peden and Fred Glahe, *The American Family and the State* (San Francisco: Pacific Institute for Public Policy Research, 1986), p. 398.
7. *1993 Green Book: Background Materials and Data on Programs Within the Jurisdiction of the Committee on Ways and Means*, Committee on Ways and Means, U.S. House of Representatives, 103rd Cong., 1st Sess., 1993, p. 714.

effects; the longer a child stays on welfare, the lower will be his or her earnings as an adult.[8]

FACT: Welfare has increased out-of-wedlock childbearing and single parenthood.

When the War on Poverty began in the mid-1960s, some 7 percent of all children were born out of wedlock. Today, the number is 33 percent. A substantial portion of that increase is due to the harmful effects of welfare.

Scientific research confirms that welfare benefits to single mothers contribute directly to the rise in illegitimate births.[9]

- A study of black Americans by Mark Fossett and Jill Kiecolt finds that higher welfare benefits lead to lower rates of marriage and greater numbers of children living in single-parent homes. In general, an increase of roughly $100 in the average monthly AFDC benefit per recipient child was found to lead to a drop of more than 15 percent in births within wedlock among black women ages 20 to 24.[10]
- Research by former Congressional Budget Office Director June O'Neill shows that, holding constant a wide range of other variables such as income, parental education, and urban and neighborhood setting, a 50 percent increase in the monthly value of welfare benefits leads to a 43 percent increase in out-of-wedlock births.[11]

---

8. For more detailed information, see Robert Rector, "Welfare: Broadening the Reform," in Stuart M. Butler and Kim R. Holmes, eds., *Issues 2000: The Candidate's Briefing Book*, (Washington, D.C.: The Heritage Foundation, 2000), pp. 294–296, at *www.heritage.org/issues/chap8.html*.
9. For a summary of studies on the effects of welfare on illegitimacy, see Robert Rector and Patrick F. Fagan, "How Welfare Harms Kids," Heritage Foundation *Backgrounder* No. 1084, June 5, 1996, at *www.heritage.org/library/backgrounder/bg1084.html*.
10. Mark A. Fossett and K. Jill Kiecolt, "Mate Availability and Family Structure Among African Americans in U.S. Metropolitan Areas," *Journal of Marriage and Family*, Vol. 55 (May 1993), pp. 288–302.
11. M. Anne Hill and June O'Neill, *Underclass Behaviors in the United States: Measurement and Analysis of Determinants* (New York: City University of New York, Baruch College, August 1993); research funded by U.S. Department of Health and Human Services Grant No. 88ASPE201A.

FACT: Illegitimacy and single parenthood harm children and society.

The collapse of marriage is the principal cause of child poverty in the United States.[12] Virtually all social and psychological problems are intensified by the absence of a father in the home.

- A child born out of wedlock and raised by a never-married mother is seven times more likely to live in poverty and 17 times more likely to be dependent on welfare than is a child raised by an intact married couple.
- Compared with children in intact two-parent families, children from single-parent families are three times more likely to engage in criminal activity, far more likely to suffer from emotional and behavioral problems and serious physical abuse, and more likely to fail and drop out of school.
- Children from single-parent homes are themselves more likely to engage in early sexual activity and have children outside marriage, perpetuating the tangle of social pathology.

FACT: Congress's 1996 welfare reform in many ways has been a remarkable success, dramatically increasing employment and decreasing child poverty.

When Congress replaced the failed AFDC program with TANF, national "work requirements" were imposed for the first time, mandating that recipients engage in constructive activities that lead to self-sufficiency in exchange for benefits. Such activities might include community service work, training, or a supervised job search. The law also required states to reduce dependence by reducing welfare caseloads. In many respects, the reform has been a success.[13]

- AFDC/TANF caseloads have been cut in half. The employment rate of disadvantaged single mothers has increased 50 percent to 100 percent. And while opponents of reform claimed that the new law (even in good economic conditions) would throw an extra million children into poverty, there are

---

12. Patrick F. Fagan and Robert Rector, "The Effects of Divorce on America," Heritage Foundation *Backgrounder* No. 1373, June 5, 2000, at *www.heritage.org/library/backgrounder/bg1373.html*.
13. Robert Rector and Patrick F. Fagan, "The Good News About Welfare Reform," Heritage Foundation *Backgrounder* No. 1468, September 5, 2001, at *www.heritage.org/library/backgrounder/bg1468.html*.

2.3 million fewer children in poverty today than there were in 1996.

- The poverty rates of both black children and children of single mothers have been cut by one-third and are now at the lowest points in U.S. history.

Some would argue that the drop in welfare caseloads is the product of the robust economy in the 1990s rather than the result of welfare reform. However, the evidence to support an economic interpretation of these changes is very weak. There were eight periods of economic expansion from 1950 to the early 1990s, yet none of these periods of growth led to a significant drop in AFDC caseloads. Only during the economic expansion of the 1990s did the caseload drop appreciably. Why was the expansion of the 1990s different from the eight prior expansions? Clearly, the answer is welfare reform.

Another way to disentangle the effects of welfare policies and economic factors on declining caseloads is to examine the differences in state performance. The rate of caseload decline varies enormously among the 50 states. If economic conditions are the main factor driving down caseloads, the variation in state reduction rates should be linked to variation in state economic conditions. On the other hand, if welfare polices are the key factors behind falling dependence, the differences in reduction rates should be linked to specific state welfare policies. Analysis shows that state workfare policies were the clear determining factor in explaining rapid rates of caseload decline. By contrast, the relative vigor of state economies had no statistically significant effect on caseload decline.[14]

A recent paper by Dr. June O'Neill, former Director of the Congressional Budget Office, examines changes in welfare caseload and employment of single mothers from 1983 to 1999. Her analysis shows that in the period after the enactment of welfare reform, policy changes accounted for roughly 75 percent of the increase in employment and decrease in dependence. By contrast, economic conditions explained only about 25 percent of the changes

---

14. Robert E. Rector and Sarah E. Youssef, "The Determinants of Welfare Caseload Decline," Heritage Foundation *Center for Data Analysis Report* No. CDA99–04, May 11, 1999, at *www.heritage.org/library/cda/cda99-04/html*.

in employment and dependence.[15] Substantial employment increases, in turn, led to large drops in child poverty.

FACT: Time limits on welfare assistance are largely irrelevant to the success of reform.

The fact that the TANF law created five-year time limits on the receipt of aid has received much attention; but while these time limits were an important public symbol, they have had little practical consequence. Very few recipients have reached the time limits. Instead, the improvements in employment and reductions in dependence and poverty were caused by the law's less publicized—but far more effective—work requirements.

FACT: Welfare reform is not "devolution."

The federal government currently pays for 72 percent of the $434 billion cost of the means-tested welfare state. Liberal state welfare bureaucrats urge "devolution" of welfare, meaning not that the states should pay for welfare, but that the federal government should collect the taxes for welfare and then hand all the funds collected over to the states without attaching meaningful principles or requirements for spending them. This type of "devolution" has always been a failure.[16] The 1996 welfare reform was not devolution in this sense. The TANF law imposed work requirements and performance standards that were far more stringent than anything in pre-reform law. Improving the reform will mean tightening, not loosening, those federal standards.

FACT: Despite its successes, welfare reform has been quite limited and incomplete.

Only one federal welfare program—AFDC—was reformed in 1996. The other 69 major means-tested programs, including food stamps, housing, and Medicaid, were left largely unchanged. In addition, not all TANF recipients are required to engage in constructive activity. In fact, of the 2 million adults currently on TANF rolls, roughly half are completely idle. Moreover, the law's

---

15. June O'Neill and M. Anne Hill, "Gaining Ground? Measuring the Impact of Welfare Reform on Welfare and Work," Manhattan Institute *Civic Report* No. 17, July 2001, p. 22, Table 4.
16. See Robert Rector, "Implementing Welfare Reform and Restoring Marriage," in Stuart M. Butler and Kim R. Holmes, eds., *Priorities for the President*, A Mandate for Leadership Project (Washington, D.C.: The Heritage Foundation, 2001.

clear goals regarding illegitimacy and marriage have been ignored by most state welfare bureaucracies.

FACT: The welfare system for children is overwhelmingly a subsidy system for single parenthood.

Of the nearly $200 billion in means-tested aid that the government gives to families with children, nearly 75 percent goes to single-parent families. Without the collapse of marriage, the welfare state as it is currently understood would not exist.

FACT: Illegitimacy and single parenthood continue to be enormous social problems.

In the 1996 welfare reform, the federal government set two national goals: reducing illegitimacy and increasing marriage. State governments were expected to use TANF funds to meet these goals. Despite nearly $100 billion in federal TANF spending over the past six years, however, the states still have done virtually nothing to increase marriage or reduce illegitimacy.

Today, one child is born out of wedlock every 35 seconds. Some 33 percent of all births occur outside marriage—a higher rate than in 1996 when welfare reform was enacted. Welfare bureaucrats at the state level are quietly hostile to the concept of marriage, which they regard as an obsolete and politically incorrect institution. They have ignored the fact that single parenthood has harmful effects on children's development and have neglected the reality that it is the principal cause of child poverty and welfare dependence. The failure of state governments to use TANF funds to develop programs to reduce illegitimacy and strengthen marriage clearly violates the intention of the federal welfare law and is the greatest single failure of welfare reform.

FACT: Welfare continues to penalize marriage.

While it is widely accepted that welfare is biased against marriage, relatively few understand how this bias operates. Many erroneously believe that welfare programs have eligibility criteria that directly exclude married couples. This is not true. Nevertheless, welfare programs do penalize marriage and reward single parenthood because of the inherent design of all means-tested programs, which reduces benefits as non-welfare income rises.

Thus, under any means-tested system, a mother will receive greater benefits if she remains single than if she is married to a working husband. Welfare not only serves as a substitute for a husband, but actually penalizes marriage because a low-income couple will experience a significant drop in combined income if they marry. For example:

- The typical single mother on TANF receives a combined welfare package of various means-tested aid benefits worth about $14,000 per year. Suppose this typical single mother receives welfare benefits worth $14,000 per year while the father of her children has a low-wage job paying $15,000 per year. If the mother and father remain unmarried, they will have a combined income of $29,000 ($14,000 from welfare and $15,000 from earnings).
- However, if the couple marry, the father's earnings will be counted against the mother's welfare eligibility. Welfare benefits will be eliminated or cut dramatically, and the couple's combined income will fall substantially.

Thus, means-tested welfare programs do not penalize marriage per se, but instead implicitly penalize marriage to an employed man with earnings. The practical effect is to significantly discourage marriage among low-income couples. This anti-marriage discrimination is inherent in all means-tested aid programs, including TANF, food stamps, public housing, Medicaid, and the Women Infants and Children (WIC) food program. The only way to eliminate it completely would be to remove means testing for the father's income from all welfare programs, making all mothers eligible without regard to their husbands' earnings, which would cost tens of billions of dollars. However, the anti-marriage bias can be reduced.

WHAT TO DO IN 2003

The TANF program will be reauthorized this year, and this offers Congress a crucial opportunity to expand and deepen the original reforms. When TANF was created in 1996, Congress established four basic goals:

- To increase work and reduce dependence;
- To reduce child poverty;
- To increase and strengthen two-parent families; and
- To reduce out-of-wedlock childbearing.

In 2002, candidates can encourage Congress to enact vigorous new policies to carry out these original goals. Specifically:

Toughen existing work requirements.

Welfare should not be a one-way handout. Welfare programs should not reward idleness and dependence. The creation of federal work requirements in TANF was a successful revolution in welfare, but it is far from complete. Currently, about half of the 2 million adults on TANF are idle on the rolls. When TANF is reauthorized, the states should be required to have at least 85 percent of adult recipients engaged in community service work, supervised job search, and/or training for at least 35 hours each week.[17]

Establish work requirements in food stamps and public housing.

These programs were largely untouched by the 1996 welfare reform. The successful principles of TANF should be applied to them as well: Able-bodied non-elderly adult recipients should be required to perform community service work, supervised job search, or training as a condition of receiving aid.

Set aside a share of future TANF funds for programs that strengthen marriage and reduce illegitimacy.

Despite the law's explicit goals of strengthening marriage and reducing out-of-wedlock childbearing, over the past five years, states have allocated only about $11 million from a total of nearly $100 billion in federal TANF funds to meet these objectives. Many welfare bureaucrats demonstrate open contempt for these goals. This neglect of marriage by the state bureaucracies is a national disgrace. A share of future federal TANF funds—2 percent in 2003, rising to 10 percent by 2008—must be set aside for pro-marriage activities. These should include education on the value of marriage for high-school students in at-risk communities, public advertising campaigns, pro-marriage counseling and relationship skills training for unmarried parents at the time of a child's birth, and pre-marital counseling for engaged couples.[18]

---

17. Part-time formal employment should also be countable toward the 30-hour-per-week performance requirement.

Reduce the anti-marriage penalties in all means-tested welfare programs.

As noted above, all means-tested programs financially penalize marriage. This lamentable public policy must be reversed. While it is not possible to eliminate the anti-marriage bias fully in the welfare system, it is possible to reduce it. The most effective way to accomplish this would be to increase the value of the Earned Income Tax Credit for married couples with children.

—*Robert Rector is Senior Research Fellow in Welfare and Family Issues at the Heritage Foundation.*

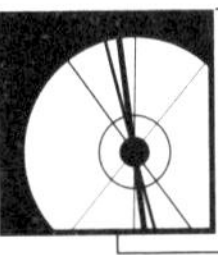

For a complete list and full-text versions of additional studies by Heritage on welfare reform, see the searchable *Issues 2002* companion CD–ROM.

EXPERTS

Heritage Foundation

Robert Rector
Senior Research Fellow in Welfare and Family Issues
The Heritage Foundation
214 Massachusetts Avenue, NE
Washington, DC 20002
(202) 608-6219
fax: (202) 544 5421
robert.rector@heritage.org

Patrick F. Fagan
William H. G. FitzGerald Research Fellow in Family and Cultural Issues
The Heritage Foundation
214 Massachusetts Avenue, NE
Washington, DC 20002
(202) 608-6207
fax: (202) 544-5421
pat.fagan@heritage.org

Other Experts

David Blankenhorn
President
Institute for American Values
1841 Broadway, Suite 211
New York, NY 10023
(212) 246-3942
fax: (212) 541-6665
iav@worldnet.att.net

Maggie Gallagher
Nationally Syndicated Columnist
53 Cedar Lane
Offining, NY 10562
(914) 762-7143
fax: (914) 762-7152

Lawrence Mead, Ph.D.
Professor of Politics
Department of Politics
New York University
715 Broadway

18. Robert Rector, "Using Welfare Reform to Strengthen Marriage," *American Experiment Quarterly*, Summer 2001, pp. 63–66.

New York, NY 10003
(212) 998-8540
fax: (212) 995-4184

June O'Neill, Ph.D.
Professor of Economics
and Finance
Center for the Study of
Business and Government
Zicklin School of Business
Baruch College,
City University of New York
17 Lexington Avenue,
Box F–1302
New York, NY 10010
(212) 802-5720
fax: (212) 802-6353

Diane Sollee
Founder and Director
Coalition for Marriage,
Family and Couples Education
5310 Belt Road, NW
Washington, DC 20015
(202) 362-3332
fax: (202) 362-0973
cmfce@smartmarriages.com

Jason Turner
Center for Self-Sufficiency
P.O. Box 11762
Milwaukee, WI 53211
(414) 962-6661
fax: (414) 906-0784
rustication@yahoo.com

Roland Warren
President
National Fatherhood Initiative
101 Lake Forest Boulevard
Suite 360
Gaithersburg, MD 20877
(301) 948-0599
fax: (301) 948-4325
nfi1995@aol.com

For continually updated and expanded information on major breaking developments on this issue over the campaign cycle, www.*heritage.org/issues/welfare.*

CITIES AND SUBURBS

Meeting Urban and Suburban Needs

Ronald D. Utt, Ph.D.

THE ISSUES

For the first time in more than 50 years, census data have revealed significant improvements in many urban areas, and the federal government will now have an opportunity to rethink its policies toward America's cities and suburbs. Between 1990 and 2000, 85 percent of U.S. cities with populations above 100,000 experienced an increase in population, reversing what had been pervasive patterns of decline. At the same time, several older cities—New York, San Francisco, Miami, and Oakland—whose borders have been unchanged through the postwar era achieved record-level populations.[1]

Historically, the federal government's involvement in urban America has focused on central cities and their declining economies, deteriorated housing, and the needs of low-income residents. But success in central-city revitalization is now allowing federal officials to think more broadly and to focus on entire metropolitan areas, extending their interest to such issues as sprawl, zoning, land use, farm preservation, and metropolitan government.

In responding to the temptation to broaden the focus of policy, candidates should keep in mind the limits of the effectiveness of federal programs and jurisdiction, the diversity of community priorities, and the importance of establishing an effective division of responsibilities between federal, state, and local governments.

---

1. U.S. Bureau of the Census, at *www.census.gov/population/cen2000/phc-t5/tab02.pdf*. For purposes of this chapter, "record-level populations" refers only to cities whose borders have been fixed since at least the 1950s. Many other American cities reached record populations in 2000, but that achievement was influenced by a pattern of annexation during the postwar era.

Among the issues that elected officials must consider are the following:

1. **Concerns regarding broader metropolitan areas should not eclipse the critical needs of central-city communities.** As Washington's focus is expanded from central cities to broader metropolitan area interests and quality of life issues, there is a risk that the needs of communities suffering the traditional, and more serious, urban problems of crime, poverty, and inadequate schools will be neglected. Former Vice President Al Gore attempted to create an intrusive Livable Communities program in Washington that shifted focus to the suburbs, and a number of federal bureaucracies are continuing this effort. Recent grant-making decisions by the Environmental Protection Agency and the U.S. Departments of Commerce and Transportation have directed funds to groups that support Clinton–Gore "smart growth" policies favoring better-off homeowners.[2]

2. **Policies that impose coercive regulations to reshape suburban communities undermine residents' choice.** New urbanists and other smart-growth advocates want to reduce housing options and lifestyle choices by forcing American families into living arrangements that meet the approval of the artistic and cultural elites. Typically, this entails an emphasis on higher density communities of apartments and townhouses, greater dependence on public transportation, and the inclusion of more commercial establishments within residential neighborhoods.

3. **Pioneering mayors and governors have shown that the keys to effective urban revitalization lie in city hall and local entities, not in Washington, D.C.** Leaders of major cities, including New York, Indianapolis, Chicago, and Milwaukee, have turned their cities around by improving the public services that are important to families—law enforcement and education. In New York City, Mayor Rudolph Giuliani reduced the murder rate to its lowest level since the mid-1960s, and Mayor Richard Daley's public school improve-

---

2. For details of a federally funded conference featuring Maryland Governor Parris Glendening, for example, see *www.outreach.psu.edu/C&I/smartgrowth*; for recent EPA grant patterns, see *www.ti.org/vaupdate20.html*.

ments have made Chicago a more attractive place to live, reversing decades of urban flight.[3]

4. **Broad-based, one-size-fits-all urban policy does not meet the unique needs of communities or enlist the skills of residents.** Existing federal urban policies, including those embodied in the Community Development Block Grant (CDBG) program in the U.S. Department of Housing and Urban Development (HUD), are premised on a myriad of false assumptions. These misguided premises include the beliefs that all central cities are in trouble; that their problems are beyond the scope of local initiatives; that critical issues are identical for every city; and that more money will cure their problems. The 50-year record of failure amassed by federal programs, contrasted with the success of locally designed solutions in such cities as Indianapolis and Chicago, demonstrates the fallacy of this view.

5. **Failed central-city policies, not the lure of the suburbs, have caused the decline of America's urban areas.** Unable to stem the flight of businesses and residents from their jurisdictions, mayors of cities where schools, police, and other public services have suffered from incompetent management have blamed their failures on suburban successes.[4]

6. **It is falsely claimed that federal urban policies and government spending, rather than local actions to improve basic services, are turning cities around.** Despite the growing number of locally based urban revitalization successes, many federal officials and advocates of expansive government often make exaggerated claims about the presumed success of Washington's programs as a way to argue for more of the same.

---

3. Ronald D. Utt, Ph.D., "What to Do About the Cities," Heritage Foundation *Backgrounder* No. 1216, September 1, 1998, at *www.heritage.org/library/backgrounder/bg1216.html*.

4. See David Rusk, *Inside Game/Outside Game* (Washington, D.C.: Brookings Institution Press, 1999), and Bruce Katz and Scott Bernstein, "The New Metropolitan Agenda: Connecting Cities to Suburbs," *Brookings Review*, Vol. 16, No. 4 (Fall 1998), p. 4.

THE FACTS

FACT: During the 1990s, many cities succeeded in reversing the process of decline.

The findings of the 2000 census reveal that, for the first time in half a century, the vast majority of American cities are improving in terms of reduced crime rates, increased employment opportunities, and population growth. New York, San Francisco, Oakland, and Miami all recorded their highest populations ever in the 2000 census.[5]

FACT: While a number of American cities have reversed a postwar depopulation trend, European, Canadian, and Japanese cities continue to lose residents to surrounding suburbs.

The growth of suburbs and the decline of the older central cities has been a global phenomenon during much of the 20th century, suggesting that universal causes such as changing technology, increased populations, and rising prosperity are key factors that have engendered the growth of the suburbs and changed the shape of our metropolitan areas. To name just a few international examples, London's population peaked in 1905, while Paris reached its peak in 1921; Toronto's population has been falling since 1971.[6]

FACT: Technological change has had an important influence on community development patterns.

The once-great American city—the model that urban officials and "experts" want to re-create—was shaped by unique social and economic arrangements that reflected the state of technology during a period that began in the late 19th century when cities were the nation's dominant economic, cultural, and political force. Whereas density was once the city's chief advantage, the advent of the automobile redefined high density as "congestion" and rendered it a major disadvantage. Enhanced mobility allowed for a

---

5. Table 2, "Incorporated Places of 100,000 or More, Ranked by Population: 2000," at *www.census.gov/population/cen2000/phc-t5/tab02.pdf*. See also note 1, *supra*.
6. For a comprehensive list of population changes in cities throughout the world, see *www.demographia.com/db-intlcitylossr.htm*.

return to the dispersed living arrangements that characterized American life before the industrial revolution.[7]

FACT: High-quality public services attracted both residents and businesses to the suburbs, and this dynamic has been recognized and imitated by successful cities.

As the families preceding them had done, entrepreneurs and established companies responded quickly to the availability of high-quality public services at lower tax rates in the suburbs and moved their businesses there. Significantly, the cities that avoided or reversed population declines also focused on providing quality services of primary benefit to their residents. The populations of New York City, Chicago, and Indianapolis increased throughout 1990s as a result of significant improvements in basic city services, not as a consequence of corporate welfare.

FACT: The "smart growth" strategies implemented in many communities will diminish homeownership opportunities among minorities and lower-income families.

Efforts to curb or redirect growth in many suburban communities often rely on restrictive regulations such as growth boundaries or on "downzoning" efforts to force large building-lot sizes. Some communities impose highly regressive taxes, known as "impact fees," of between $10,000 to $20,000 per new house. All of these regulations have the effect of raising home prices and reducing access for lower-income families. Such restrictions impose a disproportionate burden on minority households, whose homeownership rate is less than 50 percent compared to nearly 75 percent among white households.[8]

FACT: Federal "Great Society" initiatives and the programs they engendered undermined the historic role of the cities in fostering upward mobility.

Easy access to welfare replaced the drive for upward mobility and exacerbated many of the emerging problems in America's cities. Violent crime, educational decline, welfare dependency, illegiti-

7. Utt, "What to Do About the Cities," pp. 4–7.
8. Wendell Cox and Ronald D. Utt, Ph.D., "Smart Growth, Housing Costs, and Homeownership," Heritage Foundation *Backgrounder* No. 1426, April 6, 2001, at *www.heritage.org/library/backgrounder/bg1426.html*, and Matthew E. Kahn, "Does Sprawl Reduce the Black/White Housing Consumption Gap?" *Housing Policy Debate*, Vol. 12, No. 1 (2001).

macy, drug addition, infant mortality, and family dissolution—all commonly cited as measures of societal dysfunction—reached their extreme in urban areas during the 1980s. While spending on federal programs increased, these trends worsened through the mid-1990s and continue at destructively high levels today in a number of the nation's still-troubled cities.[9]

FACT: Federal urban renewal policies failed because they favored businesses and commuters rather than city residents.

In a failed attempt to improve commercial, housing, and social conditions in the inner cities, the federal urban renewal program (created as part of the 1949 Housing Act) used eminent domain to acquire entire neighborhoods that were mostly poor, black, and residential. Land was subsequently used for commercial purposes, and the social structure and cohesiveness of communities were undermined as former residents were relocated to public housing projects in distant parts of the city. Costly entertainment/commercial projects (such as Detroit's Renaissance Center, Baltimore's Harbor Place, and dozens of new convention centers and stadiums) that have been built in downtown locations have not sparked the revitalization of their respective cities. A number of recent academic studies have concluded that such costly projects may even have undermined some cities' revival by misallocating scarce resources.[10]

FACT: Cities that did not improve their services and reduce their tax burdens to retain residents and businesses bore a heavier burden of violent crime.

Several cities—both large and small, and mostly in the Northeast—continue to suffer from economic deterioration and the

---

9. Robert Rector and Patrick F. Fagan, "The Good News About Welfare Reform," Heritage Foundation *Backgrounder* No. 1468, September 5, 2001, at *www.heritage.org/library/backgrounder/bg1468.html*, and Robert Rector, "Using Welfare Reform to Strengthen Marriage," *American Experiment Quarterly*, Summer 2001, p. 63.

10. See Ronald D. Utt, Ph.D., "Cities in Denial: The False Promise of Subsidized Tourist and Entertainment Complexes," Heritage Foundation *Backgrounder* No. 1223, October 2, 1998, at *www.heritage.org/library/backgrounder/bg1223.html*; see also Dennis Coates and Brad R. Humphreys, "The Growth Effects of Sports Franchises, Stadia and Arenas," University of Maryland, Baltimore County, January 22, 1999, and "Convention Center Facts and Fictions," *Pioneer Institute's Quarterly Digest*, Vol. 3, No. 3 (Summer 2001).

flight of businesses and residents, largely because little progress has been made in improving basic public services or reducing burdensome taxes and regulations. Baltimore, Philadelphia, Detroit, Buffalo, and Cleveland, for example, continue to suffer as local officials have shown themselves to be either unable or unwilling to implement reforms that have been successful elsewhere. New York City, which gained population and jobs during the 1990s, reduced its murder rate to 8.4 per 100,000 inhabitants in 2000. At the same time, Baltimore, which lost 11.5 percent of its population throughout the 1990s, had a murder rate of 41 per 100,000, while Philadelphia, whose population shrank by 4.5 percent, saw 21 of every 100,000 citizens die by murder in 2000. The nationwide murder rate in 2000 was 5.5 per 100,000.[11]

A Guide to Smart Growth: Shattering Myths, Providing Solutions examines sprawl in detail, explaining which solutions work, which ones don't, and why. Read the entire book on the *Issues 2002* companion CD–ROM or contact Heritage's Publications office at 1-800-544-4843 to order a copy.

WHAT TO DO IN 2003

End the one-size-fits-all federal urban policy and replace HUD's Community Development Block Grants with a new incentive-based program.

Favorable findings from the recent census suggest that many of the urban problems of the postwar era are being solved through local initiatives. America should declare victory and shut down existing broad-based national urban programs. In their place, a new voluntary program, incorporating financial incentives related to achieving quantifiable performance measures, should be created to help those areas that are still in trouble. In effect, this new urban program would be similar to the *control board* type of arrangement previously imposed on New York City, Philadelphia, and Washington, D.C. The chief difference would

11. U.S. Department of Justice, Federal Bureau of Investigation, *Crime in the United States 2000: Uniform Crime Reports*, Washington, D.C., 2001, Table 6.

be that the new program would be voluntary and utilize "carrots," as opposed to the "sticks" used in the earlier takeovers.

Establish quantitative measures of performance with financial rewards for measurable improvements in the quality of life.

Under such a plan, in order to continue to receive this federal financial support, allowing wide flexibility in its use, a city would have to improve its performance against a series of measurable benchmarks agreed to by the city and the federal government with the approval of the state. These benchmark improvements could include such factors as population growth, crime rates, numbers of building permits and business licenses issued, student test scores, rates of unemployment and job creation, and other indices of the quality of life and commerce in the city.

Restructure federal law enforcement, job training, economic development, and transportation programs into block grants with maximum flexibility.

In return for a city's agreement to meet specified benchmarks and measurable performance goals within a specific time period (as well as interim goals to demonstrate progress toward that goal), a city would receive flexible block grants that it could use at its discretion. Moreover, as it met goals in one or several areas, it could reallocate funds to address other issues for which goals have not yet been achieved. Communities that failed to meet the specified goals (or interim goals) within the allotted time would forfeit their right to remain in the flexible program. They would then return to the traditional system of federal mandates, directives, and control until the goals that have been agreed upon are reached or a new contract is negotiated.

Help states to address the unique educational needs of their inner cities by block-granting all federal education spending.

As a condition of eligibility for an unrestricted educational block grant from the federal government, states and the U.S. Department of Education would agree to a testing program using either a commercially available test or one developed by the state's education department. Benchmarks would be established on the basis of initial test results, and schools would be required to raise test scores at a mutually agreed upon rate of progress. In the event of failure to meet the performance goals, a state would lose its eligibility to participate in the program and would revert to the mandate-driven process that now characterizes federal education spending.

In addition to test scores, a school system also could be required to meet other quantifiable performance objectives related to such indices as graduation and dropout rates, school violence, and the incidence of out-of-wedlock births among its students in order to maintain eligibility for unrestricted federal education grants. By requiring the testing of students and using the scores to measure both student progress and school effectiveness, the Elementary and Secondary Education Act that was reauthorized in late 2001 moves federal education spending in the direction of acknowledging the importance of performance. However, the bill's remedies for school failure are limited; it allows students in failing schools to receive money for tutorial services or to transfer to another public school within the district.[12]

—Ronald D. Utt, Ph.D., is the Herbert and Joyce Morgan Senior Research Fellow in the Thomas A. Roe Institute for Economic Policy Studies at The Heritage Foundation.

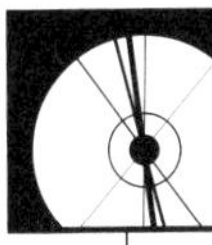

For a complete list and full-text versions of additional studies by Heritage on addressing the needs of the nation's urban and suburban communities, see the searchable *Issues 2002* companion CD-ROM.

EXPERTS

Heritage Foundation

Ronald D. Utt, Ph.D.
Herbert and Joyce Morgan Senior Research Fellow
The Heritage Foundation
214 Massachusetts Avenue, NE
Washington, DC 20002
(202) 608-6013
fax: (202) 544-5421
ron.utt@heritage.org

12. Krista Kafer, "A Small but Costly Step Toward Reform: The Conference Education Bill," December 13, 2001, at *www.heritage.org/shorts/20011213education.html.*

Robert E. Moffit, Ph.D.
Director, Domestic Policy Studies
The Heritage Foundation
214 Massachusetts Avenue, NE
Washington, DC 20002
(202) 608-6210
fax: (202) 544-5421
robert.moffit@heritage.org

Robert Rector
Senior Research Fellow
The Heritage Foundation
214 Massachusetts Avenue, NE
Washington, DC 20002
(202) 608-6213
fax: (202) 544-5421
robert.rector@heritage.org

Krista Kafer
Senior Education Policy Analyst
The Heritage Foundation
214 Massachusetts Avenue, NE
Washington, DC 20002
(202) 608-6223
fax: (202) 544-5421
krista.kafer@heritage.org

Becky Norton Dunlop
Vice President, External Relations
The Heritage Foundation
214 Massachusetts Avenue, NE
Washington, DC 20002
(202) 546-4400
fax: (202) 675-1753
bndunlop@heritage.org

Other Experts

John A. Charles
Environmental Policy Director
Cascade Policy Institute
813 Southwest Alder Street
Suite 450
Portland, OR 97205
(503) 242-0900
fax: (503) 242-3822
john@cascadepolicy.org

Wendell Cox
Principal
Wendell Cox Associates
P.O. Box 841
Belleville, IL 62222
(618) 632-8507
fax: (618) 632-8538
wcox@publicpurpose.com

Steven Hayward, Ph.D.
Senior Fellow
Pacific Research Institute
for Public Policy
755 Sansome Street, Suite 450
San Francisco, CA 94111
(415) 989-0833
fax: (415) 989-2411
hayward487@aol.com

Joel Kotkin
Olin Fellow
Pepperdine Institute
for Public Policy
8033 Sunset Boulevard, #15
Los Angeles, CA 90046
(213) 650-9054
fax: (213) 650-9072
jkotkin@earthlink.net

Samuel R. Staley, Ph.D.
Director
Urban Futures Program
Reason Public Policy Institute
3415 South Sepulveda Boulevard
Los Angeles, CA 90034-6064
(310) 391-224
fax: (310) 391-4395
sstaley@reason.org

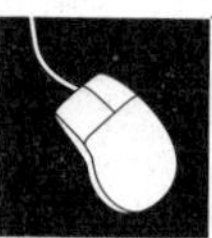

For continually updated and expanded information on major breaking developments on this issue over the campaign cycle, see www.*heritage.org/issues/citiesandsuburbs.*

EDUCATION
Opening Doors to Excellence

Krista Kafer and Jennifer J. Garrett

THE ISSUES

In inflation-adjusted dollars, Americans are paying over 72 percent more for public elementary and secondary education today than they did in 1980. Yet only a third of America's 4th graders can read proficiently, according to the U.S. Department of Education's national report card, the National Assessment of Educational Progress (NAEP). The news is even bleaker for low-income children, over half of whom cannot read or perform mathematics at even a basic level on the NAEP 2000 assessments. This is unacceptable to America's parents, and should be unacceptable to every Member of Congress and every elected and appointed official in the country.

Under the current education monopoly, there is little competition to stimulate change. To find a better school, all too often, parents must move or pay additional money to enroll their child in an independent school. Parents simply are not empowered consumers. They often lack reliable information about their schools' performance, and when they do know how their children are doing, they often lack options on which to act. Empowering parents with the information and ability to chose schools of excellence for their children, and holding public school systems accountable for their students' achievement, should be the cornerstone of true education reform.

Conservative candidates can help build a new vision for America's 21st century schools in which every child has access to excellence in a competitive market of public, private, charter, and home schools. To build a demand for such excellence and choice, candidates must emphasize the following key issues:

1. **There are no excuses for underperforming schools in America.** All children can learn regardless of their background—a

fact dramatically demonstrated in high-poverty, high-performing schools across the country. These schools—both public and private—often achieve success with fewer funds even as nearby schools wallow in mediocrity.[1]

2. **Parents have the right to know how well their children are doing in school.** The recently signed No Child Left Behind Act (P.L. 107–110) requires states to test students in grades 3 through 8 and report to the public on how well schools are performing. This is a good first step. Opponents claim the tests discriminate against poor-performing students—blaming the X-ray for the fracture. Without testing, parents cannot know whether their children need help or their schools are failing. Parents deserve a quantitative measure of their child's knowledge and skills, and standardized tests are the best tool for assessing achievement on a large scale.

3. **Parents should be able to send their children to schools that are safe and successful, and that have the best programs for their needs.** School choice, allowing parents to put their children in the best school environment, promotes academic achievement and greater satisfaction with their children's schools. It also encourages the traditional education system to improve to keep their students. Charter schools, public and private scholarships, tax incentives, and home schooling provide parents with options for making sure their children are learning. It is a win–win scenario for children.

4. **Teachers should be able to pass the tests they give to students.** Content mastery is one of the most important qualities of a successful teacher—more important than class size, computers in the classroom, and certification. Testing of teachers and teacher candidates is essential to ensuring a high-quality staff at every school and is supported by researchers across the political spectrum. Even the left-of-center Progressive Policy Institute recommends that teacher applicants pass a test of content knowledge and essential skills, as well as possess a college degree. These requirements would replace the traditional teaching degree and state-issued license.[2]

---

1. See Samuel Casey Carter, *No Excuses: Lessons from 21 High-Performing, High Poverty Schools* (Washington, D.C.: The Heritage Foundation, 2000), at *www.noexcuses.org/lessons/*.

5. **School administrators and teachers must be held accountable for student outcomes.** Many accountability systems that test achievement hold students responsible, but not their teachers and school administrators. The No Child Left Behind Act addresses this by granting funds for tenure reform, teacher testing, merit pay, and alternative certification. Whether states or school districts use these funds for these purposes, however, is up to them.

6. **NAEP achievement scores have remained flat over the past 20 years despite an unprecedented increase in spending.**[3] Total K–12 federal, state, and local spending for education, both public and private, climbed to an estimated all-time high of over $389 billion for the 1999–2000 school year.[4] Americans spent over $100 billion more on education than they did on defense.

THE FACTS

FACT: Most American children are not proficient in key academic subjects.

The recently passed No Child Left Behind Act calls for more frequent testing in both reading and math. The National Assessment of Educational Progress (NAEP) tests, given to a sample of public and private school students in 4th, 8th, and 12th grades, gauge their achievement in math, reading, science, and other subjects.[5]

- According to the 2000 NAEP assessments, only 32 percent of 4th graders are proficient in reading, while a dismal 26 percent are proficient in mathematics and 29 percent in science. Moreover, proficiency rates decline by the 12th grade.[6]

---

2. Frederick M. Hess, "Tear Down this Wall: The Case for a Radical Overhaul of Teacher Certification," Progressive Policy Institute, November 27, 2001.
3. U.S. Department of Education, National Center for Education Statistics (NCES), *NAEP 1999 Trends in Academic Progress: Three Decades of Student Performance*, 2000.
4. U.S. Department of Education, NCES, *Digest of Education Statistics 2000*, 2001, 2001, Table 32. Total includes all education spending on K–12 students.
5. Krista Kafer, "A Guide to the NAEP Academic Achievement Test," Heritage Foundation *Backgrounder* No. 1419, March 15, 2001, at *www.heritage.org/library/backgrounder/bg1419.html*.
6. U.S. Department of Education, NCES, at *http://nces.ed.gov/nationsreportcard/sitemap.asp*.

- Over half of all economically disadvantaged children scored below the basic level on these tests. On the NAEP long-term trend reading assessment, the gap between white and African–American 13-year-olds' achievement widened from 18 points in 1988 to 29 points in 1999, while the disparity in scores for 17-year-olds widened from 20 points to 31 points.[7]

FACT: The United States lags behind other countries in education performance.

Despite higher than average per-pupil expenditures, American 8th graders ranked 19th out of 38 countries on the most recent international mathematics comparison, the Third International Mathematics and Science Study–Repeat (TIMSS–R) of 1999, even falling behind Malaysia, the Russian Federation, and Bulgaria.[8] American students scored 18th out of 38 countries in science. On the TIMSS 1995 study, which tested 12th graders, American students were ranked 19th out of 21 countries in both math and science general knowledge.[9]

Because lower academic attainment affects economic competitiveness, it is no wonder that the United States has repeatedly increased the number of high-tech work visas available to attract foreign workers who have the better skills U.S. businesses are seeking.

FACT: Learning is not dependent on how much we spend.

The existence of high-poverty, high-achieving schools shows that reform is contingent not on funding, but on the will for excellence. All children can learn, regardless of background. The Heritage Foundation No Excuses project and other groups like the Education Trust have identified many such schools.[10]

---

7. U.S. Department of Education, NCES, *NAEP 1999 Trends in Academic Progress.*
8. 1999 Third International Math and Science Study–Repeat (TIMSS–R). See *TIMSS 1999 International Mathematics Report*, International Study Center, Lynch School of Education, Boston College, December 2000, p. 32.
9. See *TIMSS Highlights from the Final Year of Secondary School*, International Study Center, Lynch School of Education, Boston College, February 1998, p. 1.
10. See Carter, *No Excuses*; see also Craig D. Jerald, "Dispelling the Myth Revisited: Preliminary Findings from a Nationwide Analysis of 'High Flying' Schools," Education Trust, Inc., Washington, D.C., 2001, at *http://64.224.125.0/dtm/*.

In just one year, for example, parents of children in Bessemer Elementary School in Pueblo, Colorado, saw scores rise remarkably on state exams. Over 80 percent of Bessemer's students are eligible for the federal free and reduced-price lunch program. School policy changes resulted in students' reading scores improving from 12 percent passing to 64 percent, and in writing from 2 percent passing to 48 percent.[11] The teachers and students accomplished this without additional funding or reductions in class size. They simply devoted more time to classroom instruction and eliminated frivolous non-academic exercises.

FACT: Increased spending has not produced higher achievement.

Over the past 30 years, average per-pupil expenditures for public elementary and secondary schools have nearly doubled, rising from $3,367 in 1970 to $6,584 in 2000 in constant dollars.[12] Class sizes have decreased from 24 to 18 elementary students per teacher and 20 to 14 secondary students per teacher.[13] Yet achievement has not increased accordingly.

The evidence suggests there is little reason to expect that increasing funding will make them produce better results. In a 1999 report commissioned by the U.S. Department of Education, for example, the National Research Council concluded that "additional funding for education will not automatically and necessarily generate student achievement and in the past has not, in fact, generally led to higher achievement."[14]

In fact, private school children consistently outscore public school students on the NAEP tests, with generally far lower per-pupil costs. A 1996 Cato Institute study found that the average private school tuition nationwide was $3,116, with 67 percent of all private elementary and secondary schools charging $2,500 or less.[15] That is far less than half of the average per-pupil expenditures in public schools.

---

11. Education Leaders Council, "From Good Intentions to Results: Transforming Federal Education Policy," Washington, D.C., Winter 2000.
12. U.S. Department of Education, NCES, *Digest of Education Statistics 2000*, Table 170.
13. *Ibid.*, Table 65.
14. Helen F. Ladd and Janet S. Hansen, eds., *Making Money Matter: Financing America's Schools* (Washington, D.C.: National Academy Press, 1999), at *www.nap.edu/books/0309065283/html*.

FACT: Smaller class sizes, computers, and state certification do not correlate significantly with student achievement; teacher mastery of subject matter, however, does.

Teacher unions and their allies in government continually call for smaller classes, new computers, and more certified teachers. Research shows, however, that these approaches have little effect on student achievement.[16]

- The number of public school students per teacher nationwide decreased from 22 in 1970 to 16 in 1999.[17] The number of computers in public elementary and secondary schools increased from a ratio of over 63 students for every computer in 1985 to less than five per computer in 2000.[18] Analysis of NAEP data shows that these policies do not improve learning. The NAEP data also reveal that students whose teachers hold subject degrees in such fields as math or English, rather than education degrees, are more likely to score higher on math or reading tests, especially in the older grades.[19]
- Similarly, the Baltimore-based Abell Foundation has found a lack of correlation between student achievement and state certification, which often requires an education degree. Its October 2001 report, *Teacher Certification Reconsidered: Stumbling for Quality*, reveals that a teacher's verbal ability is the most consistent predictor of student success.

---

15. Center for Education Reform, *Nine Lies About School Choice: Answering the Critics*, September 2000, at *www.edreform.com/pubs/ninelies2000.htm*.
16. Kirk A. Johnson, Ph.D., "Do Small Classes Influence Academic Achievement? What the National Assessment of Educational Progress Shows," Heritage Foundation *Center for Data Analysis Report* No. CDA00–07, June 9, 2000, and "Do Computers in the Classroom Boost Academic Achievement?" *Center for Data Analysis Report* No. CDA 00–08, June 14, 2000, at *www.heritage.org/library/cda/cda00-07.html* and */cda00-08.html*.
17. In 1999, the average K–12 student–teacher ratio was 16 to 1; the ratio for elementary school was 18 to 1, and the ratio for secondary school was 14 to 1. See *http://nces.ed.gov/pubs2001/digest/dt065.html*.
18. U.S. Bureau of the Census, *Statistical Abstract of the United States* (Washington, D.C.: U.S. Government Printing Office, various years).
19. Kirk A. Johnson, Ph.D., "The Effects of Advanced Teacher Training in Education on Student Achievement," Heritage Foundation *Center for Data Analysis Report* No. 00–09, September 14, 2000, at *www.heritage.org//library/cda/CDA00-09.html*.

FACT: School choice is gaining more allies from Main Street to Pennsylvania Avenue.

A richer and more impressive body of research demonstrates that choice improves academic performance of at-risk students, promotes parental involvement, and fosters competition and accountability in public school systems. A recent survey conducted on behalf of the National Education Association found strong support for such programs: 63 percent of those polled favored legislation that would provide parents with tuition vouchers of $1,500 a year to send their children to any public, private, or charter school.[20] Because of such support, options for parents to put their children in a better school environment are increasing around the country.[21]

- 37 states and the District of Columbia have enacted charter school laws.[22] As of fall 2001, more than 2,300 charter schools nationwide serve over half a million children.[23]
- 10 states have publicly sponsored private school choice programs, from vouchers to tax credits.
- Under a law signed by President Bush, parents can now save for their children's education expenses in tax-free educational savings accounts.
- More than 50,000 students have benefited from almost 100 privately funded scholarship programs that allow them to attend a school of choice, and another 12,000 have benefited from five publicly funded programs.
- During the 2000–2001 school year, almost 2 million children in grades K-12 were being home schooled.

---

20. Greenberg Quinlan Research, Inc., and the Tarrance Group, National Education Association Survey, March 2001.
21. Robert E. Moffit, Ph.D., Jennifer J. Garrett, and Janice A. Smith, eds., *School Choice 2001: What's Happening in the States* (Washington, D.C.: The Heritage Foundation, 2001).
22. A charter public school agrees to meet certain performance standards in exchange for exemptions from public school regulations (other than those governing health, safety, and civil rights); it accepts accountability for results in exchange for autonomy in choosing methods to achieve those results. States determine further specificity of the law. Depending on state law, parents, teachers, universities, or businesses may charter a school and design its curriculum.
23. See Center for Education Reform, "Charter School Highlights and Statistics," at *www.edreform.com*.

FACT: The academic performance of low-income children improves under school choice.

More and more studies indicate that private schools produce far better student achievement than does the public school system.

- A March 2001 report commissioned by New York University found that New York City's Catholic school students achieve higher scores than their public school peers on New York's 4th and 8th grade standardized tests. Moreover, students in Catholic schools pass their exams at a higher rate. "The study demonstrates that Catholic Schools are more effective in severing the connection between race or income and academic performance," said Professor Joseph Viteritti, co-chair of the university's Program on Education and Civil Society.[24]
- In August 2000, Harvard University's Paul Peterson and his colleagues released the results of a study of privately funded voucher programs in New York; Dayton, Ohio; and the District of Columbia. They found that African–American children who used vouchers to attend private schools exhibited significant academic improvement. Black students in their second year at a private school improved their test scores by 6.3 percentile points—a striking advance at a time when public schools are showing an inability to close the achievement gap between white and black students.[25]

FACT: School choice introduces competitive market forces into the system and compels public schools to work harder to attract and retain students.

- A Manhattan Institute study on Florida's school choice program finds that poor-performing public schools in danger of losing students to other schools under the state's school choice policy experienced higher academic gains relative to the other government schools. Schools on the verge of losing students saw test scores jump over twice as high as did the other schools.[26]

---

24. Press release, "Catholic Schools Outperform Public Schools on State English and Math Exams: New Study Says," New York University, March 22, 2001, at *www.nyu.edu/publicaffairs/newsreleases/b_CATHO.shtml*.
25. William G. Howell *et al.*, "Test Score Effects of School Vouchers in Dayton, Ohio, New York City, and Washington D.C.: Evidence from Randomized Field Trials," Harvard University, August 2000.

- According to a February 2001 study on "School Choice and School Productivity" by Harvard University economist Caroline Hoxby, Milwaukee's public elementary schools improved as a result of competition from the private school choice program.[27]

FACT: School choice does not drain any money away from public schools and enables public schools to use their money more effectively.

The amount of most vouchers is significantly less than the per-student amount spent by the local public school district on students. In most cases, when a student uses a voucher to transfer to another school, the school districts keep the remaining per-pupil funds not spent on that voucher.

- A December 2000 report on the benefits of school choice conducted by Caroline Hoxby notes that, while reducing per-pupil costs, school choice improves educational performance. In "Does Competition Among Public Schools Benefit Students and Taxpayers?" Hoxby reports that improvements in public school performance because of competition from choice also decrease the overall demand for private schools. Policies that reduce choice, by comparison, are likely to increase the share of students who go to private schools and reduce the share of voters who approve of the job the public education system is doing.[28]

FACT: School choice programs, far from "skimming" the best students, serve the very students who need them most.

Thousands of children with severe disabilities are educated by private schools at public expense through the Individuals with Disabilities Education Act (IDEA) and through state funding. Over 3,000 private schools now serve over 100,000 students with disabilities.[29] Private schools serve children who have fallen

---

26. Jay P. Greene, Ph.D., "An Evaluation of the Florida A-Plus Accountability and School Choice Program," Center for Civic Innovation, Manhattan Institute, February 2001, at *www.manhattan-institute.org/html/cr_aplus.htm*.
27. Caroline Hoxby, "School Choice and School Productivity," Harvard University, February 2001.
28. Caroline Hoxby, "Does Competition Among Public Schools Benefit Students and Taxpayers?" *American Economic Review*, December 2000; see also "The Difference That Choice Makes," *Economist*, January 27, 2001.
29. See Janet R. Beales, "Meeting the Challenge: How the Private Sector Serves Difficult to Educate Students," Reason Foundation, 1996.

behind academically. The families of struggling students are more likely to seek an alternative school than are those whose students are thriving. John Witte, an evaluator of the Milwaukee Parental Choice Program, explained it this way:

> The students in the Choice program were not the best, or even average students from the Milwaukee [public] system.... Rather than skimming off the best students, the program seems to provide an alternative education environment for students who are not doing particularly well in the public school system.[30]

As a 2000 report by Wisconsin's Legislative Audit Bureau found, despite fears of "creaming" and segregation, Milwaukee's school choice program served a student population that was demographically identical to the city's public school students. It concluded that most of the schools participating in the program provided high-quality academic programs.[31]

FACT: School choice does not violate church–state principles and follows the same guidelines as federal student loans and grants.

Following World War II, Congress passed the G.I. Bill, which allowed thousands of returning servicemen to use taxpayer money to attend colleges of choice, including religious schools. In response, the number of colleges and universities increased to meet the growing demand. Federal student loans and Pell grants are also redeemable at religious institutions. Also, many disabled K–12 students already use taxpayer money to attend private schools.

The U.S. Supreme Court has ruled that laws do not violate the Establishment Clause if they do not aid one religion over another. A school choice program must not have a religious purpose, advance religion, or cause a government entanglement with religion. State supreme courts have ruled that several voucher and

---

30. Daniel McGroarty, "Voucher Wars: Strategy and Tactics as School Choice Advocates Battle the Labor Leviathan," Milton and Rose D. Friedman Foundation, April 1998, p. 5.
31. See Wisconsin Legislative Audit Bureau Web site at *http://www.legis.state.wi.us/lab/reports/00-2full.pdf.*

tax credit programs are constitutional because they meet these guidelines.[32] In 2002, the U.S. Supreme Court will review a federal appeals court decision in *Simmons–Harris* v. *Zelman* that struck down the Cleveland voucher program as unconstitutional.

No Excuses: Lessons from 21 High-Performing, High-Poverty Schools examines the common practices of 21 principals of low-income schools who set the standard for high achievement. The lessons uncovered in these case studies provide a valuable resource for anyone interested in providing increased educational opportunities for low-income children. Read the entire book on the *Issues 2002* companion CD–ROM or contact Heritage's Publications office at 1-800-544-4843 to order a copy.

WHAT TO DO IN 2003

Enact choice legislation and grant families access to schools of excellence.

On January 8, 2002, President Bush signed the No Child Left Behind Act, requiring states to test students and report to parents on the quality of their schools. These reports will provide parents with a rich source of data on their schools. Additionally, students in persistently failing schools will be granted intra-district school choice. Poor students in failing schools will be given access to tutorial services. However, the law does not provide access to quality out-of-district schools or private schools. Nor does it address the needs of failing students at mediocre institutions.

Information is only as good as the ability to act on it. The No Child Left Behind Act takes a modest first step toward providing more opportunities for students. State and national leaders must take the next step by enacting measures such as vouchers or tax incentives to provide families with access to better schools. Additionally, states should adopt charter school laws

---

32. Center for Education Reform, *Nine Lies About School Choice: Answering the Critics*.

and open enrollment policies to enable students to have greater access to other public schools.

Establish a demonstration reform project using the District of Columbia's public schools.

The nation's capital is home to some of the worst-performing schools in the United States. From decrepit public school buildings and schools plagued by violence and drugs to poor academic performance and a huge bureaucracy, the District of Columbia exemplifies what can happen when years of ineffective management and the lack of competition combine. The result has been a bleak future for the city's youth. Changes are being made, but the problems are immense.

The evidence is growing that choice can make a significant difference. A recent Heritage analysis compared the District's African–American children in public and Catholic schools. It found that, after holding demographic and socioeconomic factors constant, the Catholic school children performed better in math. In fact, the average 8th grade African–American Catholic school student in the District outscored 72 percent of his or her public school peers.[33]

Because of its authority over District education spending, Congress has a responsibility and the opportunity to reform the schools in its backyard. It can enact legislation to introduce competition to give students at failing schools access to schools of excellence through vouchers. Competition in the system will help all D.C. schools to improve.

Focus federal funds on promoting sound research and solutions that work.

Congress should always ensure that the federal government is spending America's education resources on research-based programs that produce measurable achievement in the classroom. In 2002, Congress will reauthorize the U.S. Department of Education's research and information dissemination department, the Office of Educational Research and Improvement (OERI), which provides research findings and instructional

---

33. Kirk A. Johnson, Ph.D., "Comparing Math Scores of Black Students in D.C.'s Public and Catholic Schools," Heritage Foundation *Center for Data Analysis Report* No. CDA99–08, October 7, 1999, at *www.heritage.org/library/cda/cda99-08.html*.

materials to schools across the country. Research with the department's stamp of approval can have a strong effect on instruction and student achievement. In the past, OERI has made little distinction between quality research and education fads.[34] Congress should make sure that OERI's research is relevant, accurate, and objective.

Require full evaluations of all federal education programs and end those that are failing.

Many education programs continue to be given ever-larger federal budgets without undergoing any serious evaluation of their performance. During the 106th Congress, legislators mandated a long-overdue evaluation of Head Start using methodologies approved by the U.S. General Accounting Office (GAO). Other programs should be subjected to a similar requirement as a condition of funding. Programs should be required to meet specific goals for academic improvement. If a GAO-approved evaluation shows that a program has failed, that program should be eliminated or drastically reformed. The U.S. Department of Education should provide specific information about where funds are going and how programs improve academic achievement.

Reform the Individuals with Disabilities Education Act (IDEA).

Over the past 25 years, IDEA has succeeded in helping millions of disabled children gain a free and appropriate education. Despite such success, lingering issues need to be resolved. Parents, teachers, and administrators continue to voice concern over such issues as discipline, paperwork burdens, and over-identification. The President's newly formed IDEA Reform Commission will make its report to Congress by July 2002, providing Congress with an opportunity to reform the legislation when it considers IDEA reauthorization. If the process is not finished in 2002, lawmakers will have an opportunity to revisit the act in 2003.

---

34. Nina Shokraii Rees, "Why Congress Should Overhaul the Federal Regional Education Laboratories," Heritage Foundation *Backgrounder* No. 1200, July 2, 1998, at *www.heritage.org/library/backgrounder/bg1200/html*.

Ensure that Head Start helps poor children enter school ready to learn.

In 2003, Congress will have the opportunity to reauthorize Head Start. Taxpayers have spent over $30 billion on Head Start since 1965 to provide comprehensive health, social, educational, and mental health services to disadvantaged students.

According to the GAO, the early childhood development program has continued to operate without any valid, useful study of how well it works.[35] Some studies indicate that it has not, in fact, given children a head start. Children enrolled in Head Start graduate knowing on average only one or two letters of the alphabet.[36] Further, such cognitive gains as are made tend to fade away by the 2nd grade.[37] The study of Head Start mandated by the 106th Congress should be finished this year. If Head Start is shown to have no sustained effects on children's educational attainment, it should be reformed or eliminated in favor of programs that help students succeed.

—Krista Kafer is Senior Policy Analyst for Education, and Jennifer J. Garrett is a Research Assistant in Domestic Policy Studies, at The Heritage Foundation.

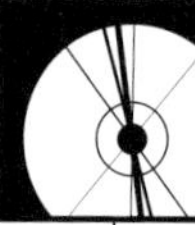

For a complete list and full-text versions of additional studies by Heritage on education reform, see the searchable *Issues 2002* companion CD–ROM.

35. U.S. General Accounting Office, *Head Start: Research Provides Little Information on Impact of Current Program*, GAO/HEHS–97–59, April 15, 1997, p. 4.
36. Chester E. Finn, Jr., Bruno V. Manno, and Diane Ravitch, "Education 2001—Getting the Job Done: A Memorandum to the President-Elect and the 107th Congress," Thomas B. Fordham Foundation, December 14, 2000.
37. Grover J. Whitehurst, "Much Too Late," *Education Next* (Stanford, Cal.: Hoover Institution, 2001).

EXPERTS

Heritage Foundation

Krista Kafer
Senior Policy Analyst
for Education
The Heritage Foundation
214 Massachusetts Avenue, NE
Washington, DC 20002
(202) 608-6223
fax: (202) 544-5421
krista.kafer@heritage.org

Jennifer J. Garrett
Research Assistant
The Heritage Foundation
214 Massachusetts Avenue, NE
Washington, DC 20002
(202) 608-6239
fax: (202) 544-5421
jennifer.garrett@heritage.org

Megan Farnsworth
Education Fellow
The Heritage Foundation
214 Massachusetts Avenue, NE
Washington, DC 20002
(202) 608-6173
fax: (202) 544-5421
megan.farnsworth@heritage.org

Kirk A. Johnson, Ph.D.
Senior Policy Analyst
Center for Data Analysis
The Heritage Foundation
214 Massachusetts Avenue, NE
Washington, DC 20002
(202) 608-6226
fax: (202) 544-5421
kirk.johnson@heritage.org

Other Experts

Jeanne Allen
President
Center for Education Reform
1001 Connecticut Avenue, NW,
Suite 204
Washington, DC 20036
(202) 822-9000
fax: (202) 822-5077
cer@edreform.com

Dr. William J. Bennett
Director
Empower America
1701 Pennsylvania Avenue, NW
Suite 900
Washington, DC 20006
(202) 452-8200
fax: (202) 833-0388
bennett@empower.org

Clint Bolick
Vice President and Director for
State Chapter Development
Institute for Justice
1717 Pennsylvania Avenue, NW
Suite 200
Washington, DC 20006
(202) 955-1300
fax: (202) 955-1329
cbolick@ij.org

Matt Brouillette
President
The Commonwealth Foundation
3544 North Progress Avenue
Suite 102
Harrisburg, PA 17110
(717) 671-1901
fax: (717) 671-1905
mbrouillette@
commonwealthfoundation.org

Kaleem Caire
President and CEO
Black Alliance for Educational
Options (BAEO)
501 C Street, NE, Suite 3
Washington, DC 20002
(202) 544-9870
fax: (202) 544-7680
kaleemc@aol.com

Robert C. Enlow
Vice President, Programs and
Public Relations
Milton and Rose Friedman

Foundation
1 American Square, Suite 1750
Indianapolis, IN 46282
(317) 681-0745
fax: (317) 681-0945
rcenlow@friedmanfoundation.org

William Evers
Research Fellow
Hoover Institution
Stanford University
Stanford, CA 94305
(650) 723-4148
fax: 650-723-1687
evers@hoover.stanford.edu

Chester E. Finn, Jr.
President
Thomas B. Fordham Foundation
1627 K Street, NW, Suite 600
Washington, DC 20006
(202) 223-5450
fax: (202) 223-9226
cefinnjr@aol.com

Mary F. Gifford
Director of Leadership Development
Mackinac Center for Public Policy
140 West Main Street
P.O. Box 568
Midland, MI 48640
(989) 631-0900
fax: (989) 631-0964
gifford@mackinac.org

Jay P. Greene
Senior Fellow
Manhattan Institute for Policy Research
1257 Allamanda Way
Weston, FL 33327
(954) 349-2322
fax: (954) 384-8790
jaygreene@earthlink.net

Eric Hanushek, Ph.D.
Hanna Senior Fellow on Education Policy
Hoover Institution
Stanford University
Stanford, CA 94305-6010
(650) 736-0942
fax: (650) 723-1687
hanushek@hoover.stanford.edu

Caroline M. Hoxby
Morris Kahn Associate Professor of Economics
Department of Economics
Harvard University
Cambridge, MA 02138
(617) 496-3588
fax: (617) 495-8570
choxby@harvard.edu

Lisa Graham Keegan
Chief Executive Officer
Education Leaders Council
1225 19th Street, NW, Suite 400
Washington, DC 20036
(202) 822-6903
fax: (202) 822-5077
info@educationleaders.org

Andrew T. LeFevre
Director of Criminal Justice and Education Task Forces
American Legislative Exchange Council
910 17th Street, NW, 5th Floor
Washington, DC 20006
(202) 466-3800
fax: (202) 466-3801
alefevre@alec.org

Mark R. Levin
President
Landmark Legal Foundation
445-B Carlisle Drive
Herndon, VA 20170
(703) 689-2370
fax: (703) 689-2373
markrlevin@aol.com

Terry Moe
Senior Fellow
Hoover Institution
Stanford University
Stanford, CA 94305
(650) 723-1754
fax: (650) 723-1687
moe@hoover.stanford.edu

Paul E. Peterson, Ph.D.
Henry Lee Shattuck Professor of Government
Director, Program on Education Policy and Governance
John F. Kennedy School of Government
Harvard University
79 John F. Kennedy Street
Cambridge, MA 02138
(617) 495-8312
fax: (617) 496-4428

Michael Poliakoff
President
National Council for Teacher Quality
1225 19th Street, NW, Suite 400
Washington, DC 20036
(202) 261-2621
fax (202) 261-2138
MPoliakoff@nctq.org
MBPoliakoff@aol.com

Diane Ravitch, Ph.D.
Research Professor
New York University
Nonresident Senior Fellow
Brookings Institution
1775 Massachusetts Avenue, NW
Washington, DC 20036
(202) 797-6000
fax: (202) 797-2495

For continually updated and expanded information on major breaking developments on this issue over the campaign cycle, see *www.heritage.org/issues/education*.

CRIME

Making America Safer

Edwin Meese III, David B. Muhlhausen, and Robert E. Moffit, Ph.D.

THE ISSUES

State and local officials are the front-line forces making America safer. They are implementing effective policies to get violent criminals off the streets and behind bars. Combined with aggressive and intelligent local police methods, these efforts are helping to reduce crime across America. In the first six months of 2001, despite upward spikes in homicide in several major cities, both violent crime and overall crime declined.

Nevertheless, Americans still believe we can make our cities, neighborhoods, and suburban communities much safer. To continue reducing crime, law enforcement officials and federal and state policymakers must recognize several key principles.

1. **Controlling violent crime is largely a state and local responsibility.** Congress's past willingness to federalize crimes that traditionally were the responsibility of states and local authorities has been strongly criticized by, for example, the American Bar Association's Task Force on the Federalization of Criminal Law.[1] State and local officials need to be aggressive in targeting hard-core criminals who commit a disproportionate share of crimes by implementing tough policies that put them behind bars and keep them there. Mounting evidence shows that this approach works.

2. **Federal crime prevention programs have been wasteful, ineffective, and unproven.** Many of the more than 500 fed-

---

1. Task Force on the Federalization of Criminal Law, *The Federalization of Criminal Law: Defending Liberty, Pursuing Justice* (Washington, D.C.: American Bar Association, 1998). The task force was chaired by former U.S. Attorney General Edwin Meese III.

eral crime prevention programs throw tax dollars where they are least needed, yet they are not subject to rigorous and regular evaluation.[2] A 1997 report by the U.S. Department of Justice, which had analyzed the evaluations of federal crime programs costing a total of over $3 billion annually, noted that many of the programs had been evaluated as ineffective or had escaped scrutiny altogether.[3] Another study determined that the vaunted Community Oriented Policing Services (COPS) program, enacted as a centerpiece of the 1994 crime bill, was unlikely to achieve its goal of putting an additional 100,000 police officers on the streets.[4]

3. **Repeat violent offenders are still public enemy number one.** Despite official reports of a continuing decline in the overall crime rate, repeat offenders continue to be the most serious threat to Americans' personal safety. Persons with a criminal record—often a relatively small number of repeat offenders—are disproportionately responsible for serious crimes. In a recent analysis of crime in Philadelphia, as many as half of all murderers in the city's highest-crime police district were found to be on probation or parole, or awaiting trial or sentencing, at the time they killed their victims.[5]

4. **Improved police management can reduce crime and prevent excessive use of police force.** The performance of the police, as demonstrated in cities such as Garden Grove and San Diego, California, New York City, and Lowell, Massachusetts, can control crime, reduce fear, and improve the quality of life for local citizens. It is not the sheer number of police but how

---

2. Lawrence W. Sherman, Chairman, Department of Criminology and Criminal Justice, University of Maryland, testimony before the Subcommittee on Youth Violence, Committee on the Judiciary, U.S. Senate, 105th Cong., 1st Sess., November 5, 1997, p. 1.

3. Lawrence Sherman *et al.*, *Preventing Crime: What Works, What Doesn't, What's Promising* (Washington, D.C.: U.S. Department of Justice, Office of Justice Programs, 1997).

4. Gareth Davis *et al.*, "The Facts About COPS: A Performance Overview of the Community Oriented Policing Services Program," Heritage Foundation *Center for Data Analysis Report* No. CDA00–10, September 25, 2000, at *www.heritage.org/library/cda/cda00-10.html.* See also U.S. Department of Justice, Office of Justice Programs, *National Evaluation of the COPS Program*, 2000.

5. Joseph Tierney, Wendy McClanahan, and Bill Hangley, *Murder Is No Mystery: An Analysis of Philadelphia Homicide, 1996–1999* (Philadelphia, Pa.: Public/Private Ventures, 2001), p. 15.

they are managed and deployed that determines their effectiveness.

5. **The real root cause of crime is family breakdown.** Fatherless children—regardless of socioeconomic and racial background—are most likely to commit violent crimes as teenagers and adults. The rising rate of illegitimacy in the United States means that teenage crime will likely continue to plague American communities.[6]

6. **The President should nominate and the Senate should promptly confirm federal judges with a strong record of fidelity to the Constitution and the rule of law.** State and local officials have primary responsibility for fighting violent crime, but activist federal judges often interfere with effective law enforcement and have a detrimental effect on public safety. Among the important issues federal courts address are (1) what constitutes an unreasonable search and seizure; (2) the applicability of the exclusionary rule; (3) prison overcrowding; (4) state and federal death penalty procedures; (5) the constitutionality of state and federal criminal laws (such as anti-pornography and anti-loitering laws); and (6) procedures that govern arrests and criminal trials. A number of federal judges have shown undue leniency toward criminal defendants and insensitivity toward victims of crime in their activist rulings. Regrettably, however, the Senate Judiciary Committee has stalled hearings and votes on many of President Bush's nominations to fill vacant judgeships.

THE FACTS

FACT: Overall crime rates and the violent crime rate continue to fall, largely as a result of local and state initiatives.

According to the Federal Bureau of Investigation (FBI), in the first six months of 2001, overall crime fell by 0.3 percent, and despite upward spikes in homicide in several major cities, violent crime declined by another 1.3 percent.[7] This news reflects the

---

6. See John J. DiIulio, Jr., "The Coming of the Super-Predators," *The Weekly Standard*, November 27, 1995, pp. 23–28.
7. U.S. Department of Justice, Federal Bureau of Investigation, "FBI Releases CIUS 2001 Preliminary Report," press release, December 17, 2001, at *www.fbi.gov/pressrel/pressrel01/01prelimcius.htm.*

pattern of crime reduction over the past 10 years, with murders dropping a stunning 37.2 percent since 1991.[8]

FACT: The highly touted federal COPS program to put 100,000 more police officers on the street is falling far short of its goal.

In 1994, President Clinton launched a federal initiative known as Community Oriented Policing Services to deploy 100,000 more police officers on America's streets. The COPS program provides federal funding to state and local police agencies for the hiring and redeployment of officers for community policing purposes. From fiscal year 1994 to FY 2002, over $10 billion has been spent on this effort, but major studies have documented that the COPS program has failed to meet its objectives. For example:

- A study by Heritage Foundation analysts in the Center for Data Analysis (CDA) examined the hiring of officers after the COPS program was initiated in 1994, compared with the historical hiring trend of officers from 1975 to 1993. By 1998—far from the 100,000 officers promised—the COPS grants appeared to have deployed only an additional 40,000 officers above the number that would have been hired anyway.[9]
- An evaluation of the COPS program conducted by Urban Institute scholars and published by U.S. Department of Justice program officials in 2000 estimated that the number of officers placed on the streets by COPS nationwide would peak at most around 57,000 by 2001—again, far less than the 100,000 promised.[10] The COPS program office still claims to have "funded" more than 100,000 officers, including officers who may not have been hired or deployed.[11]

---

8. "Section II: Crime Index Offenses," in *Crime in the United States 2000, Uniform Crime Reports*, October 2001, p. 15, at *www.fbi.gov/ucr/cius_00/contents.pdf*.
9. Davis *et al.*, "The Facts About COPS."
10. U.S. Department of Justice, *National Evaluation of the COPS Program*, 2000, p. 163.
11. U.S. Department of Justice, Office of Inspector General, *Special Report, Police Hiring and Redeployment Grants, Summary of Audit Findings and Recommendations*, Report No. 99–14, April 1999. See also Michael R. Bromwich, *Management and Administration of the Community Oriented Policing Services Grant Program*, U.S. Department of Justice, Office of Inspector General, Audit Division, Report No. 99–21, July 1999.

FACT: COPS grants have not helped to reduce violent crime.

CDA analysts examined the impact of COPS grants on violent crime rates in 752 counties from 1995 to 1998.[12] After taking into account socioeconomic factors and local law enforcement expenditures that could influence crime, they found that the grants for hiring additional police officers and for the Making Officer Redeployment Effective (MORE) program had no statistically significant effect on reducing violent crime rates. These grants are major components of the COPS program. Clearly, funding without a clear crime-fighting objective is unlikely to reduce violent crime.

FACT: Compared with grants that go into general funds, federal grants targeted to specific local problems are somewhat effective in reducing violent crime.

A small portion of COPS grants that target specific activities—like domestic violence, youth firearms violence, and gang violence—are more effective than COPS hiring and redeployment grants in reducing violent crime.[13] This difference in effectiveness may be explained by the differences in the grants. Narrowly targeted grants are intended to help law enforcement agencies tackle specific problems, compared with hiring and redeployment grants that simply pay for operational costs. But local law enforcement agencies are not dependent on federal funds to develop innovative responses to violent crime.

FACT: Federal spending on conventional anti-crime programs has exceeded spending on counterterrorism and the FBI's national security programs by more than 22 to 1.

Grants from the Office of Justice Programs and the COPS Office are given to state and local governments for police, juvenile justice, and other criminal justice programs. From FY 1996 to FY 2000, these combined streams of funding cost American taxpayers a total of $23 billion. During that same period, Congress appropriated $1 billion for the FBI's counterterrorism and national security efforts.[14]

---

12. David B. Muhlhausen, "Do Community Oriented Policing Services Grants Affect Violent Crime Rates?" *Center for Data Analysis Report* No. CDA01–05, May 25, 2001, at *www.heritage.org/library/cda/cda01-05.html*.

13. *Ibid.*

FACT: Problem-oriented policing, when used correctly, is effective in reducing crime.

The concept of problem-oriented policing is often discussed under the broad umbrella of community policing, but it is a distinct tactic. Police officers engaged in problem-oriented policing do not simply respond to calls for service by making an arrest. Rather, they identify, define, and analyze the causes of a crime in order to work to prevent re-occurrences.[15] Rigorous research shows the impact the police can have on reducing crime when police officers critically analyze the occurrence of crime and develop clear strategies to reduce it.

Anthony A. Braga of Harvard University selected 24 high-activity, violent-crime Jersey City, New Jersey, neighborhoods and matched them into 12 pairs.[16] Each neighborhood's particular crime problems and characteristics were identified by officers using crime-mapping technology and on-site visits. By random assignment, one of the matched pairs received problem-oriented policing techniques, while the other received traditional police patrols of the neighborhood. Specific plans were developed for each neighborhood under the problem-oriented policing model, including aggressive order maintenance and preventive changes in the physical environment. The control neighborhoods received conventional police patrols. Criminal incidents and calls for service significantly decreased in the neighborhoods subject to problem-oriented policing, compared with the control neighborhoods.[17]

---

14. See David B. Muhlhausen, "Where the Justice Department Can Find $2.6 Billion for Its Anti-Terrorism Efforts," Heritage Foundation *Backgrounder* No. 1486, October 5, 2001, at *www.heritage.org/library/backgrounder/bg1486.html*.

15. Herman Goldstein, *Problem-Oriented Policing* (New York: McGraw–Hill, 1990).

16. Anthony A. Braga *et al.*, "Problem-Oriented Policing in Violent Crime Places: A Randomized Controlled Experiment," *Criminology*, Vol. 37, No. 3 (1999), pp. 541–580.

17. *Ibid.*

FACT: A disproportionate number of violent crimes are committed by a small number of criminals with a history of repeat offenses.

- An ambitious analysis of 1.7 million criminal offenses conducted by researchers at the Bureau of Justice Statistics found that

> A small fraction of offenders were responsible for a disproportionate number of these 1.7 million charges. An estimated 5 percent of the prisoners were charged with 45 or more offenses each before and after their release in 1983. This group of high rate offenders accounted for nearly 20 percent of all arrest charges. Offenders with 25 or more charges represented 18.6 percent of all offenders but accounted for 47.8 percent of all charges.[18]

- The Bureau of Justice Statistics also found that two-thirds of prisoners released from state prisons are rearrested within three years, but only about 40 percent of them are again committed to prison.[19]

- A recent analysis of Philadelphia homicide arrests in the city's highest-crime police district found that about half of the district's murderers had histories of violent crime and drug and weapons arrests. As many as half of them were actually on probation or parole, or awaiting trial or sentencing, at the time they killed their victims.[20]

FACT: Too many probationers and parolees waste little time before committing another crime.

- Dangerously high caseloads and lack of monitoring allow parolees to violate the terms of their supervision or commit further offenses.[21] The Bureau of Justice Statistics estimates

18. Allen J. Beck and Bernard E. Shipley, "Recidivism of Prisoners Released in 1983," *Bureau of Justice Statistics Special Report*, U.S. Department of Justice, Office of Justice Programs, NCJ–116261, April 1989, p. 4.
19. *Ibid.*, p. 1.
20. Tierney, McClanahan, and Hangley, *Murder Is No Mystery: An Analysis of Philadelphia Homicide, 1996–1999.*
21. Joan Petersilia, "When Prisoners Return to the Community: Political, Economic, and Social Consequences," in *Sentencing and Corrections: Issues for the 21st Century*, National Institute of Justice, No. 9, November 2000.

that "24 percent of those serving time in state prisons for rape and 19 percent of those serving time for sexual assault had been on probation or parole at the time of the offense for which they were in state prison in 1991."[22]

- A 1991 U.S. Department of Justice study of 162,000 probationers found that 6,400 were sent back to state prisons for committing murder, 7,400 for committing rape, 10,400 for committing an assault, and 17,000 for committing robbery.[23]
- Several studies found that about half of all probationers do not comply with the terms of their sentences, but only 20 percent of those who violate the terms of their probation are incarcerated for non-compliance.[24]

FACT: When police brutality occurs, it is horrific, but incidents of excessive use of police force are rare.

In 1999, the Bureau of Justice Statistics surveyed Americans aged 16 and over about police contact during the previous year.[25] The survey found that, of the 21 percent of U.S. residents who had contact with the police, 52 percent reported being stopped for traffic violations; 21 percent merely asked for or provided the police with some assistance; and 22 percent reported a crime, either as a witness or as a victim. Less than half of 1 percent of respondents experienced the use or threatened use of force by the police; and more than half of those who reported experiencing such force also admitted that they had argued, disobeyed, resisted, or assaulted the police or had been under the influence of alcohol or drugs. Although excessive police force is unacceptable, the problem is indeed much smaller than many persons assume.

---

22. Lisa Price-Grear, "Bureau of Justice Statistics Fiscal Year 1998: At a Glance," U.S. Department of Justice, Office of Justice Programs, revised May 1998, p. 16, at *www.ojp.usdoj.gov/bjs/pub/pdf/bjsfy98.pdf.*
23. Robyn L. Cohen, "Probation and Parole Violators in State Prison, 1991," *Bureau of Justice Statistics Special Report*, U.S. Department of Justice, Office of Justice Programs, NCJ–149076, August 1995, p. 1.
24. Reinventing Probation Council, "Broken Windows," in *Probation: The Next Step in Fighting Crime*, Manhattan Institute Center for Civic Innovation, No. 7, August 1999, p. 2, at *www.manhattan-institute.org/html/cr_7.htm.*
25. Patrick A. Langan *et al.*, *Between Police and the Public: Findings from the 1999 National Survey*, U.S. Department of Justice, Bureau of Justice Statistics, NCJ–184957, February 2001, pp. 1–3.

FACT: Additional federal legislation prohibiting "racial profiling" is unnecessary, and the proposed legislation would do more harm than good.

Government discrimination based on race, religion, and national origin is prohibited by the U.S. Constitution and a number of state and federal statutes. Moreover, various federal laws allow anyone subjected to unlawful discrimination by state or federal officials to sue for monetary damages and injunctive relief.[26] Illegitimate racial profiling occurs when a particular racial or ethnic group is targeted for increased stops or arrests simply by virtue of its race or ethnic origin. If an individual police officer or police agency intentionally engaged in such conduct, that would be illegal and would subject that officer or agency to liability under existing anti-discrimination laws. However, much of what has been labeled "racial profiling" by activists and the press is not profiling at all.

- The use of racial characteristics to describe or identify particular criminal suspects is often necessary in law enforcement and is neither racial profiling nor unlawful. Police officers must take such physical descriptions into account when narrowing the range of potential suspects, especially when they arrive at the scene soon after a crime occurs. For example, if a rape victim reported that her attacker was an overweight white man, it would be counterproductive and a waste of valuable time and resources for the police to focus on anyone that did not meet that physical description.

- Those who say that illegal racial profiling is widespread base their claim almost entirely on arrest statistics that, at most, show a disparate number of arrests by race. That type of statistic says *absolutely nothing* about whether the particular rate of arrests is too high, too low, or the result of improper police practices. Serious social science studies, which control for crime as reported by victims and other relevant variables, confirm that illegitimate racial profiling is rare.[27]

26. See, for example, 42 U.S.C. §§ 1981–1983.

- Proposed congressional legislation to fix the alleged problems would do far more harm than good.[28] Americans who live in high-crime areas need and often demand additional police patrols and other resources in their neighborhoods. Most crime in America is intra-racial, with minority criminals preying on members of their own race. If the police and local officials are effective in meeting the demands of citizens in high-crime areas, this will likely correlate with an increased arrest rate for a particular racial group (or a "disparate impact" on arrests by race) and a reduction in crime. The proposed federal legislation would presume there was discrimination from such a crime reduction success story. Law-abiding citizens in high-crime areas could be the most severely hurt, as politicians and police officials refuse to increase police resources where they are most needed.

- Under some proposed federal legislation, individual police officers might also be reluctant to pursue suspicious conduct if doing so would adversely affect their stop or arrest statistics for that reporting period and subject them to unwarranted investigation. It is absurd to expect that every police officer on every beat will stop and arrest an exact microcosm of the jurisdiction's racial or ethnic population during each reporting period, but legislation that requires the collection of arrest statistics in every jurisdiction is based on the notion that unlawful discrimination is the most likely explanation for any disparity.

- The community policing model relies on experienced officers, regardless of race, to know what behavior is so out of place in their beat that it merits additional attention. Stopping cars along a highway based solely or even largely on the driver's perceived race—sometimes referred to as "driving while black"—is illegitimate.[29] But in a special setting, race

27. See, for example, U.S. General Accounting Office, *Racial Profiling: Limited Data Available on Motorist Stops*, B–283949, GAO/GGD–00–41: "We found no…source of information that could be used to determine whether race has been a key factor in motorist stops. [The existing studies] have not provided conclusive empirical data from a social science standpoint to determine the extent to which racial profiling occurs. See also James Q. Wilson and Richard J. Herrnstein, *Crime & Human Nature* (New York: Simon and Schuster, 1985), pp. 459–486.

28. The legislation introduced in the 106th Congress that received the most attention was H.R. 3981/S. 989.

sometimes may be one of several supporting factors that lead a police officer to examine a situation more closely. In the movie *Traffic*, the character played by Michael Douglas spots some white teenagers dressed in prep school uniforms in an inner-city minority neighborhood, and concludes they are there to buy drugs. An experienced beat cop who never observed white teens living in such a neighborhood, who knew there were no prep schools in the area, and who knew that an open-air drug market was in the immediate direction in which the teens were heading might have even more reason to be suspicious and to monitor their behavior.

- Although unlawful racial profiling is rare, police forces across the country have responded to the real and, in some cases, perceived need to better educate and monitor police officers about unlawful racial profiling. The Police Executive Research Forum (PERF) has been particularly active in trying to ensure that the nation's police departments have clear and effective policies against unlawful racial profiling. Its *Racially Biased Policing* report is especially helpful because it provides a comprehensive set of recommendations to eliminate bias in policing rather than simply addressing erroneous notions of "racial profiling" in particular settings.[30]

- Finally, the Supreme Court has explained that racial and ethnic classifications are not unconstitutional if they are narrowly tailored to serve a compelling government interest. This exacting test is almost never satisfied, and justifiably so. But the prevention of terrorist attacks in America is a compelling government interest. There may be instances in which officials determine that airport screeners and anti-terrorism units must take national origin into account to provide an adequate level of security against future terrorist attacks. In such cases, the federal courts would be open to consider the challenged procedures and the stated grounds that justified them. That is a much better protection of personal liberty than a blunt federal statute that would flatly prohibit the consideration of national origin under any circumstances.

---

29. It should be re-emphasized, however, that the above-cited GAO study found no convincing evidence that this practice is widespread.
30. Lorie Fridell, Robert Lunney, Drew Diamond, and Bruce Kubu, *Racially Biased Policing: A Principled Response*, Police Executive Research Forum, Washington, D.C., 2001. The report is available by contacting PERF.

FACT: Aggressive order-maintenance policing, as practiced by New York City, has reduced crime without resulting in an increase in excessive use of force.

Perhaps the most dramatic example of police success in combating crime and reducing the use of excessive force is in New York City. Serious crime dropped a stunning 54.7 percent between 1993 and 1999, and murder rates declined by 65.4 percent.[31] At the same time, even as the size of the force grew, the number of police shootings declined by 50.5 percent, and the numbers of allegations of excessive use of force and civilian complaints per police officer also declined.[32]

A Manhattan Institute study of the performance of the New York City Police Department estimates that over 60,000 violent crimes were prevented between 1989 and 1998 because of a strategy called "broken windows" policing, which focuses on improving the quality of life in the city's diverse neighborhoods.[33]

Despite certain highly publicized and tragic events in New York City, objective measures of police performance indicate that the NYPD does not have a rampant police brutality problem. Among police departments in Chicago, Dallas, Houston, Miami, New York, Philadelphia, and Washington, D.C., the NYPD's fatal shooting rate of 0.28 per 1,000 officers was the lowest in 1999.[34] Police agencies in Miami, Houston, and Washington, D.C., had fatal shooting rates that were, respectively, 10.7, 6.0, and 4.1 times the NYPD's.[35]

---

31. New York Police Department, "Executive Summary," *NYPD Response to the Draft Report of the United States Commission on Civil Rights*, 2000, p. 1, at *www.ci.nyc.ny.us/html/nypd/html/dclm/exsumm.html*.
32. *Ibid.*, p. 2.
33. George L. Kelling and William H. Sousa Jr., "Do Police Matter? An Analysis of the Impact of New York City's Police Reforms," Manhattan Institute *Civic Report* No. 22, December 2001, p. 1.
34. New York Police Department, "Executive Summary," *NYPD Response to the Draft Report*, p. 5.
35. Based on calculations of data provided in *ibid.*

FACT: Putting each repeat or violent offender in prison substantially increases public safety.

Steven Levitt of the University of Chicago found that for each prisoner released from prison, the result was an increase of almost 15 reported and unreported crimes per year.[36]

The results of two studies by Thomas B. Marvell and Carlisle E. Moody of the College of William and Mary support these findings of the effects of incarceration:

- In a 1994 study of 49 states' incarceration rates from 1971 to 1989, Marvell and Moody found that for each additional prisoner put behind bars, about 17 crimes (mainly property crimes) were averted.[37]
- In another study using national data from 1930 to 1994, the scholars found that a 10 percent increase in the total prison population is associated with a 13 percent decrease in homicide, after controlling for socioeconomic factors.[38]

FACT: Family structure, not race, is a determining factor of crime.

Heritage Foundation studies show that a chaotic broken community stems from broken families.[39] Although race appears to be an important factor in crime rates, studies find that the difference is attributable to widely different marriage rates among various ethnic groups. The evidence simply does not support the view that a criminal's race is causally linked to crime rates. When social scientists control for family structure, the rates for blacks and whites are not statistically different.[40]

---

36. Steven D. Levitt, "The Effect of Prison Population Size on Crime Rates: Evidence from Prison Overcrowding Litigation," *The Quarterly Journal of Economics*, May 1996, pp. 319–351.
37. Thomas B. Marvell and Carlisle E. Moody, Jr., "Prison Population Growth and Crime Reduction," *Journal of Quantitative Criminology*, Vol. 10, No. 2 (1994), pp. 109–140.
38. Thomas B. Marvell and Carlisle E. Moody, Jr., "The Impact of Prison Growth on Homicide," *Homicide Studies*, Vol. 1, No. 3 (1997), pp. 205–233.
39. For additional information, see the chapter on the family. For a detailed account of the relationship between broken families and the rise in violent crime as described in social science literature, see Patrick F. Fagan, "The Real Root Causes of Violent Crime: The Breakdown of Marriage, Family, and Community," Heritage Foundation *Backgrounder* No. 1026, March 17, 1995, at *www.heritage.org/library/backgrounder/bg1026.htm*.
40. *Ibid.*, p. 4.

WHAT TO DO IN 2003

Candidates for Congress have an opportunity to focus voters' attention on policies that make America's communities, neighborhoods, and cities much safer. The best policies would:

Reduce federal intrusion into state and local crime-fighting activities.

Members of Congress should affirm the division of authority between the federal government and the states in combating violent crime. Federal officials have enough to do in fighting international terrorism, illegal narcotics trafficking, and powerful organized crime syndicates without taking on street crime. Therefore, Congress should undertake a systematic review of every federal law dealing with violent crime, determine which provisions interfere with or undermine legitimate state and local law enforcement authority, and repeal those provisions.

At the very least, Congress and the Administration should make sure that taxpayers' money is targeted toward local anti-crime programs that work. Before any federal grants are awarded, applicants must be required to present a clear plan on how they intend to use the funds to prevent crime. The plan should be based on programs that have been empirically demonstrated to be effective in other jurisdictions. Applicants also must have in place a system to measure and evaluate the effectiveness of the federal grants. And after the funds have been spent, the federally funded activities must be evaluated for their effectiveness in reducing crime.

Examples of the kind of program that would qualify for this assistance are the problem-oriented policing programs implemented in Jersey City, New Jersey, and Boston, Massachusetts, which have reduced crime substantially.[41]

---

41. Braga *et al.*, "Problem-Oriented Policing in Violent Crime Places." See also Anthony A. Braga *et al.*, "Problem-Oriented Policing, Deterrence, and Youth Violence: An Evaluation of Boston's Operation Ceasefire," *Journal of Research in Crime and Delinquency*, Vol. 38, No. 3 (2001), pp. 195–225.

End wasteful and ineffective grant programs administered by COPS and the Office of Justice Programs, and use the money to bolster counterterrorism efforts.

From FY 1996 to FY 2000, the federal government allocated over $23 billion in Office of Justice Programs and COPS grants to state and local governments for police, juvenile justice, and other criminal justice programs. As noted above, however, during that same period, Congress appropriated only $1 billion for the FBI's counterterrorism and national security efforts—a ratio of more than 22 to1.[42] The threat to America from terrorism demands that Congress and the Bush Administration reorder the federal government's crime-fighting priorities and start channeling funds away from ineffective programs, such as COPS, and into efforts to counter terrorism. For fiscal year 2002, Congress appropriated $4 billion in funding for COPS and OJP programs that are often wasteful, unproven, or demonstrably ineffective.

For FY 2003, the Administration has proposed the elimination of COPS hiring grants and the consolidation of the Byrne Formula Grant and Local Law Enforcement Block Grant programs into a smaller Justice Assistance Grant Program.[43] These changes would make $430 million available for the more urgent task of counterterrorism. While these changes represent progress, however, the Administration still does not require applicants for the $800 million in Justice Assistance Grant Program funding to demonstrate that they are going to use federal taxpayer dollars effectively.

Oppose funding for federal crime programs if at least 10 percent of it is not earmarked for scientific evaluations of effectiveness.[44]

For more than four decades, Congress has enacted numerous social programs aimed at crime prevention. Congress should review these programs and require their directors to present impact evaluation data on effectiveness.[45] No congressional

---

42. See Muhlhausen, "Where the Justice Department Can Find $2.6 Billion."
43. *Budget of the United States Government, Fiscal Year 2003—Appendix* (Washington, D.C.: U.S. Government Printing Office, 2002), pp. 650–651.
44. This recommendation was made originally by Professor Lawrence Sherman, now with the University of Pennsylvania. See Sherman *et al., Preventing Crime: What Works, What Doesn't, What's Promising.*

funding for any federal crime prevention program should be appropriated without also funding rigorous program evaluations. Anecdotal examples are simply not sufficient direct evidence that a program has reduced crime. Every dollar wasted is a dollar lost to public safety.

Target law enforcement policies to remedy abuses of probation and parole, which contribute to the problem of repeat offenders.

States, which are responsible for curbing the abuses of probation and parole, should subject parolees to intense supervision. Offenders must be held to the terms of their probation or parole and face increasing penalties for non-compliance. Those who violate the terms of their parole or probation should be promptly reincarcerated. States should incarcerate violent offenders and require them to serve their full sentences. States should abolish parole for violent repeat offenders. Some violent offenders—particularly those that prey on children and law enforcement personnel—pose too great a risk to let out on parole and should remain incarcerated.

Nominate and confirm judges to serve on the Supreme Court and other federal courts whose records demonstrate a sensitivity to public safety and fidelity to the Constitution and the rule of law.

As the federal judges appointed by Presidents Ronald Reagan and George H. W. Bush retire, a number of federal courts are becoming dominated by activist judges who substitute their own views on criminal law for what is provided in criminal statutes and the U.S. Constitution. President George W. Bush has responded by nominating a number of outstanding candidates to fill more than 100 vacancies on the federal bench.[46] The judicial vacancy rate is now double what Senate Judiciary Committee Chairman Patrick Leahy (D–VT), said constituted a "judicial vacancy crisis" just a few years ago. Nevertheless, Senator Leahy has stalled confirmation hearings and is falling fur-

---

45. An "impact evaluation" is defined as an evaluative study that measures a program's outcomes on the social conditions that it is intended to improve. Process measures, such as how much funding was dispersed and how many people were served, are not measures of a program's effectiveness in improving the targeted social condition.

46. See *www.usdoj.gov/olp/judicialnominations.htm*.

ther and further behind in his obligation to act on the President's judicial nominations.[47]

President Bush should continue to nominate candidates with a strong record of sensitivity to public safety and fidelity to the Constitution and the rule of law. The Senate should act promptly on those nominations and apply the same criteria in its deliberations—instead of the political litmus tests advanced by some liberal activist groups and some members of the Senate Judiciary Committee.

Raise hiring standards for police officers and improve management of police departments.

The Attorney General should work with state and local officials to implement policies that will reduce the incidence of excessive use of police force. A bad person cannot make a good police officer. In the hiring and promotion of police officers, state and local officials should require that candidates meet high mental, moral, and physical standards of performance. In addition, police commanders should be held accountable for effective policing methods in their jurisdiction.

—Edwin Meese III is Ronald Reagan Distinguished Fellow in Public Policy and Chairman of the Center for Legal and Judicial Studies, David B. Muhlhausen is a Policy Analyst in the Center for Data Analysis, and Robert E. Moffit, Ph.D., is Director of Domestic Policy Studies at The Heritage Foundation. Todd Gaziano, Senior Fellow in Legal Studies and Director of the Center for Legal and Judicial Studies at The Heritage Foundation, and Research Assistant Jennifer Garrett assisted with this chapter.

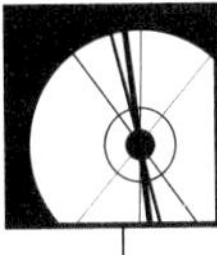

For a complete list and full-text versions of additional studies by Heritage on crime prevention issues, see the searchable *Issues 2002* companion CD–ROM.

47. See Alberto Gonzales, "The Crisis in Our Courts," *The Wall Street Journal*, January 25, 2002, p. A18.

EXPERTS

Heritage Foundation

David B. Muhlhausen
Policy Analyst
Center for Data Analysis
The Heritage Foundation
214 Massachusetts Avenue, NE
Washington, DC 20002
(202) 546-6209
fax: (202) 675-1772
david.muhlhausen@heritage.org

Robert E. Moffit, Ph.D.
Director of Domestic Policy Studies
The Heritage Foundation
214 Massachusetts Avenue, NE
Washington, DC 20002
(202) 546-6211
fax: (202) 544-5421
robert.moffit@heritage.org

Edwin Meese III
Ronald Reagan Distinguished Fellow in Public Policy and
Chairman, Center for Legal and Judicial Studies
The Heritage Foundation
214 Massachusetts Avenue, NE
Washington, DC 20002
(202) 608-6181
fax: (202) 547-0641
edwin.meese@heritage.org

Todd Gaziano
Senior Fellow in Legal Studies
and Director, Center for Legal and Judicial Studies
The Heritage Foundation
214 Massachusetts Avenue, NE
Washington, DC 20002
(202) 608-6181
fax: (202) 547-0641
todd.gaziano@heritage.org

Other Experts

George Kelling
Professor, School of Criminal Justice
Rutgers University
15 Washington Street
Newark, NJ 07102
(973) 353-5923
fax: (973) 353-5896

Andrew T. Lefevre
Director of Criminal Justice and Education Task Forces
American Legislative Exchange Council
910 17th Street, NW, 5th Floor
Washington, DC 20006
(202) 466-3800
fax: (202) 466-3801
alefevre@alec.org

James Q. Wilson
Professor Emeritus
The Anderson School
University of California Los Angeles
110 Westwood Plaza
Box 951481
Los Angeles, CA 90095
(310) 825-2840

For continually updated and expanded information on major breaking developments on this issue over the campaign cycle, see *www.heritage.org/issues/crime.*

THE FAMILY

Improving Marriage, Strengthening Society

Patrick F. Fagan

THE ISSUES

The family is the building block of society. It is the organism through which the very life of a nation is nurtured and passed on to future generations. Without stable marriages as the basis of the family unit, this organism is weakened, and children are the most seriously affected. Thus, future generations of Americans will bear the brunt of the family's weakness today.

The effects, however, go beyond the family. When marriages and families are healthy, communities thrive; when marriages break down, communities break down. And the more this happens, the more government is asked to step in to address this collateral damage—even though its record at solving the social problems that arise from broken families has been poor.[1]

1. **As marriage declines, the demand for government intervention with social programs rises.** Many studies show that when the state of marriage in a community is healthy, the demand for government social programs is low. But when the state of marriage is poor, the need for state spending is high—to address everything from poverty, drug addiction, crime, court services, remedial education services, crisis pregnancies, foster care, child support enforcement, health problems, and mental health needs.

   To reduce the need for such programs, policymakers should build on what they know about the beneficial effects of healthy marriages. Marriage is not a panacea for all personal

1. For additional information and charts illustrating many of the problems that result from family breakdown, see *www.heritage.org/issues/family*.

or social problems, but the work involved in producing healthy marriages will transform family and community life so that the number of people supported by government falls significantly. Spending resources in this way is a far more effective investment in the future.

2. **A strong family is built on wedlock, worship, and work.** Research is showing that not only does marriage benefit a family and its children; so too does regular worship of God. And when marriage and worship combine with full-time work by just one parent (at any income level), the probability that the family will fall victim to social problems virtually disappears. Families that are not characterized by wedlock, worship, and work are more likely to suffer from drug abuse, child abuse, out-of-wedlock births, teenage abortions, school dropouts, violent juvenile crime, mental illness, poverty, and dependence on government.

   Simply put, faith, family, and work provide a safety net that government cannot match.[2] While America's political freedoms protect the right of citizens to choose their own lifestyles, they cannot protect them from the consequences of their choices. Public programs should provide conditions that permit society's basic institutions to do their work; they should not ignore these institutions, much less undermine them.

3. **The federal government penalizes marriage, especially among the poor.** As the chapter on welfare reform explains in more detail, the current welfare system includes disincentives to marriage; low-income couples that marry tend to lose a larger portion of their benefits than they otherwise would. Since the beginning of the War on Poverty in the mid-1960s, the proportion of children in the lowest-income quintile that are being raised by single parents has risen from 60 percent to 80 percent. And although the welfare reform act of 1996 called on the states to use a portion of their federal Temporary Assistance to Needy Families (TANF) funds to promote marriage, few have done so. In 2000, the states budgeted merely 0.16 percent of the $7.3 billion in surplus TANF

---

2. See, for example, the research papers on the effects of marriage and worship presented by sociologists at a May 2001 Princeton University conference, at *http://crcw.princeton.edu/CRCW/religionandfamily.htm*.

money available nationally.[3] The Earned Income Tax Credit (EITC) is another program that, because of its current structure, discriminates against working parents who marry.

THE FACTS

FACT: The environment that allows children to thrive the most is provided by the natural family.

A natural family is one in which mother and father live together to care for the children they bring into existence. Married family life is associated in research studies with better health and longer life spans. Married couples have consistently lower death rates from disease and suicide. Divorce causes reductions in household income and wealth, often forcing single mothers onto the poverty rolls. In households with children, the drop in household income immediately following a divorce may be as high as 42 percent. Frequent housing moves often follow, disrupting both learning and friendships. Divorce is tied to higher rates of crime, abuse, neglect, and drug use. In fact, divorce increases the juvenile crime rate by up to 12 times.[4]

Other than the widowed family, all other forms of the family unit—aside from the natural family—involve some form of personal rejection, whether between the mother and father (in divorce and some out-of-wedlock births) or in the form of an ambivalence of affection and commitment (in most out-of-wedlock births and cohabitation).[5] An analysis of available data shows that nearly one-third of all children conceived today will be aborted;[6] one-third of those that are not will be born out-of-wedlock; and 40 percent of those born to married parents will experience the divorce of their parents before age 18.[7]

---

3. See Ed Lazere, "Welfare Balances After Three Years of Temporary Assistance to Needy Families Block Grants," Center on Budget and Policy Priorities, January 2000, pp. 14–15.
4. Patrick F. Fagan, "Encouraging Marriage and Discouraging Divorce," Heritage Foundation *Backgrounder* No. 1421, March 26, 2001, at *www.heritage.org/library/backgrounder/bg1421.html.*
5. Except where death causes the end of the marriage.
6. Over 80 percent of abortions occur outside of marriage; see Stanley K. Henshaw and Kathryn Kost, "Abortion Patients in 1994–1995: Characteristics and Contraceptive Use," *Family Planning Perspectives*, Vol. 28, No. 4 (1996), pp. 104–147.

FACT: The safest place for children is living in an intact married family; the most dangerous is a home where the mother lives with a boyfriend.

Children raised outside of the always-intact married family are at greater risk of serious child abuse—six times more likely in a step family; 13 times more likely in the single-mother-living-alone family; 20 times more likely in the cohabiting-natural-parent family; and 33 times more likely when the mother lives with a boyfriend. Abuse resulting in death is 73 times more likely when a mother lives with a boyfriend.[8]

FACT: The safest relationship for women is marriage; the most dangerous is cohabitation.

Federal survey data found domestic violence against women to be almost three times higher among cohabiting couples than among couples who have ever been married (that is, married, separated, and/or divorced), and almost five times higher than among currently married couples.[9]

FACT: The intact married family is the best mental health, school preparation, and drug prevention "program" there is.

Children born or raised outside of marriage are more likely to suffer mental health problems; they suffer depression[10] and commit suicide[11] more often. Children whose parents were not married have showed an increased likelihood of having lower verbal IQ, lower school performance, and lower school attendance, all leading to lower job attainment and lower income.[12] Teenagers

7. Analysis of data on birth, divorce, and abortion from U.S. Department of Health and Human Services, National Center for Health Statistics, 1950–1995.

8. See charts from Robert Whelan, *Broken Homes & Battered Children*, Family Education Trust, Great Britain, 1993, at *www.heritage.org/issues/family*.

9. U.S. Department of Justice, National Crime Victimization Survey, 1999. For more information, see chart at *www.heritage.org/issues/family*.

10. Deborah A. Dawson, "Family Structure and Children's Health and Well Being: Data from the 1988 National Health Interview Survey of Child Health," *Journal of Marriage and the Family*, Vol. 53 (August 1991). Data from U.S. Department of Health and Human Services, Centers for Disease Control, National Center for Health Statistics, National Health Survey, Series 10, No. 178, June 1991.

11. Patricia L. McCall and Kenneth Land, "Trends in White Male Adolescent, Young-Adult, and Elderly Suicide: Are There Common Underlying Structural Factors?" *Social Science Research*, Vol. 23 (1994), pp. 57–81.

whose parents have divorced have used cocaine almost twice as much as children in intact married families, and children in single-parent families have used cocaine almost three times as much.[13]

FACT: One-third of all children are born out of wedlock, and much more often to adult women than to teens.

The out-of-wedlock birth rate has leveled off at around 33 percent of all births for the past five years, but this is the result of two opposing trends: a decrease in teenage out-of-wedlock births[14] and a continued rise in the number of older adults giving birth out of wedlock.[15]

Recent survey data from the Fragile Families Survey conducted by Princeton and Columbia Universities show that the majority of the fathers and mothers of children born out of wedlock are romantically involved. Most of these couples also reported a 50–50 chance of getting married.[16] One major obstacle: federal welfare and tax policy.

FACT: Divorce affects about 1 million children each year.

Following the "no fault" change in divorce laws in the 1970s, the number of children suffering the divorce of their parents peaked at 1.2 million per year in the early 1980s.[17] Today, the picture is more complex: Children see their married parents split, but so do the children of cohabiting parents. Good data on the latter are not

---

12. See Patrick F. Fagan, "Rising Illegitimacy: America's Social Catastrophe," Heritage Foundation *F.Y.I.* No. 19, June 29, 1994, at *www.heritage.org/library/archives/fyi/fyi_19.pdf*.
13. U.S. Department of Health and Human Services, National Longitudinal Survey of Adolescent Health, Wave 2, University of NC/NICHD/HHS; see chart at *www.heritage.org/issues/family*.
14. The recent steady decrease can be attributed in large part to the introduction of abstinence education programs.
15. Data from U.S. Department of Health and Human Services, Centers for Disease Control and Prevention, National Center for Health Statistics, *Vital Statistics*, relevant years (cited hereafter as NCHS *Vital Statistics*).
16. Sara McLanahan, Irving Garfinkel, *et al.*, "The Fragile Families and Child Well Being Study, Baseline Report," August 2001, at *http://crcw.princeton.edu/fragilefamilies/nationalreport.pdf*.
17. For an overview of the literature, see Patrick F. Fagan and Robert Rector, "The Effects of Divorce on America," Heritage Foundation *Backgrounder* No. 1373, June 3, 2000, at *www.heritage.org/library/backgrounder/bg1373.html*.

available. Thus, the number of children affected by the breakup of their parents is still likely to be around 1.2 million per year.

FACT: One generation of broken marriages feeds the next generation of broken marriages.

Social research shows that, among the children of broken marriages, there are more out-of-wedlock births,[18] more cohabitation, and more divorce.[19] Social scientist Deborah Dawson has described it this way: "Women who spend part of their childhood in single parent families are more likely to marry and bear children early; to give birth before marriage; and to have their own marriages break up."[20]

FACT: The rate of divorce among couples who have lived together before they marry is twice the rate of divorce among those who have not lived together before marriage.

Cohabitation is a fragile living arrangement. Not only are couples more likely to divorce if they live together first, but those who cohabit, split, and then marry someone else eventually divorce at four times the rate of those who do not cohabit before marriage.[21]

FACT: Children in broken families are more likely to commit juvenile crime.

When it comes to juvenile crime rates, marriage matters a lot. For instance, in Wisconsin—the only government entity to have published family background data—teenagers of always-single-parent families are 22 times more likely to end up in jail[22] than are those from two-parent families.[23]

---

18. See Fagan, "Rising Illegitimacy, America's Social Catastrophe"; see also Andrew J. Cherlin, Kathleen E. Kiernan, and P. Lindsay Chase-Lansdale, "Parental Divorce in Childhood and Demographic Outcomes in Young Adulthood," *Demography*, Vol. 32 (1995), pp. 299–316.
19. See Cherlin *et al.*, "Parental Divorce in Childhood"; Paul Amato and Alan Booth, *A Generation at Risk*, (Cambridge: Harvard University Press, 1997), pp. 109–112; and Pamela S. Webster *et al.*, "Effects of Childhood Family Background on Adult Marital Quality and Perceived Stability," *American Journal of Sociology*, Vol. 101 (1995), pp. 404–432.
20. Dawson, "Family Structure and Children's Health and Well Being," pp. 573–584.
21. Larry L. Bumpass, Teresa Castro Martin, and James A. Sweet, "The Impact of Family Background and Early Marital Factors on Marital Disruption, *Journal of Family Issues*, Vol. 12, No 1 (March 1991), pp. 22-42.
22. Or other forms of detainment, such as group homes.

The huge differences in rates of crime among black and white teenagers virtually vanish when one controls for family background.[24] In other words, black teenagers and white teenagers from broken families have similar rates of juvenile crime: They are high. Black teenagers and white teenagers from intact married parents also have similar rates of juvenile crime: They are low.

Finally, fairly recent findings from a U.S. longitudinal study of more than 6,400 boys conducted over 20 years show that children who grow up without their biological father in the home are roughly three times more likely to commit crimes that lead to incarceration than are children from intact families.[25] Other studies have found that children of divorced parents are up to six times more likely to be delinquent than are children from intact families.[26]

FACT: A child is 50 percent more likely to die during infancy if born out of wedlock.

Children born outside of marriage have 1.5 times the risk of low birthweight;[27] and low birthweight increases their susceptibility to neonatal illnesses, which make a baby significantly more likely to die in infancy.[28]

FACT: Marriage also provides the safest environment for a child before birth.

Both national surveys conducted by the Alan Guttmacher Institute, the research institute used by Planned Parenthood, show

23. See Patrick F. Fagan, "Congress's Role in Improving Juvenile Delinquency Data," Heritage Foundation *Backgrounder* No. 1351, March 10, 2000, at *www.heritage.org/library/backgrounder/bg1351.html.*
24. Douglas Smith and G. Robert Jarjoura, "Social Structure and Criminal Victimization," *Journal of Research in Crime and Delinquency*, Vol. 25, No. 1 (February 1988), pp. 27–52; see also Robert J. Sampson, "Urban Black Violence: The Effect of Male Joblessness and Family Disruption," *American Journal of Sociology*, Vol. 93 (1987), pp. 348–382.
25. Cynthia Harper and Sara S. McLanahan, "Father Absence and Youth Incarceration," findings presented at 1998 meeting of the American Sociological Association, San Francisco.
26. See David B. Larson, James P. Swyers, and Susan S. Larson, *The Costly Consequences of Divorce* (Rockville, Md.: National Institute for Healthcare Research, 1995), p. 123.
27. Nicholas Eberstadt, *The Tyranny of Numbers: Mismeasurement and Misrule* (Washington, D.C.: AEI Press, 1995), p. 33, Table 1-4; based on 1960 federal survey data from HHS/NCHS.
28. *Ibid.*, p. 32.

that being conceived outside of marriage quadruples the chances of a child being aborted.[29]

FACT: Civic and church leaders now know how to do a better job of preparing people for marriage.

Over the past two decades, marriage research experts[30] have contributed to an increase in the knowledge of precisely which skills and habits build better marriages, as well as assessment tools and proven preparation courses.[31] Engaged couples enrolled in marriage preparation courses are better able to identify the difficulties that lie ahead for them; many, in fact, decide *not* to marry.

Cities that have instituted a "marriage-savers" policy have seen their divorce rates drop over the past decade. Marriage Savers, a faith-based, non-denominational movement, has spread to over 180 cities across the country.[32] Its presence is linked to decreased divorce rates citywide in 32 cities. Modesto, California, for example, has had a 47.6 percent drop in divorces, while its marriage rate has risen by 13.1 percent. Between 1995 and 1999, Kansas City, Kansas, and its suburbs saw divorces decrease by 44 percent on this program.

There is even one pilot program in which 50 percent of those already in divorce court seeking a divorce will turn around to rebuild their marriages successfully if given the chance to take "Focused Thinking Mediation."[33]

---

29. Heritage Foundation calculations based on Alan Guttmacher Institute data; from Stanley K. Henshaw *et al.*, "Characteristics and Private Contraceptive Use of U.S. Abortion Patients," *Family Planning Perspectives*, Vol. 20, No. 4 (1989), and Henshaw and Kost, "Abortion Patients in 1994–1995: Characteristics and Contraceptive Use."
30. Such as Dr. Howard Markman and Dr. Scott Stanley, Directors of the Center for Marital and Family Studies at the University of Denver; David Olson of the University of Minnesota, at *http://fsos.che.umn.edu/olson/default.html*; and other academics active in this field. See *www.smartmarriages.com/*.
31. See PAIRS at *www.pairsfoundation.com*; PREP at *www.prepinc.com*; and PREPARE/ENRICH at *www.lifeinnovations.com*; see also *www.marriagesavers.org/public/in_brief.htm*.
32. See *www.marriagesavers.org*.
33. See Fagan, "Encouraging Marriage and Decreasing Divorce," pp. 12–13; see also *www.beyondwinwin.org*.

FACT: Churches that offer a full range of marriage resources virtually eliminate divorce.[34]

Part of the reason for this is that up to 20 percent of couples who take the course decide to part before marriage. The rates of divorce in areas near these churches appear to have fallen significantly.[35] Clearly, many people would save themselves and their children the grief of divorce by approaching marriage more cautiously and deliberately. When church and government cooperate in offering a mixture of faith-based and secular approaches to strengthening marriage, the rebuilding of a culture of marriage follows.[36]

FACT: Abstinence programs are working—especially among teenagers.

Overall, teen abortion rates are down, teen out-of-wedlock birth rates are down,[37] and teenage virginity is rising significantly again. But out-of-wedlock birth rates continue to climb among those in their late twenties and thirties.[38]

FACT: Regular worship increases health, wealth, and happiness.

Children from inner-city poor families who worship weekly are most likely to reach the middle class as adults.[39] Adults who worship weekly are more likely to have happy intact marriages, live longer, be happier, be healthier, and earn more money throughout their lifetime.[40] Families that worship weekly are most likely to

---

34. A full-service program includes seven activities; see Fagan, "Encouraging Marriage and Discouraging Divorce." At the Fourth Presbyterian Church of Bethesda, Maryland, 30 of 175 couples in the program broke their engagement or relationship to avoid a bad marriage—double the national average. Of the 145 couples who did marry between 1992 and 1997, only three separations have occurred. See *www.marriagesavers.com/public/create_ms_church.htm*.
35. See *www.marriagesavers.com/public/divorcerates.htm*.
36. See *www.marriagesavers.com/public/three_governors_invite_marriage.htm*.
37. The rate per thousand has dropped continuously since 1991; see Child Trends, "Facts at a Glance," August 2001, p. 4, at *www.childtrends.org/*.
38. NCHS *Vital Statistics*, relevant years; see chart at *http://issues.heritage.org/family*.
39. Richard B. Freeman, "Who Escapes? The Relation of Church-Going and Other Background Factors to the Socio-Economic Performance of Black Male Youths from Inner-City Poverty Tracts," National Bureau of Economic Research *Working Paper* Series No. 1656, 1985.

raise children who do better at school, commit fewer crimes, have fewer out-of-wedlock births, and marry more often.[41]

FACT: Poverty is predominantly a phenomenon of the broken family.

Children living in always-single-parent families are six times more likely to live in poverty than are children in married families.[42] Of all black children in America, only 3 percent live with married parents and are in poverty.[43] The two-parent family puts much more into the marketplace and gets much more out of it.[44]

FACT: Government welfare programs still penalize poor parents for marrying and spur the growth of poor single-parent families.

- Despite welfare reform, when a single mother marries a poor working man, the federal and state governments will penalize them by reducing their total income resources by as much as 22 percent. Eugene Steuerle of the Urban Institute reports that if a single working man who earns $8 per hour were to marry a single mother of one child, and if she also earns the minimum wage, they will lose $7,500 in income transfers, or roughly 22 percent of their combined income.[45] An equivalent penalty in loss in annual income for a middle-class couple earning $30,000 each per annum who decide to marry would be about $13,000.
- The proportion of single-parent families has grown continually in the past few decades. In 2000, 80 percent of children in the bottom quintile of income lived in single-parent fami-

---

40. See Patrick Fagan, "Why Religion Matters: The Impact of Religious Practice on Social Stability," Heritage Foundation *Backgrounder* No. 1064, January 25, 1996, at *www.heritage.org/library/categories/family/bg1064.html*.
41. *Ibid.*, pp. 11–16.
42. Federal Reserve Board, Survey of Consumer Finance, 1995; see Chart 2 at *www.heritage.org/library/cda/cda01-04.html*.
43. Data from U.S. Bureau of the Census, *Current Population Survey*, 1998; see chart at *www.heritage.org/issues/family*.
44. Federal Reserve Board, Survey of Consumer Finance, 1995; see chart at *www.heritage.org/issues/family*.
45. C. Eugene Steuerle, Senior Fellow, Urban Institute, before the Subcommittee on Human Resources, Committee on Ways and Means, U.S. House of Representatives, 107th Cong., 1st Sess., May 22, 2001, at *http://waysandmeans.house.gov/humres/107cong/5-22-01/5-22steu.htm*, Table 1, Example 4.

lies. In 1990, it was 72 percent; in 1980, it was 62 percent.[46] That is a growth of 30 percent in just two decades.

FACT: The federal government will penalize more and more middle-class families with children by gradually undoing recently enacted family-friendly tax provisions.

Recent reforms in the federal tax code, especially the child tax credit, seem like a boon to families; but Congress devised a way to take it all back. The alternative minimum tax (AMT) year by year takes back more and more of the tax relief offered to middle-class families raising children.

This strategy is a replay of the congressional bracket-creep tax strategy of the 1960s, 1970s, and 1980s that financed the expansion of the welfare state from the mid-1960s. Initially designed to ensure that wealthy individuals could not avoid paying income taxes, the AMT is now used as a tax cudgel against ordinary families with children. Since inflation will likely increase the effect of the AMT by itself, this current tax policy is a way to undo the reform the federal government appeared to give families in the child tax credit. Even with this credit, the family is still enjoys far less protection from taxes to raise children than it received in the 1950s.[47]

FACT: Congress still spends more on programs that promote sex outside of marriage than it spends on those that promote sex within marriage.[48]

Congress spends about $145 million more on programs that promote sex outside of marriage (such as Title X of the Public Services Health Act[49] and related programs) than it spends on those that promote abstinence until marriage (such as Section 510, Title V, of the Social Security Act[50] and related programs). Both strategies require investments of time, education, and resources to shape people's values, habits, and skills, especially young peo-

46. Data from U.S. Bureau of the Census, *Current Population Surveys*, published in March of each year; see chart at *www.heritage.org/issues/family*.

47. See testimony of Eugene Steuerle, Urban Institute, at *www.urban.org/TESTIMON/steuerle2.htm*.

48. The President's FY 2003 budget proposes to equalize the spending on both sets of programs.

49. P.L. 91–572.

50. 42 U.S.C. 710.

ple's attitudes toward marriage. Given the social problems associated with broken families, Congress should choose to fund programs that promote marriage and families.

FACT: The welfare state spends virtually nothing on restoring marriage among the poor.

The welfare reform act of 1996 mandated that states use a portion of their federal Temporary Assistance to Needy Families funds to promote marriage. With only a few exceptions, however, the states have not done so. In 2000, the states budgeted only 0.16 percent of the $7.3 billion surplus TANF money that had accumulated nationally.[51]

FACT: The United States, for good reasons, has not ratified two U.N. treaties that are hostile to the natural family.

The United Nations Convention on the Rights of the Child and the Convention on the Elimination of All Forms of Discrimination Against Women (CEDAW), despite their many good goals, set forth a number of objectives that undermine the role of parents and the strength of families. They, for example, seek to have laws enacted in every country that would guarantee a child's right to privacy in all matters, to full freedom of expression whether at home or at school, to an abortion without regard to age, and to legal mechanisms that allow the child to challenge his parent's authority.[52]

WHAT TO DO IN 2003

Work to restore a culture of stable, healthy marriages.

The role of government is to ensure the conditions under which civil society (family, church, school, and the marketplace) can flourish. Americans must be empowered to build

---

51. See Lazere, "Welfare Balances After Three Years of Temporary Assistance to Needy Families," pp. 14–15.

52. For a review with examples of such U.N. policies, see Patrick F. Fagan, "How U.N. Conventions on Women's and Children's Rights Undermine Family, Religion, and Sovereignty," Heritage Foundation *Backgrounder* No. 1407, February 5, 2001, at *www.heritage.org/library/backgrounder/bg1407.html*; see also CEDAW Committee, 21st Sess., "Concluding Observations of the Committee on the Elimination of Discrimination Against Women: Ireland," 1999, paragraphs 193, 325, and 361, at *www.unhchr.ch/tbs/doc.nsf/*.

communities that support healthy marriages—communities in which parents live by the three fundamental principles of wedlock,[53] worship,[54] and work.[55] This often means getting government out of the way and reducing government social engineering.

Even liberal family sociologists now report that children thrive when their fathers and mothers have stable marriages and worship regularly.[56] No one can refute the data: Children and adults in intact married families are happier, healthier, and better off financially than are children in single-parent families.[57]

Stop punishing the working poor for marrying.

Current policy is destroying the culture of marriage among the poor.[58] At a minimum, Congress should move quickly to begin to level the playing field for the poor so that those who marry get the same support as those who do not. One way to take care of the marriage penalty in government programs would be to implement a supplemental Earned Income Tax Credit for working parents who marry. States should shoulder the burden for their proportion of this supplement.

Some will object that this is too expensive, but government would pay no more money; it would just rearrange the subsidy it now gives to people who cohabit so that the "penalty portion" of it is transformed into a compensating subsidy for those who choose to marry. While some would rather pay for an expanding welfare state than shore up marriage, conservatives would rather build strong children than repair broken adults.

---

53. For three overviews of the relationship between marriage and social effects, see Patrick F. Fagan: "How Broken Families Rob Children of Their Chances for Future Prosperity," Heritage Foundation *Backgrounder* No. 1283, June 11, 1999, at *www.heritage.org/library/backgrounder/bg1283.html*; Fagan, "Rising Illegitimacy: America's Social Catastrophe," at *www.heritage.org/library/archives/fyi/fyi_19.pdf*; and Fagan and Rector, "The Effects of Divorce on America," at *www.heritage.org/library/backgrounder/bg1373.html*.
54. See Fagan, "Why Religion Matters."
55. Patrick F. Fagan, "Time for Instruction in the Three W's," op-ed, at *www.heritage.org/views/2001/ed061801.html*.
56. See *http://crcw.princeton.edu/CRCW/papers/cityreports/nyc08-01.pdf*.
57. Linda J. Waite and Maggie Gallagher, *The Case for Marriage: Why Married People Are Happier, Healthier, and Better Off Financially* (New York: Doubleday, 2000), pp. 47–64, 67, 110–123, and 130.
58. Data from U.S. Bureau of the Census, *Current Population Surveys*, March of each year; see chart at *www.heritage.org/issues/family*.

Move program funds toward those programs that explicitly promote marriage.

Even if unintended, current federal policy has had a devastating effect on marriage among the poor. Government should dedicate its time and effort to finding ways to restore marriage among the poor. Media coverage, education, research, and state marriage programs such as those launched in Oklahoma[59] are allowing officials to begin to repair the years of damage done by the disincentives to marriage.

Governors and states predictably will appeal to the principle of federalism, asking to be left alone. However, all but a few states ignored the 1996 welfare reform mandate to begin efforts to restore marriage; by 2001, they collectively had spent only 0.16 percent of their TANF surplus dollars on this objective. Governors expect Washington to pay 70 percent of their welfare budgets. If they wish to receive aid, they should accept the corresponding responsibility of funding programs that prepare couples for stable marriages.

"Healthy Marriage" programs in the states would steer many of the couples in them *away* from marrying and, subsequently divorcing, because they are not really suited for each other. Federal healthy marriage programs should implement and report performance measurements, accepting accountability for the work they purport to do. Such measurements also would provide those who distribute the funds, and the public from whom the tax dollars were exacted, with a means for assessing the programs' value.[60]

Sunset programs that promote sex outside of marriage, and in the interim, give a dollar-for-dollar match to those that promote abstinence.

The U.S. General Accounting Office has never evaluated well-funded federal family planning programs, but the few abstinence education programs have been monitored closely since their inception. The playing field should at least be leveled. The implementation of abstinence programs has coincided

---

59. See *www.governor.state.ok.us/marriageconf.htm*.

60. See Patrick F. Fagan and Claudia Horn, "The Nature and Good Uses of Outcome Based Evaluation for Faith-Based Initiatives," Heritage Foundation *Backgrounder*, forthcoming.

with a significant drop in abortions and out-of-wedlock births as well as evidence of increased and prolonged virginity. These successful programs should be expanded. The next step would be a dollar-for-dollar match for the total funds going to programs that promote sex outside of marriage. That change alone would mean an increase of $145 million for the abstinence education budget—a good boost for a good policy that invests in tomorrow's children.

Modify the American Community Survey to track wedlock and worship.

The American Community Survey[61] is likely to replace the long form of the decennial census—a development welcomed by all social scientists familiar with the issue, whether liberal or conservative. Yet its survey findings will fail to illuminate the problems affecting the nation's *communities* until it is designed to measure the social infrastructure of the nation, including religious worship and family structure, accurately. Without these data, scholars cannot identify the fundamental patterns that form America's social capital: its community life. Leaving out those data would be like having the Federal Reserve Board's Survey of Consumer Finance neglect to gather individual income and expenditure data. The time to act is now, as the final form of this survey is in process.

Require data on work, wedlock, and worship in all federal social surveys.

To lay the groundwork for a new brand of social policy that rebuilds families, the data on work, wedlock, and worship must be gathered in social surveys conducted by the U.S. Departments of Health and Human Services, Labor, Housing and Urban Development, and Education. Work, wedlock, and worship are the fundamental elements upon which a strong nation is built. Surveys that do not gather these data can only point to problems. But without solid information, politicians normally look to government, not civil society, for solutions.

Congress should require these departments to gather data on family structure and religious worship in all surveys related to crime, addiction, mental health, educational attainment, and

61. See *www.census.gov/acs/www/About/*.

performance. Similar data need to be collated by the international division of the Census Bureau for international comparisons. Such data would demonstrate the need to reverse current U.N. social policies, which are clearly destructive.

—Patrick F. Fagan is William H. G. FitzGerald Research Fellow in Family and Cultural Issues at The Heritage Foundation.

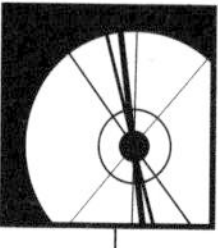

For a complete list and full-text versions of additional studies by Heritage on issues affecting the family, see the searchable *Issues 2002* companion CD–ROM.

EXPERTS

Heritage Foundation

Patrick F. Fagan
William H. G. FitzGerald Research Fellow in Family and Cultural Issues
The Heritage Foundation
214 Massachusetts Avenue, NE
Washington, DC 20002
(202) 608-6211
fax: (202) 544-5421
pat.fagan@heritage.org

Robert Rector
Senior Research Fellow
The Heritage Foundation
214 Massachusetts Avenue, NE
Washington, DC 20002
(202) 608-6211
fax: (202) 544-5421
robert.rector@heritage.org

Joseph Loconte
William E. Simon Fellow for Religion and a Free Society
The Heritage Foundation
214 Massachusetts Avenue, NE
Washington, DC 20002
(202) 608-6164
fax: (202) 546-8328
joe.loconte@heritage.org

Other Experts

David Blankenhorn
President
Institute for American Values
1841 Broadway, Suite 211
New York, NY 10023
(212) 246-3942
fax: (212) 541-6665

Alan Carlson
President
The Howard Center
934 North Main Street
Rockford, IL 61103
(815) 964-5819

Janice Crouse, Ph.D.
Senior Fellow
Beverly LaHaye Institute
Concerned Women for America
1015 15th Street, NW, Suite 1100
Washington, DC 20005
(202) 488-7000

Bill Pierce
President
International Association of Vol-

untary Adoption Agencies and NGOs
2001 S Street, NW, Suite 302
Washington, DC 20009
(202) 299-0050

David Popenoe, Ph.D.
Director
Institute for Family Strengths
Rutgers University
New Brunswick, NJ 08903-5051
(732) 932-8435

Roland Warren
President
National Fatherhood Initiative
101 Lake Forest Boulevard
Suite 360
Gaithersburg, MD 20877
(301) 948-0599

For continually updated and expanded information on major breaking developments on this issue over the campaign cycle, see *www.heritage.org/issues/family.*

ISSUES 2002

Foreign Policy

HOMELAND SECURITY

Strengthening Capabilities to Protect America

Michael Scardaville

THE ISSUES

Since the September 11, 2001, terrorist attacks, America's security has become the top priority of government at every level. The attacks have exposed numerous deficiencies in homeland security, challenging policymakers to reconsider both the vulnerabilities within their jurisdictions and the levels of preparedness for other attacks on the American homeland.[1] However, the speed with which this issue was forced upon them and the economic turmoil that followed have had a down side. In attempting to respond to the vulnerabilities made clear by the attacks, many Members of Congress have downplayed, overlooked, or simply ignored these key issues.

1. **In heightening security, the challenge for Washington will be to maintain fiscal responsibility while balancing security and civil liberties.** Washington's tendency to broaden its reach in the effort to improve security opens the door for fiscal irresponsibility. For example, three months after the attacks, Senator Charles E. Schumer (D–NY) declared that "The tectonic plates beneath us are inexorably moving us to larger federal involvement." Implying that only Washington could improve security, he asserted that, "For the foreseeable future, the federal government will have to grow."[2] But big-

---

1. For an in-depth study of the priorities for security of the homeland, see *Defending the American Homeland: A Report of the Heritage Foundation Homeland Security Task Force Chaired by L. Paul Bremer III and Edwin Meese III* (Washington, D.C.: The Heritage Foundation, 2002), at *www.heritage.org/homelanddefense/*.
2. Senator Charles E. Schumer, "Big Government Looks Better Now," op-ed, *The Washington Post*, December 11, 2001, p. A33.

ger government is not the solution. Homeland security must start from the ground up; the terrorist attacks showed that the first responders to an attack will always be local emergency crews and health officials.

The national priority on homeland security is no excuse for wasteful spending, and filling in the gaps exposed in the attacks will require shifting funds from lesser priorities. Franklin D. Roosevelt followed this model in 1942 in slashing New Deal big government programs to pay for World War II. Security protects liberty, and to provide the level of security needed to protect the homeland and constitutional freedoms, policymakers must be cautious that their homeland security initiatives do not threaten civil liberties.

2. **The best homeland defense is a strong offense.** The U.S. war on global terrorism is the front line in rooting out terrorists who would attack the homeland. Working closely with America's allies in the war to improve intelligence and to build the momentum for dissuading regimes and states from supporting terrorists in any way also is key.

3. **The nation's intelligence assets must be improved to thwart terrorists.** While the al-Qaeda terrorists took advantage of security gaps to attack the U.S. homeland, the inability of the intelligence community to discover the plot beforehand was the result of many factors, including insufficient information sharing among government agencies and inadequate resources. According to John Gannon, former head of the National Intelligence Council, a "cultural divide" exists between the Central Intelligence Agency (CIA) and the Federal Bureau of Investigation (FBI): "Whereas the FBI collects information to bring into court as evidence, the CIA does threat assessments."[3] Such differences inhibit information sharing. At least five of the September 11 terrorists were already on federal terrorist watch lists. The decline of human intelligence (HUMINT) capabilities over the past two decades and the lack of sufficient numbers of Arabic linguists in the intelligence community made intelligence collection regarding the terrorists even more difficult. Such deficiencies must be corrected.

---

3. Intellibridge Global Intelligence Solutions, "Intelligence Agencies Cooperate on Supercomputer," *Homeland Security Monitor*, February 19, 2002.

4. **The nation must prepare against terrorism using weapons of mass destruction (WMD).** The anthrax attacks in 2001 should remove any doubt that terrorists not only can obtain chemical, biological, radiologic, or nuclear (CBRN) materials to use as weapons against American civilians, but that they have the will to use them. According to the Centers for Disease Control and Prevention (CDC) Web site, biological agents are easily disseminated and cause high mortality rates, strain on public health systems, massive panic, and social disruption. It is well-known that rogue regimes and terrorist networks such as al-Qaeda seek CBRN weapons to use against the United States. Special action and funding are needed to prepare first responders at the local level for such terrorism.

5. **An effective homeland defense strategy must focus on controlling America's borders.** The best way to increase homeland security is to prevent terrorists and their weapons from ever entering the United States. Improving information sharing, planning, and resources to ensure that those watching America's borders are able to identify and detain suspected terrorists or weapons is crucial to homeland security. Yet as one government commission reported, "The state of security in U.S. seaports generally ranges from poor to fair, and, in a few cases, good."[4] The same can be said of other ports of entry. Programs for scrutinizing and approving the entry of people and products via air, land, and sea must be implemented rapidly by numerous federal agencies and departments.

6. **The National Guard must be freed from cumbersome military support duties and international peacekeeping activities to focus on homeland defense.** The Guard's unique role in disaster relief, combined with its military training, makes it a valuable tool for homeland security. However, over the past two decades, because of force reductions, many U.S. Air Force and Army support activities have been transferred to the Guard. In addition, National Guard units have been deployed more often as part of international peacekeeping missions to such areas as Bosnia and Kosovo, where the

---

4. *Report of the Interagency Commission on Crime and Security in U.S. Seaports*, Fall 2000, p. V.

United States has no strategic interest. These roles inhibit the Guard's ability to serve homeland defense adequately.

7. **For homeland security policy to be effective, the federal government must work more closely with state and local agencies and the private sector.** In nearly all scenarios, state and local agencies will have responsibility for orchestrating the immediate response to a terrorist attack. In addition, most of the nation's infrastructure assets that terrorists would attack are owned or operated by private industries. Washington must build a new partnership with all levels of government and the private sector to remove obstacles that stand in the way of securing the homeland.

   The new Office of Homeland Security (OHS) must bring all federal homeland security programs in line with the national strategy it is to complete by mid-2002. OHS will also have to work closely with federal, state, and local officials and the private sector to ensure that programs, data, intelligence, and other resources are compatible. With over 40 federal agencies and scores of state and local agencies involved in homeland security policy, this task could be daunting, but the National Security Council provides a model, balancing the initiatives of a diverse group of federal agencies on national security policy.

THE FACTS

FACT: The key to responding to terrorist attacks using chemical, biological, or radiologic weapons is early detection.

No national surveillance system exists to recognize that a biological attack may have occurred;[5] nor are America's hospitals prepared for such an eventuality. According to Senator Bill Frist (R–TN), "only one in five hospitals even has a bioterrorism plan."[6] Likewise, even though there are National Guard units in every

---

5. Daniel J. Dire, "CBRNE–Biological Warfare Agents," *eMedicine Journal*, Vol. 2, No. 7 (July 3, 2001), Sec. 3.
6. Statement of Senator Bill Frist, M.D., before the Subcommittee on Labor, Health and Human Services, Education and Related Issues, Committee on Appropriations, U.S. Senate, 107th Cong., 1st Sess., October 3, 2001, at *www.senate.gov/~frist/Press/News_Releases/01-201/01-201.html.*

state, the majority lack Civil Support Teams that can respond to chemical and biological attacks.[7]

FACT: Biological terrorism is not new, the toxins available for use are not few, and their potential for widespread deaths is great.

- Since the mid-1300s, armies around the world have used biological warfare to weaken their enemies.[8]
- In the past 20 years, terrorist organizations have attempted to use biological agents at least six times, three of these on American soil.[9]

Terrorists who wish to conduct an attack with biological weapons have numerous options. Some toxins such as anthrax can be produced relatively easily, while others such as smallpox require more advanced production capabilities. Terrorists also may have access to biological weapons-grade material produced by a number of states, particularly Iran, Iraq, Libya, North Korea, and Syria—all of which are on the U.S. list of state sponsors of terrorism.

Biological agents can be delivered in many ways that are more deadly than through the mail. A 1993 Office of Technology Assessment report, for example, estimated that 250 pounds of anthrax spores spread efficiently over the Washington, D.C., metropolitan area could cause up to 3 million deaths—more than from a 1-megaton hydrogen bomb.[10]

---

7. Testimony of Maj. Gen. Paul D. Monroe, Jr., before the Subcommittee on Technology, Terrorism, and Government Information, Committee on the Judiciary, U.S. Senate, 107th Cong., 1st Sess., December 13, 2001.
8. Jack Spencer and Michael Scardaville, "Understanding the Bioterrorist Threat: Facts and Figures," Heritage Foundation *Backgrounder* No. 1488, October 11, 2001, at *www.heritage.org/library/backgrounder/bg1488.html.*
9. This figure counts the anthrax attacks in September and October 2001 as one coordinated attack. In addition to the anthrax attacks, in 1984, the Rajneeshee religious cult sprayed salmonella on salad bars in Oregon in an attempt to prevent people from voting in local elections; and in 1995, two members of a Minnesota militia were convicted of possessing ricin, which they planned to use against law enforcement officers who had served legal papers on other members of their group.
10. Office of Technology Assessment, "Proliferation of Weapons of Mass Destruction: Assessing the Risks," OTA–ISC–559, August 1993, pp. 53–54.

FACT: "Dirty bombs" and radiologic incidents are also attractive to terrorists.

According to a recent article in *The Washington Post*, the U.S. intelligence community has concluded that Osama bin Laden's al-Qaeda network may have made significant progress on developing a radiological "dirty bomb."[11] But other forms of radiologic attack are also likely. Terrorists could attack the nation's nuclear power plants or any of the 70 sites used to store nuclear waste in 31 states.[12]

The destruction caused by a radiologic explosion for the most part would be secondary to the number of deaths and illnesses caused by exposure to extreme radiation. The Center for Defense Information estimates that the number of people who would die from a dirty bomb released at noon in Manhattan would approach 2,000.[13]

FACT: Deficiencies in U.S. immigration programs and consular services allow terrorists to enter the United States more easily.

Current immigration and consular policies represent a gaping hole in security that terrorists can use to infiltrate American society. At least 13 of the September 11 hijackers entered the United States on legal visas, although at least five of them were on federal government watch lists; three of the terrorists used the visa express program; but three were in the country illegally, having overstayed their visas. The United States does not have the means to determine whether visa holders leave once their visas expire.

- The U.S. Bureau of the Census recently reported that 8,705,421 people were living in the United States illegally in 2000.[14]
- The Immigration and Naturalization Service (INS) maintains an Automatic Biometric Identification System, known as

---

11. Bob Woodward, Robert G. Kaiser, and David B. Ottaway, "U.S. Fears Bin Laden Made Nuclear Strides," *The Washington Post*, December 4, 2001, p. A1.
12. Center for Defense Information, "What If the Terrorists Go Nuclear," October 1, 2001, at *www.cdi.org/terrorism/nuclear.cfm*.
13. *Ibid.*
14. August Gribbin, "Census Report Finds Illegals Threat to U.S. Security," *The Washington Times*, January 23, 2001.

IDENT; but according to the Justice Department, the system has been mismanaged.[15] In addition, the data are not cross-referenced with records in other law enforcement or intelligence agency databases.

- The INS has issued over 5 million advance green cards using biometric (fingerprint) technology since 1998 but has never installed the machines that can read them.[16] Similarly, it has initiated a biometric program using hand scans to accelerate entry into the United States for pre-approved passengers at seven airports.

The database of biometric green cards is not linked to the federal government's other watch lists, even though the 2001 Uniting and Strengthening America by Providing Appropriate Tools Required to Intercept and Obstruct Terrorism Act (USA PATRIOT Act)[17] requires the Attorney General and the Director of the Federal Bureau of Investigation to give the U.S. Department of State's Consular Affairs division access to information in its National Crime Information Center.

FACT: Border security involves numerous federal agencies and departments.

The Coast Guard is primarily responsible for securing America's ports and maritime approaches and maintains prevention, response, and consequence management roles in all areas of maritime security. The INS regulates permanent and temporary immigration to the United States and operates the U.S. Border Control program. The Customs Service is charged with ensuring that products entering the United States do not present a security risk and therefore maintains a presence at air, land, and sea points of entry. In many ways, the Consular Service is the first line of homeland defense against terrorism because it is responsible for determining who should and should not receive travel documents to enter the United States.

---

15. Jonathan Peterson, "High Tech, Low Effort at INS Security," *The Los Angeles Times*, November 19, 2001.
16. *Ibid.*
17. P.L. 107–56.

FACT: Current maritime security programs are insufficient to prevent terrorists and their weapons from entering the United States.

- Only 3 percent of the 16 million cargo containers that enter the United States each year are inspected, and only then upon arrival in American ports.[18] Any one of those containers could contain a WMD carrying nuclear, chemical, radiological, or biological material.

- Because it is both a military organization and a civil law enforcement agency, the Coast Guard is particularly well-positioned to conduct maritime homeland security missions; but it is hampered by outdated equipment and a small budget. The average age of its fleet is 28 years, with some ships having been built before World War II.[19] Nonetheless, after September 11, the Coast Guard increased the percentage of its assets dedicated to homeland security functions from 2 percent to over 50 percent. President Bush's FY 2003 Coast Guard budget request of $7.1 billion, with $500 million for the Coast Guard's Integrated Deepwater Project, will help alleviate the burden, but it cannot be a one-time boost. A sustained commitment will be necessary for the Coast Guard to complete all the vital missions it is assigned.

FACT: The National Guard is involved in a number of new missions that inhibit its ability to prepare for homeland defense.

The National Guard offers certain advantages for homeland security.[20] Its units are locally based in 2,700 communities across the nation,[21] enabling them to respond more quickly to local events than is possible for military forces dispersed around the nation, and are already familiar with local infrastructure. America's 4,500 Guardsmen report directly to their states' governors unless nationalized by the President. This exempts them from the provi-

18. Ron Laurenzo, "Senator Seeks Port Legislation to Plug Gap in Homeland Defense," *Defense Week*, November 5, 2001, p. 7.
19. Steve Olafson, "Safeguarding the Shore; Coast Guard's Endeavor Against Terrorism Threat Hurt by Aging Fleet," *The Los Angeles Times*, December 23, 2001.
20. See *Defending the American Homeland*, Chapter 4, pp. 77–80.
21. National Guard Bureau, *Responding to Acts of Terrorism, Role of the National Guard*, July 17, 2001, at *www.ngb.dtic.mil/links/links.shtml*.

sions of the Posse Comitatus Act, which has prohibited the nation's armed forces from engaging in law enforcement functions on United States soil since Reconstruction.[22]

The National Guard also can supply their localities with unique capabilities during emergencies, including communications and logistics as well as chemical or biological response capabilities. To meet the CBRN threat, the Guard currently has 24 certified Weapon of Mass Destruction Civil Support Teams designed to support the states in the event of an attack with WMD; an additional eight have been authorized by Congress but are not yet operational.

- During the 1980s and 1990s, activities that support military deployments, such as communications, logistics, intelligence, and food services, were transferred to the National Guard to reduce the size of the active-duty forces. In recent years, National Guard units also were deployed as part of international peacekeeping operations to reduce the strain on the active-duty military. During 2000 alone, some 235,000 Guardsmen and Reservists were deployed oversees.[23] These missions detract from the Guard's ability to defend the homeland or respond to emergencies.

FACT: Vital national infrastructure is vulnerable to a number of terrorist threats.

Vulnerabilities exist, albeit in varying degrees, in nearly every type of infrastructure that is critical to the nation's operations. The critical infrastructures identified by President Clinton in Presidential Decision Directive 63 (PDD–63, "Critical Infrastructure Protection") include information and telecommunications networks, banking and finance systems, the water supply, transportation nodes, emergency law enforcement services, emergency fire services, public health services, electric power, and oil and gas production and storage. Missing from this list is the Global Positioning System (GPS), including both its signal and its network of satellites, upon which many other infrastructure and military systems now rely.[24]

---

22. See *Defending the American Homeland*, Chapter 4.
23. See *www.defenselink.mil/pubs/dod101/busiest.html*.
24. See *Defending the American Homeland*, Chapter 1.

Any number of forms of attack are possible. Terrorists can use conventional explosives to destroy a facility, conduct a cyber attack to disrupt vital information systems, or threaten an attack to disrupt services. The former chairman of the President's Commission on Critical Infrastructure Protection testified in 1997 that "an adversary can utilize readily-available cyber tools to effectively bypass our national defense forces to directly access the infrastructures that underpin our national economic strength."[25] The private Internet security firm Riptech estimates that at least 128,678 cyber attacks on businesses occurred in the last six months of 2001.[26]

FACT: The private sector has major incentives to promote security.

Bottom lines and consumer and shareholder confidence already provide major incentives to industries that own and operate critical infrastructure. Increasing government regulation is usually not the answer to increasing security in these industries.[27] In fact, many government initiatives, such as the Freedom of Information Act (FOIA), antitrust legislation, liability concerns, and current tax policies, inhibit the development of a true partnership for security between the private sector and the government.

Defending the American Homeland is a comprehensive study incorporating the recommendations of The Heritage Foundation Homeland Security Task Force. Read the entire book on the *Issues 2002* companion CD–ROM or contact Heritage's Publications office at 1-800-544-4843 to order a copy.

---

25. "Statement of Robert T. Marsh, Former Chairman, President's Commission on Critical Infrastructure Protection," Subcommittee on Technology of the Committee on Science, U.S. House of Representatives, November 6, 1997.
26. Renae Merle, "Computer Attacks on Companies Up Sharply," *The Washington Post*, January 28, 2002, p. A8.
27. For a discussion of security measures in European and Israeli airports and privatization of security, see Robert W. Poole, Jr., "Learn from Experience on Airport Security," Heritage Foundation *Backgrounder* No. 1493, October 15, 2001, pp. 2–3, at *www.heritage.org/library/backgrounder/bg1493*.

WHAT TO DO IN 2003

Improve intelligence and information sharing among all levels of government with homeland security responsibilities.

A number of national commissions and independent task forces have called for the inter- and intra-departmental sharing of government intelligence and information related to terrorism.[28] The first step should be the creation of a federal-level intelligence fusion center to which all information on suspected terrorists and terrorist activities collected by federal agencies and state and local law enforcement agencies can be sent and from which it is disseminated on a need-to-know basis.[29] The Office of Homeland Security should create new mechanisms for information sharing and dissemination, looking to the High-Intensity Drug Trafficking Area (HIDTA) program for inspiration.

Give state and local governments the tools they need to assess the threat, monitor their areas of jurisdiction, and improve response.

The federal government and state and local agencies all have a stake in compiling an accurate inventory of vulnerable assets. A single common vulnerability assessment model that the agencies could use to determine what needs to be improved immediately and what can be addressed at a later time would enhance coordination efforts among federal, state, and local officials.

No universally accepted national standard for assessing the extent to which a state or local area is prepared for a CBRN attack currently exists. The OHS should work with state and local agencies to develop national standards for preparedness, vulnerability assessment checklists, and a comprehensive manual of civil defense exercises. It also should prepare response exercises that encompass all levels of government, from Washington to local town offices, to simulate responses to WMD and more conventional attacks. These exercises would enhance both planning and communications, and would test the nation's ability to respond to attacks.

---

28. See *Defending the American Homeland*, Chapter 3.
29. *Ibid.*, esp. pp. 62–64.

Build a national surveillance network for early detection of chemical, biological, and other attacks on the homeland.

In the event of a CBRN attack, early detection is pivotal for effective consequence management. It is not now possible for state and local officials to recognize that an attack has just occurred. By the time a trend of reactions has been established, the terrorists are likely to be far removed and many Americans ill or dead. Technology must be developed to detect attacks; more immediately, however, monitoring and reporting systems should be established to help speed detection of CBRN attacks.

A national surveillance system should be built from the ground up. Local surveillance networks that collect information on, for example, the number of hospital admissions, school absences, and state employee absences each day should provide these data regularly to the states, and the states should then compile this information and make regular reports to the federal government. The federal government should help the states develop guidelines for reporting requirements and help ensure that health officials can recognize the symptoms of a CBRN attack. The CDC should establish a nationwide system for collecting and analyzing relevant data on possible CBRN events from state and local networks.[30]

Reform the procedures for allowing people and products to enter the United States.

The September 11 attacks showed that terrorists can easily enter the United States through consular and immigration channels. If these loopholes are to be closed, the culture of the consular services must change. Visa decisions should be based first and foremost on whether an applicant is likely to pose a security risk, not on whether he or she is likely to return home. This will require the government to share information on suspected terrorists with consular and immigration officials. Advanced tamper-proof passports, visas, and immigration documents also should be developed.

A system should be developed and quickly deployed to cross-check airline reservation systems against government-wide databases of known and suspected terrorists—similar to the Advanced Passenger Information System (APIS) administered

---

30. *Ibid.*, Chapter 2, pp. 33–36.

by Customs, the INS, and the Animal and Plant Health Inspection Service (APHIS). However, it should function in real time, allowing airport security personnel to apprehend suspected terrorists *before* they enter the United States. The system should be used on domestic originating flights as well. Information on passengers' travel habits should not be collected; and only limited information, such as a warning to put a hold on a ticket, should be shared with the airlines.

To increase maritime security, a pilot point-of-origin inspection program for cargo could be implemented in three geographically diverse nations. If the pilot program proves effective and cost-efficient, arrangements for point-of-origin inspection programs should be included in international trade agreements.

Free the National Guard for homeland security duties.

The National Guard must be freed from the support services it was assigned after the end of the Cold War to reduce the size of the active forces as well as international peacekeeping duties. The Secretary of Defense should add more active-duty personnel to the active forces for these support missions and reduce America's peacekeeping commitments so that they do not detract from the Guard's homeland security and warfighting missions.

The Secretary should ensure that the National Guard has in place appropriate standing operational plans to support state and local officials in the event of an attack. The National Guard Bureau, the National Guard State Area Commands (STARCs), and the State Adjutants General should be involved in developing each state's consequence management plans. Relevant National Guard Bureau regulations should be updated to reflect the new environment, and State Adjutants General should update their state crisis action plans as necessary.

Improve federal efforts to protect critical infrastructure.

PDD–63 assigned responsibility for protecting each identified critical infrastructure to an individual or agency within the federal government but failed to instill methods for accountability, oversight, and a chain of command. President Bush can correct these deficiencies by issuing a new directive. He should require responsible government agencies and parties to report as soon as possible, and thereafter annually, to the Director of OHS on the status of infrastructure security under their purview.[31] The President should also designate the Global Positioning System frequency and constellation of satellites as a critical infrastructure and designate the Department of Defense as the lead agency responsible for coordinating government security programs for GPS. Like the Internet, GPS has been integrated into many other infrastructures, enabling them to function more efficiently and more securely. Because its disruption could have serious economic and physical consequences, security must extend beyond protecting its role as a navigational aid.[32]

Unleash market forces to mobilize the private sector to promote infrastructure security.

Congress should remove legislative roadblocks that prevent closer cooperation between industry and the government on infrastructure protection. It should address the private sector's FOIA concerns about sharing information on their operations, provide narrow anti-trust exemptions for companies that share information to promote security, and reduce the tax liability of those who adopt best security practices. Each federal lead agency should publish a biannual "honor roll" of the top 100 companies that have improved security. Such a competitive atmosphere would increase consumer, investor, and insurer interest in those companies and heighten incentives to invest in security among other industries.

Revising the tax code to allow infrastructure owners to deduct the full cost of security-related spending in the year that it was incurred would be a good step in encouraging private-sector investment in security. Depreciating security-related purchases creates a tax on investment and increases costs—disincentives to security spending that Congress can remove. Washington also should help industry develop model security standards and private-sector vulnerability assessment programs.

—Michael Scardaville is Policy Analyst for Homeland Defense in the Kathryn and Shelby Cullom Davis Institute for International Studies at The Heritage Foundation.

---

31. *Ibid.*, Chapter 1, pp. 13–19.

32. *Ibid.*, pp. 19–21.

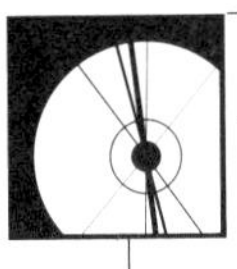

For a complete list and full-text versions of additional studies by Heritage on homeland security, see the searchable *Issues 2002* companion CD–ROM.

EXPERTS

Heritage Foundation

Michael Scardaville
Policy Analyst for Homeland Defense
Kathryn and Shelby Cullom Davis Institute for International Studies
The Heritage Foundation
214 Massachusetts Avenue, NE
Washington, DC 20003
(202) 608-6057
fax: (202) 544-5421
michael.scardaville@heritage.org

Jack Spencer
Policy Analyst for Defense and National Security
The Heritage Foundation
214 Massachusetts Avenue, NE
Washington, DC 20003
(202) 608- 6124
fax: (202) 544-5421
jack.spencer@heritage.org

Kim R. Holmes, Ph.D.
Vice President
Director, Kathryn and Shelby Cullom Davis Institute for International Studies
The Heritage Foundation
214 Massachusetts Avenue, NE
Washington, DC 20003
(202) 608-6111
fax: (202) 544-5421
kim.holmes@heritage.org

Daniel W. Fisk
Deputy Director, Kathryn and Shelby Cullom Davis Institute for International Studies
The Heritage Foundation
214 Massachusetts Avenue, NE
Washington, DC 20003
(202) 608-6114
fax: (202) 544-5421
dan.fisk@heritage.org

Edwin Meese III
Ronald Reagan Distinguished Fellow in Public Policy and
Chairman, Center for Legal and Judicial Studies
The Heritage Foundation
214 Massachusetts Avenue, NE
Washington, DC 20003
(202) 608-6181
fax: (202) 547-0641
ed.meese@heritage.org

Other Experts

Ambassador L. Paul Bremer III
Senior Advisor, Political and Emerging Risks
MMC Enterprise Risk
1255 23rd Street, NW, Suite 400
Washington, DC 20037
(202) 263-7860
fax: (202) 263-7861

Daniel Goure, Ph.D.
Lexington Institute
1655 North Fort Myer Drive
Arlington, VA 22209
(703) 522-5828

Major General David Grange
McCormick Tribune Foundation
435 North Michigan Avenue,
Suite 770
Chicago, IL 60611
(312) 222-3027

Colonel Joseph Muckerman
2103 Woodmont Road
Alexandria, VA 22307
(703) 522-5828

Bob Warshaw
Warshaw & Associates
348 Wabash Drive
Sylva, NC 28779
(828) 586-1843

For continually updated and expanded information on major breaking developments on this issue over the campaign cycle, see *www.heritage.org/issues/homelandsecurity.*

DEFENSE

Maintaining U.S. Military Strength

Jack Spencer

THE ISSUES

On September 11, 2001, America was caught by surprise and suffered a deliberate and coordinated terrorist attack on its soil, even though numerous warnings had predicted that terrorists would attack the U.S. homeland and despite significant increases in counterterrorism spending in the past decade. The hijacking and steering of the passenger jets into the Pentagon and World Trade Center exposed America's surprising vulnerability to attack, even after terrorists had successfully bombed American embassies in Kenya and Tanzania, military installations in Saudi Arabia, the U.S.S. *Cole*, and (eight years earlier, in 1993) the World Trade Center.

Policymakers can no longer ignore the fact that new threats to America's interests are emerging around the world; nor can they ignore the deficiencies of America's armed forces, the vulnerability of its vital space assets, and the proliferation of ballistic missiles and weapons of mass destruction that could one day target American civilians. Defending America is the government's first responsibility, and Washington must take the necessary steps to ensure that the U.S. military can continue to defend the country and transform into the world's premier fighting force of the 21st century.

1. **U.S. armed forces must always be ready to fight and win America's wars.** The terrorist attacks showed how difficult it is to predict where and when America may have to use military force to protect its people and interests. To protect America from the devastation its enemies seek, it is vitally important that America's fighting forces are maintained at high states of readiness, fully functioning and well equipped, with modern materiel, adequate facilities for real-life training

exercises, and appropriate policies to sustain high morale. Operations other than warfighting that detract from readiness must be kept to a minimum.

2. **The armed forces must be prepared to respond to a variety of contingencies in an unpredictable future.** The September 11 attacks demonstrate the unpredictable and dangerous future that lies ahead for the leader of the free world. Forces that were designed to fight the Cold War must be transformed to meet all possible emerging threats. The U.S. Department of Defense's 2001 Quadrennial Defense Review (QDR) lays out a strategy to achieve this objective,[1] but it will not proceed without the full support of the President and Congress.

3. **Only robust and sustained funding can sustain the type of 21st century soldiers, airmen, sailors, and Marines that the nation needs.** The President has submitted a defense budget adequate to fund the war on terrorism. However, to prepare the armed forces for future phases of the war, as well as for more unpredictable and emerging threats, this level of defense spending must be sustained for many years. Congress, which has wasted the surplus on special-interest projects that have nothing to do with the war on terrorism or the recession,[2] needs to make a long-term commitment to defense for the future security of the nation.

4. **Social experiments have no place in the armed forces.** The purpose of the U.S. military is to defend America from aggression by fighting and winning wars, not to be a proving ground for social experimentation. In recent years, the forces have been subjected to a host of policies that promote the agenda of special interests rather than the professionalism of the forces and the warrior ethos and military ethic among all members of the service branches. This has damaged not only morale and retention, but military preparedness.

---

1. For the 2001 Quadrennial Defense Review, see *www.defenselink.mil/pubs/qdr2001.pdf*.
2. See, for example, Ronald D. Utt, Ph.D., "Lobbyists Continue to Use Tragedy to Raid American Taxpayers: An Update," Heritage Foundation *Backgrounder* No. 1502, November 13, 2001, at *www.heritage.org/library/backgrounder/bg1502.html*.

5. **Force modernization and transformation require the Pentagon to eliminate waste.** The Pentagon wastes billions of dollars each year on outdated weapons systems, inefficient business practices, unnecessary missions, excess infrastructure, and non-defense spending—often to advance a political agenda. That money should be used to fund the war on terror and to transform the U.S. military into a 21st century fighting force.

THE FACTS

FACT: The U.S. armed forces must transform from a Cold War force to a 21st century military.

The primary difference between today's armed forces and those of 15 years ago is size: Today's force is about two-thirds that of the U.S. military in 1986. Though significant advances have been made in precision-guided munitions and communications, the military still relies on the tactical fighters, tanks, ships, bombers, and organizations that it developed to contain the Soviet Union. Effective use of these forces requires that the United States have access to an extensive network of forward-deployed bases, committed allies, and prepositioned weaponry.

Since the end of the Cold War, many nations have become less willing to give the United States unhindered access to their soil. Furthermore, adversarial nations are developing tactics to deny the United States access to many of those forward-basing areas.[3]

U.S. armed forces should be capable of conducting worldwide operations to attack and destroy widely distributed targets rapidly, such as terrorist cells anywhere in the world. This type of force requires advanced cruise missiles; unmanned combat aircraft and "space bombers"; new submarines to replace those that are becoming obsolete; low-visibility surface ships; directed-energy weapons, such as lasers and microwaves; and space-control assets. Such revolutionary capabilities would maximize the advantages that are provided by technology advances in robotics, miniaturization, and automation.

---

3. The problem of access is discussed in detail in the 2001 Quadrennial Defense Review.

Central to such a military revolution are networks of land, air, sea, and space sensors that collect targeting data and other information with which to monitor enemy activities in real time or detect the presence of chemical, nuclear, or biological contaminants. In addition, they would be used for developing new navigation tactics for all forces. Human intelligence (HUMINT) is needed to support these technological means, allowing forces to sustain a rapid pace of operations with little logistical support. Development of this type of force will require significant investments in space-based reconnaissance, surveillance, and communications, as well as innovative and flexible logistical options, secure command-and-control networks, and expanded basing options.

FACT: The Department of Defense will need sustained budget increases to pay for its force modernization and transformation.

The previous Administration lacked the political will to battle for defense spending, but the events of September 11 prove that defense must be a high priority in Washington.

- Between 1989 and 1998, the national defense budget dropped over $100 billion in constant inflation-adjusted dollars. Even with the recent increases, the budget remains less than it was in 1989—despite rapidly aging equipment, increased missions, and deteriorating infrastructure.[4]
- President Bush has requested a budget of $379 billion for defense in fiscal year 2003, and Congress seems willing to fund larger defense budgets to fight the war on terrorism, at least for now. But the Pentagon will need to sustain budgets of $400 billion to $420 billion throughout the Future Years Defense Plan (FYDP)[5] to fund a robust R&D program, to recapitalize infrastructure, and to begin modernizing the aging forces. Even these additional increases beyond the President's FY 2003 budget request equate to only around 3.5 percent of the nation's GDP.

---

4. U.S. Department of Defense, *National Defense Budget Estimates for 2002*, March 1999, p. 193.
5. The Future Years Defense Plan is a five-year plan laid out by the Department of Defense.

FACT: The Pentagon wastes billions of dollars annually that should be used to finance the modernization of the armed forces.

- In the 2002 defense budget, over $2 billion was wasted on non-defense spending, such as environmental cleanup and support for the International Sporting Competition. Additionally, the Department of Defense operates approximately 25 percent excess base capacity, which could yield significant savings if closed, and spends billions each year on "new" weapons systems that largely were developed during the Cold War. While these systems would make a contribution to the nation's overall defense, their costs are too high in terms of what they take away from the transformation effort.

- Money is also wasted on unnecessary missions. For example, the armed forces spend approximately $3 billion per year on peace operations in the Balkans. According to Secretary of Defense Donald Rumsfeld, the Pentagon could save 5 percent of its budget ($19 billion) by eliminating waste through operational efficiencies. Similarly, a panel of experts appointed by the Secretary has estimated that the Department could save $15 billion to $30 billion each year by overhauling its financial practices.

FACT: Other nations—including terrorist states—are investing heavily in systems designed to attack U.S. vulnerabilities.[6]

China, for example, expressly designed its military strategy to oppose the United States, and its recent ICBM tests and nuclear modernization suggest that it is building its nuclear deterrent to undermine U.S. power in the region.[7] But China is not alone.

The best defense is a strong offense, and America's military strength must be projected to regions around the world by air, by sea, and increasingly by space. It is reasonable to assume that nations that see themselves as America's enemies will invest in

6. See *Report of the Commission to Assess United States National Security Space Management and Organization*, Pursuant to Public Law 106–65, January 11, 2001; National Intelligence Council, *Foreign Missile Development and the Ballistic Missile Threat to the United States Through 2015*, September 1999; and National Defense Panel, *Transforming Defense: National Security in the 21st Century*, December 1997.

7. See also the chapter on Asian Security.

technologies, such as sophisticated air defenses, that limit the ability of the United States to project its power around the world.

The United States does not have adequate defenses against ballistic missiles and is increasingly vulnerable to advanced cruise missile technology, as are its troops stationed abroad and its allies. These more accurate technologies are proliferating rapidly to rogue regimes, some of which support terrorist groups. Potential adversaries, such as China and Iran, are investing heavily in increasingly lethal weapons that could be used against America's large and highly visible ground and sea forces.[8] As these states' technological capabilities continue to grow—qualitatively and quantitatively—the U.S. military will become less able to protect America and its interests abroad until it effectively transforms to counter them.[9]

FACT: America must enhance its space capabilities for strategic superiority.

The United States first used advanced space capabilities to its advantage in the 1991 Gulf War. Since then, it has continued to develop its space assets. Today, America's military depends on space for surveillance and reconnaissance; guiding smart bombs; command, control, and communications; and intelligence.

While utilization of space gives America an unparalleled advantage over potential adversaries, it also opens up vulnerabilities as dependence on space grows, and this creates incentives for hostile states to develop ways to disrupt America's access to space. Iran and North Korea are developing space programs, and other nations like India and China are actively pursuing them.

The commercialization of space is giving many nations inexpensive and unlimited access to this new frontier, with growing numbers of companies launching satellites for third parties or giving them access to existing satellites. Potentially hostile nations will use their increasing knowledge of space to support their own military capabilities.

---

8. Bill Gertz, "Russia Readies Warship for China; Missiles Will Threaten U.S. Carriers," *The Washington Times*, July 12, 2000, p. A1.
9. For a detailed analysis of cruise missile proliferation and the difficulty of defending against that threat, see Dave Tanks, "Assessing the Cruise Missile Puzzle: How Great a Defense Challenge?" Institute for Foreign Policy Analysis, October 2000.

FACT: Military readiness is compromised by using U.S. forces on missions that do not advance U.S. interests.

- Both people and equipment wear out faster under frequent use. For example, according to a Congressional Budget Office (CBO) survey, the units deployed in Somalia in 1992 needed 10 months to restore their equipment to predeployment readiness levels.[10]
- A CBO survey of U.S. Army leaders who participated in various peace missions found that almost two-thirds felt their units' training readiness had declined.[11]
- The U.S. General Accounting Office (GAO) recently concluded that "long deployments can adversely affect morale and retention."[12] The stress of frequent and unexpected deployments also jeopardizes the military's ability to retain high-quality, experienced personnel. Before the war on terrorism began, understaffed units were deployed on more missions for longer periods. Some 58 percent of U.S. troops are married, and long deployments put great strain on their families, causing many service members to leave the services as soon as they can.

FACT: Women, who make up approximately 15 percent of the armed forces, often serve in potentially dangerous combat support units.

Although women do not serve in direct combat positions in the infantry, armored, or field artillery units or submarines, many are being assigned to combat support units, combatant ships, and pilot billets that put them in harm's way. These assignments inevitably would put women in combat during a war. During the Persian Gulf War, female U.S. soldiers were taken prisoner for the first time in U.S. history and were sexually abused by their Iraqi captors. The possibility that women prisoners would be raped and tortured, or that large numbers of women would be killed and wounded in action, could have dramatic and negative effects

---

10. Congressional Budget Office, *Making Peace While Staying Ready for War: The Challenges of U.S. Military Participation in Peace Operations*, December 1999, Chapter 3.
11. *Ibid.*
12. U.S. General Accounting Office, *Contingency Operations: Providing Critical Capabilities Poses Challenges*, GAO/NSIAD–00–164, July 6, 2000, p. 3.

on the country's ability to conduct a war. Indeed, Marine Sergeant Jeannette Winters became the first female casualty of the war in Afghanistan in January 2002.

WHAT TO DO IN 2003

America's fighting men and women are prevailing in the war on terror not because of the defense policies instituted during the past decade, but in spite of them. Their exemplary showing demonstrates the high quality of their character more than anything else. If they are to continue to perform in this fashion, certain policies and actions are essential.

Maintain adequate defense spending to restore America's military strength and prepare it for an unpredictable future.

Even today, U.S. forces are undermanned and fighting with aging equipment. As of mid-December, the aircraft of the carrier USS *Roosevelt* spent more time in the air than they had at any previous time. The tactical fighters spend up to nine hours in the air per mission, compared with less than three hours during the Gulf War. Pilot shortages have caused airmen to get special medical clearances to allow them to exceed their limit of 65 hours of flight time per month. The carrier's mechanic crews have seen a 30 percent to 40 percent increase in work due to failing spare parts. Just between September 19 and December 14, 2001, the maintenance crews had to replace seven engines in tactical fighters.[13]

The reason for these unacceptable circumstances is twofold: The United States is fighting a war with aging equipment and using this equipment in a way that it was never meant to be used. To prepare for both the near- and long-term threats, Congress should support the President's Future Years Defense Plan as described in the 2003 Department of Defense budget materials.[14] This total amount of spending will be necessary for the U.S. military to conduct the war on terrorism and to recon-

---

13. Andrew England, "Planes, Pilots and Carrier Crew Pushed to the Limit in Afghanistan Campaign," Associated Press, December 14, 2001.
14. U.S. Department of Defense, news release, "Details of Fiscal 2003 Department of Defense (DOD) Budget Request," February 4, 2002. In the coming weeks, the Department of Defense will release a more in-depth description of its budget in the coming weeks that will be accessible at *www.dtic.mil/comptroller/fy2003budget/*.

stitute its forces while investing in a premier fighting force for tomorrow. It also will support the personnel accounts that until recently were grossly underfunded.

Increase America's capabilities to fight a global war on terror.

Aircraft carriers and the U.S. Marine Corps are fundamental to the ability of the United States to defend its interests worldwide, but the United States must seek new ways to use its military power as nations develop methods of countering its traditional forces.

- The U.S. Navy should develop a more stealthy missile-intensive platform, such as the arsenal ship or a missile submarine, to augment the current fleet. This platform should be able to operate independently, thereby avoiding many of the threats that surface ships face while also requiring far less support.
- The Pentagon should move forward with a plan to convert no more than four of its ballistic missile submarines to cruise missile platforms.
- The U.S. Air Force should diversify its air-to-ground strike options and procure enough tactical aircraft over the next 10 years to ensure a modern force, similar in size to today's force, to meet near-term threats. It should minimize the long-term procurement of aircraft that only marginally improve its current capabilities and invest instead in a reliable unmanned combat aerial vehicle (UCAV). Additionally, it must modernize its bomber force and develop a new long-range air-launched cruise missile.

Strengthen America's space assets and space presence.

Access to space is essential for conducting operations during a conflict. Information about enemy activities provided by satellite intelligence, for example, has been key in the war in Afghanistan. Such dependence means that space control or even space dominance may prove decisive in future conflicts. The United States must defend its satellite system, making it more survivable and deploying anti-satellite (ASAT) capabilities, which will be necessary to enable the military to control space in times of conflict if adversaries use satellites to conduct their operations.

To ensure the survivability of America's space-based systems, the United States should deploy distributed military satellite networks—smaller and widely dispersed satellites with duplicative functions. The government also will need to develop a military space plane that can replace damaged or old satellites and possibly conduct military operations.

Restore the combat focus of deployments and modernization.

On balance, peacekeeping and other long-term non-combat missions detract from warfighting readiness. The reason: When troops are participating in non-combat missions, they are not training for combat.

As the September 11 attack demonstrates, the U.S. military must always be at a high state of readiness because no one can predict when it will be called upon to defend the nation. The United States also may have to fight major wars in Iraq, Korea, or some other region where large, heavy land forces may be needed. A warfighting-ready Army is America's insurance policy against near-term failures in force transformation. At the same time, the Army must not remain technologically stagnant. Every Defense program should enhance the ability of the U.S. military forces to fight and win wars.

Over the past decade, however, defense resources have been drained by non-combat missions. The equipment used in these missions was not built for peacekeeping, and this has caused deficiencies in application. Disturbingly, the deficiencies of the U.S. warfighting forces for non-combat missions have been used to define the requirements for the Army's force modernization. Instead of reflecting the changing security environment, recent modernization efforts have tended to reflect America's past commitment to non-combat operations. This may be changing under the new Administration, but that is not yet clear. Continuing along this path would be folly because deterring aggression requires a strong combat capability, not an ability to conduct non-combat operations.

Preserve the credibility of America's nuclear deterrent.

The world has changed dramatically in the past decade, but nuclear deterrence is still strategically important. The United States needs a strategic nuclear posture that is safe, reliable, and effective—and this can be assured only with periodic testing. America's nuclear force must be large enough to counter the strategic nuclear forces deployed in Russia, China, and rogue states such as North Korea in the future.

Proposed levels of around 2,000 warheads should be sufficient for this mission as long as certain conditions are met: that effective missile defenses are deployed; that Russia builds down to the agreed upon levels; that China's deliverable nuclear warheads do not exceed the 200 to 400 level; that emerging nuclear powers do not exceed 50 deliverable warheads; and that the United States retains the right to test its warheads through explosive testing. For these reasons, it is imperative that the Administration and Congress refrain from revisiting the Comprehensive Test Ban Treaty (CTBT) defeated by Congress in 1999.[15]

Eliminate waste by closing excess military bases, procuring weapons that advance transformation, and reforming the Pentagon's business practices.

Congress should support the President's plan to close excess military bases as soon as possible. Currently, the Pentagon maintains 20 percent to 25 percent excess base capacity. Significant savings could be generated by eliminating this excess. The cumulative savings from the four previous rounds of base closures approaches $16 billion.[16]

The Department of Defense must reduce or halt the production of some of its major weapons that draw important funds away from other priorities. It is essential that the Pentagon begin the transformation of forces now, and making a clean break from these systems will make that transformation process easier. This will mean focusing on acquiring new technology that allows weapons to operate with less support. The development of hybrid engines and fuel cells, for example, would reduce the number of fuel vehicles needed to support field operations. Additionally, sensors and networked information systems would allow smaller numbers of people to cover larger swaths of territory.

---

15. Baker Spring, "The Comprehensive Test Ban Treaty and U.S. Nuclear Disarmament," Heritage Foundation *Backgrounder* No.1330, October 6, 1999, at *www.heritage.org/library/backgrounder/bg1330.html*.
16. For more on the base infrastructure issue, see U.S. Department of Defense, *Base Structure Report: Fiscal Year 2001 Baseline*, 2001.

Congress should work with the Defense Department to eliminate waste. On the personnel side, for example, the staffs of many higher-ranking military officials could be reduced with no loss of functionality. Numerous other opportunities to eliminate duplicative services at the department also exist.

Refrain from making the military a social experiment.

The purpose of the U.S. military is to fight and win America's wars, not to be a proving ground for social experimentation. President Bush's recent 2002 military budget increases are rightly focused on arresting the decline in U.S. military readiness, but the problem demands more than additional funding. Washington must rethink its social policies that affect the readiness of the armed forces to the detriment of national security. A first step should be to end gender-integrated officer and enlisted basic training, which numerous studies have found to result in lower standards, increased misconduct, and declining morale.[17]

Congress also should defund the Defense Advisory Committee on Women in the Service (DACOWITS), which was set up after the Korean War to advise the Chiefs of Staff on women's issues in the services. Over the years, the committee has become a vehicle for promoting the legislative agenda of special-interest groups. The focus should be on the challenge of maintaining equality and professionalism while promoting the warrior ethos and military ethic among all members of the services, not using the military as a social experiment.

—Jack Spencer is Policy Analyst for Defense and National Security in the Kathryn and Shelby Cullom Davis Institute for International Studies at The Heritage Foundation.

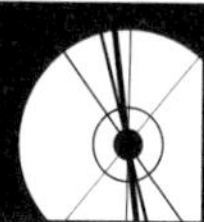

For a complete list and full-text versions of additional studies by Heritage on defense policy, see the searchable *Issues 2002* companion CD–ROM.

---

17. See *Report of the Federal Advisory Committee on Gender-Integrated Training and Related Issues to the Secretary of Defense*, December 16, 1997, and Stephanie Gutmann, *The Kinder, Gentler Military* (New York: Scribner, 2000).

EXPERTS

Heritage Foundation

Jack Spencer
Policy Analyst for Defense and National Security, Kathryn and Shelby Cullom Davis Institute for International Studies
The Heritage Foundation
214 Massachusetts Avenue, NE
Washington, DC 20002
(202) 608-6124
fax: (202) 675-1758
jack.spencer@heritage.org

Baker Spring
F. M. Kirby Research Fellow in National Security Policy, Kathryn and Shelby Cullom Davis Institute for International Studies
The Heritage Foundation
214 Massachusetts Avenue, NE
Washington, DC 20002
(202) 608-6112
fax: (202) 675-1758
baker.spring@heritage.org

Daniel W. Fisk
Deputy Director, Kathryn and Shelby Cullom Davis Institute for International Studies
The Heritage Foundation
214 Massachusetts Avenue, NE
Washington, DC 20002
(202) 608-6114
fax: (202) 675-1758
dan.fisk@heritage.org

Kim R. Holmes, Ph.D.
Vice President
Director, Kathryn and Shelby Cullom Davis Institute for International Studies
The Heritage Foundation
214 Massachusetts Avenue, NE
Washington, DC 20002
(202) 608-6111
fax: (202) 675-1758
kim.holmes@heritage.org

Larry M. Wortzel, Ph.D.
Director, Asian Studies Center
The Heritage Foundation
214 Massachusetts Avenue, NE
Washington, DC 20002
(202) 608-6081
fax: (202) 675-1779
larry.wortzel@heritage.org

Other Experts

Angelo Codevilla, Ph.D.
Professor, International Relations
Boston University
156 Bay State Road
Boston, MA 02215
(617) 353-6417
info@iwp.edu

Kenneth de Graffenried, Ph.D.
Institute of World Politics
1521 16th Street
Washington, DC 20036
(202) 462-2101

Elaine Donnelly
President
Center for Military Readiness
P.O. Box 2324
Livonia, MI 48151
(313) 646-9430
info@cmrlink.org

Frank Gaffney, Jr.
President
Center for Security Policy
1920 L Street, NW, Suite 210
Washington, DC 20036
(202) 835-9077
info@centerforsecuritypolicy.org

Phillip Gold, Ph.D.
Senior Fellow
Discovery Institute
1402 Third Avenue, Suite 400
Seattle, WA 98101
(206) 292-0401

Daniel Goure, Ph.D.
Senior Fellow
Lexington Institute
1655 North Fort Myer Drive, Suite 325
Arlington, VA 22209
(703) 522-5828
mail@lexingtoninstitute.org

Fred C. Iklé, Ph.D.
Distinguished Scholar
Center for Strategic and International Studies
1800 K Street, NW
Washington, DC 20006
(202) 775-3155
IkleOfc@csis.org

Sven F. Kraemer
President
Global Challenge 2000
1521 16th Street, NW
Washington, DC 20036
(202) 986-6224
fax: (202) 462-6045

Colonel Robert Maginnis, Sr.
Policy Analyst and Director
Military Readiness Project
Family Research Council
801 G Street, NW
Washington, DC 20001
(202) 393-2100
rlm@frc.org

Mackubin T. Owens
Professor of Strategy and Force Planning
U. S. Naval War College
686 Cushing Road
Newport, RI 02841
(401) 841-6454
fax: (401) 841-3893
owensm@nwc.navy.mil

Richard Perle
Resident Scholar
American Enterprise Institute
1150 17th Street, NW
Washington, DC 20036
(202) 862-5849
fax: (202) 862-5924
richard@perle.org

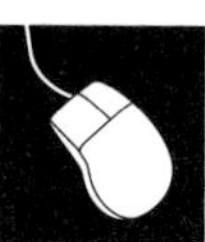

For continually updated and expanded information on major breaking developments on this issue over the campaign cycle, see *www.heritage.org/issues/defense.*

MISSILE DEFENSE

Ending America's Vulnerability to Ballistic Missiles

Baker Spring

THE ISSUES

President Bush, in announcing last year that the United States would withdraw from the 1972 Anti-Ballistic Missile (ABM) Treaty, took the first important step toward deploying an effective system to protect Americans and their allies from missile attack. That treaty, a relic of the Cold War between America and the Soviet Union, was based on the belief that its two parties would not launch nuclear weapons against each other for fear of retaliation—in effect, basing strategic stability on a principle known as mutually assured destruction (MAD). The ABM Treaty effectively ended when the Soviet Union disintegrated in 1991 because none of the resulting 15 nations, either by itself or together with the others, could fulfill its obligations.

Nevertheless, the Clinton Administration continued to adhere to the treaty's restrictions on missile defenses for U.S. territory. Supporters of that policy claim that terminating the treaty is wrong; but their arguments simply do not resonate with the American public, who realize that they are utterly vulnerable to attack. There is no system that could protect U.S. civilians today from the devastation wrought by a ballistic missile carrying nuclear, chemical, biological, or radiologic weapons.

Protecting the country is the federal government's first and most important constitutional function. The growing threat of ballistic missile attack—a threat that derives directly from the proliferation of missile technology and weapons to states that are hostile to the United States and the West—is the key reason Congress passed the National Missile Defense Act (P.L. 106–38) in July 1999.

Americans' sense of vulnerability became palpable after the terrorist and anthrax attacks last fall. Polls continue to show strong public support for deploying a missile defense system as soon as technologically possible.[1] To achieve this goal, several issues must first be addressed.

1. **Identifying those systems necessary to an effective layered missile defense system design (or "architecture") based on a full array of tests is the next key step.** Without the constraints on research and testing imposed by the ABM Treaty, the President can now start to identify those systems necessary for the desired architecture. The Bush Administration has said that it supports a global, layered system with air, sea, land, and space components. But instead of choosing an architecture now, it has chosen to conduct more tests. As testing progresses, the Administration should be able to identify those systems that it will include in its architecture.
2. **Fielding an effective defense will require proper funding of missile defense programs.** Withdrawing from the ABM Treaty will allow a more efficient and effective missile defense program to proceed, but no important program can succeed if it is starved for funds. Since September 11, even though the nation understands the urgency of defending America from those who would do it great harm, Congress has spent valuable resources on special-interest projects that are unrelated to defending America, or even to addressing the recession. Such irresponsible spending is a threat to national security.
3. **While Russia's cooperation on missile defense issues is desirable, it is not necessary.** The decision to withdraw from the ABM Treaty does not mean that the United States is curtailing diplomacy with Russia over shared interests and shared threats regarding missile defenses. Russian President Vladimir Putin clearly recognized, in the attacks on America, that the proliferation of weapons of mass destruction threatens global and regional security. Russia's cooperation would help ensure international support for America's deployment of a global system of missile defense to deter and defeat terror in every region.

---

1. Richard Benedetto, "Public Cautious, Not Panicked, About Bioterrorism," *USA Today*, October 23, 2001.

4. **Deploying missile defenses will not undermine strategic stability.** Arms control advocates assert that deploying missile defenses could lead to a new nuclear arms race. Even though no other nation is bound by the restrictions the ABM Treaty would impose on America's missile defense programs, they want the United States to abide by them unilaterally. This makes no sense. History proves that deterrence and defense are far more effective than vulnerability in preventing aggression and assuring strategic stability.

5. **America must work quickly to catch up with the expanding threat.** The capabilities of the U.S. military to defend against a ballistic missile launched against U.S. territory already lag behind the threat, largely because of the ABM Treaty's restrictions.[2] Among the possible hostile states that already have ballistic missiles are Iran, Iraq, Libya, North Korea, and Syria. National security rests on how effectively the U.S. Department of Defense manages the acquisition of missile defense systems that can disable or "kill" any missile launched intentionally or accidentally, from land or sea, against the United States.

THE FACTS

FACT: Missile defense is a vital part of homeland defense.

Since the September 11, 2001, attacks, all Americans—and indeed all of America's allies and supporters in the war on terrorism—have come to recognize that protecting the U.S. homeland is an urgent priority. To do so, the U.S. government must defend against weapons of mass destruction (WMD), such as ballistic missiles carrying chemical, biological, radiologic, or nuclear (CBRN) warheads. Currently, the United States cannot defend against even one such missile.

FACT: The Administration and Russia have agreed to reduce their offensive nuclear weapons arsenals even further.

Arms control advocates claimed that deploying missile defenses would jeopardize the international effort to reduce nuclear arms, but that has not been the case. At the same time that President

2. Baker Spring, "Missile Defense Programs Lag Behind the Threat," Heritage Foundation *Executive Memorandum* No. 642, January 12, 2000.

Bush announced the U.S. withdrawal from the ABM Treaty last December, he announced that he had reached an agreement in principle with Russian President Putin to reduce the number of deliverable strategic nuclear warheads to roughly 2,000 on each side. Each country possesses roughly 6,000 such warheads today.

FACT: Proliferation of ballistic missiles is an international scourge.

The story of the Soviet Scud–B missiles is a stark example. The first Soviet Scud–B missile, with a range of almost 200 miles, was introduced in 1961. Since then, the Scud missile technology has proliferated to at least 29 other countries, including Afghanistan, Cuba, the Democratic Republic of the Congo, Egypt, Iran, Iraq, Libya, North Korea, Pakistan, Syria, and Vietnam.[3]

North Korea is reportedly working to develop an intercontinental ballistic missile, the Taepo Dong–2, with an expected range of up to 6,210 miles. Because North Korea is a known proliferator of weapons, some fear this technology will soon appear in other countries. The Gulf War and various intelligence estimates make clear that rogue regimes would use ballistic missiles against their enemies to cause massive casualties of civilians.

FACT: Terrorist groups are capable of obtaining ballistic missiles and willing to launch them at U.S. territory.

Nation states are not the only entities capable of obtaining ballistic missiles. Well-organized terrorist groups can obtain them as well. The 1998 *Report of the Commission to Assess the Ballistic Missile Threat to the United States* (known as the Rumsfeld Commission after its chairman, Donald Rumsfeld) noted how shorter-range missiles, which are widely available, can be launched from ships off U.S. coasts.[4] Critics of missile defense have tried to argue that the September 11 attacks show that the threat to America from terrorism is greater than from missile attack, as if the two threats were mutually exclusive. The Rumsfeld Commission report makes clear that this is not the case. Both threats are clear,

---

3. Jack Spencer, *The Ballistic Missile Threat Handbook* (Washington, D.C.: The Heritage Foundation, 2000).
4. Executive Summary, *Report of the Commission to Assess the Ballistic Missile Threat to the United States*, Published Pursuant to Public Law No. 104–201, July 15, 1998, pp. 20–21.

present, and growing rapidly, and need to be addressed in a comprehensive homeland defense strategy.

FACT: From 1984 through mid-2001, the U.S. military's "hit-to-kill" tests of missile defense technology destroyed the target missile successfully 15 times in 17 attempts.[5]

The Defense Department's primary technology for countering ballistic missiles uses kinetic energy in what is known as "hit-to-kill" systems. Since 1983—even including tests in which the booster or other basic equipment failed to launch the interceptor—these missile defense systems have destroyed test targets 21 times out of 39 attempts.[6] Moreover, the rate of success has been improving, with two successful tests of the ground-based system for countering long-range missiles last year and a successful test of a sea-based interceptor early in 2002. Contrary to the claims of opponents, not only is the technology to hit a ballistic missile before it reaches U.S. territory "feasible," but it is improving with every test.

FACT: As a program, missile defense has consumed less than 2 percent of the national security budget annually in recent years.

Critics of missile defense claim that it is simply too expensive. The missile defense budget, however, has consumed less of the national security budgets in recent years than the Defense Department wastes because of poor financial practices.[7] President Bush has stated that he plans to increase missile defense funding levels, but these are not expected to exceed 3 percent of national security budgets each year (around $8 billion), on average.

FACT: Far from being alone on this issue, America enjoys the support of its allies in pursuing its missile defense program.

The Bush Administration has successfully organized a broad coalition of nations to confront the terrorist threat. A number of U.S.

---

5. Lt. Gen. Ronald T. Kadish, "Statement Before the House Armed Services Committee's Subcommittee on Military Research and Development," June 14, 2001.
6. According to the Missile Defense Agency, formerly the Ballistic Missile Defense Organization (BMDO).
7. Gerry J. Gilmore, "Overhauling Financial System May Save DoD $30B Yearly," American Forces Press Service, July 11, 2001.

allies are also participating in America's missile defense project, including Israel, Japan, and select NATO members.

WHAT TO DO IN 2003

As progress in testing permits, start to identify the elements necessary for a global, layered missile defense system with air, land, sea, and space components.

As progress in testing permits, the Bush Administration should start identifying the specific elements of an architecture for a layered missile defense system in 2002 and 2003. It has already indicated its preference for a layered system that is capable of protecting U.S. friends and allies as well as U.S. territory. Such a system, using satellites and other space-based assets, as well as land-based and sea-based defenses, should be capable of countering ballistic missiles in the boost, mid-course, and terminal phases of flight. The boost phase is most desirable to destroy a missile aimed at U.S. territory as soon after launch as possible. All Members of Congress should support such a system.

Space is the best place for deploying missile defense systems, such as sensors and kill weapons, because ballistic missiles must transit space. Sea-based defenses—for example, aboard 22 of the Navy's Aegis cruisers—conceivably could be deployed within the next three to four years.

Support full funding for missile defense programs.

No important weapons program can proceed if it is not properly funded. Congress should fund the missile defense program at between $8 billion and $10 billion annually—almost half the annual amount the Administration plans to spend to improve Medicare through 2011.[8] Congress should also ensure that the Defense Department has considerable discretion in spending that money.

---

8. U.S. Office of Management and Budget, *A Blueprint for New Beginnings: A Responsible Budget for America's Priorities*, February 28, 2001, at *www.whitehouse.gov/news/usbudget/blueprint/budtoc.html.*

Seek a streamlined management approach similar to that of the military's successful Polaris project to facilitate the rapid deployment of missile defenses.

Congress often slows and even hobbles important weapons development and acquisition programs by imposing restrictive management requirements on the Department of Defense. Members of Congress should make sure this is not the case when it comes to missile defense. The Defense Department needs wide-ranging authority to manage its missile defense programs responsibly and efficiently so that these programs proceed to deployment more quickly. America's missile defense program already lags behind the threat. A streamlined acquisition system would help it to meet the threat.

Encourage Russia's participation in missile defense programs to address shared threats.

Missile defense no longer is an albatross in U.S.–Russian relations. The Administration should be engaging Russia in cooperative efforts to field missile defense systems—since Russia also faces a growing threat from proliferation of WMD. Congress should support the President's efforts by refusing to ratify any agreement that seeks to revive the defunct ABM Treaty or tie its revival to other efforts to reduce strategic arms, which the Administration is discussing with Russia.

—Baker Spring is F. M. Kirby Research Fellow in National Security Policy in the Kathryn and Shelby Cullom Davis Institute for International Studies at The Heritage Foundation.

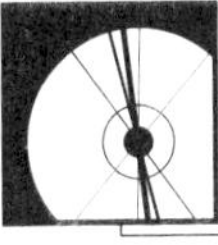

For a complete list and full-text versions of additional studies by Heritage on missile defense, see the searchable *Issues 2002* companion CD–ROM.

EXPERTS

Heritage Foundation

Baker Spring
F. M. Kirby Research Fellow in National Security Policy
Kathryn and Shelby Cullom Davis Institute for International Studies
The Heritage Foundation
214 Massachusetts Avenue, NE
Washington, DC 20002

(202) 546-6112
fax: (202) 675-1758
baker.spring@heritage.org

Jack Spencer
Policy Analyst, Kathryn and Shelby Cullom Davis Institute for International Studies
The Heritage Foundation
214 Massachusetts Avenue, NE
Washington, DC 20002
(202) 546-6124
fax: (202) 675-1758
jack.spencer@heritage.org

Kim R. Holmes, Ph.D.
Vice President
Director, Kathryn and Shelby Cullom Davis Institute for International Studies
The Heritage Foundation
214 Massachusetts Avenue, NE
Washington, DC 20002
(202) 546-6111
fax: (202) 675-1758
kim.holmes@heritage.org

Daniel W. Fisk
Deputy Director, Kathryn and Shelby Cullom Davis Institute for International Studies
The Heritage Foundation
214 Massachusetts Avenue, NE
Washington, DC 20002
(202) 546-6404
fax: (202) 675-1758
dan.fisk@heritage.org

Other Experts

Ambassador Henry F. Cooper
Visiting Fellow
The Heritage Foundation
Director
High Frontier
2800 Shirlington Road, Suite 405
Arlington, Virginia 22206
(703) 671-4111
fax: (703) 931-6432
hifront@erols.com

Frank Gaffney, Jr.
Director
Center for Security Policy
1920 L Street, NW, Suite 210
Washington, DC 20036
(202) 835-9077
fax: (202) 835-9066
gaffney@security-policy.org

Daniel Goure, Ph.D.
Senior Fellow
Lexington Institute
1655 North Fort Myer Drive, Suite 325
Arlington, VA 22209
(703) 522-5828
fax: (703) 522-5837
goure@lexingtoninstitute.org

Dr. Fred Iklé
Distinguished Scholar
Center for Strategic and International Studies
1800 K Street, NW
Washington, DC 20006
(301) 951-0176
fax: (301) 951-0286
IkleOfc@csis.org

For continually updated and expanded information on major breaking developments on this issue over the campaign cycle, see *www.heritage.org/issues/missiledefense*.

INTERNATIONAL TERRORISM

Containing and Defeating the Axis of Evil

James Phillips and Larry M. Wortzel

THE ISSUES

In the worst terrorist atrocity in U.S. history, the September 11, 2001, attacks killed more than 3,000 Americans and citizens of many other nations. International terrorism—a deadly cancer that has plagued Western democracies for decades—has metastasized into a more lethal threat to national security and international stability. Since the Cold War, when the Soviet Union and its allies supported terrorist groups in the West and around the Third World to undermine the stability and strength of democratic governments, the West too often has preferred to respond to international terrorist threats through diplomacy or appeasement. The effort clearly has failed.

With the decline of communist-supported terrorism, the chief terrorist threats to the United States have emanated increasingly from rogue states, such as Afghanistan,[1] Iraq,[2] and Iran,[3] and from Islamic extremist movements, such as Osama bin Laden's al-

---

1. See James Phillips, "Keys to the Endgame in Afghanistan," Heritage Foundation *Backgrounder* No. 1507, December 6, 2001, at *www.heritage.org/library/backgrounder/bg1507.html*.
2. See James Phillips, "Target Iraq's Terrorist Regime, Not Just Osama bin Laden, to Win War on Terrorism," Heritage Foundation *Executive Memorandum* No. 780, October 2, 2001, at *www.heritage.org/library/execmemo/em780.html*.
3. See James Phillips, "Stay the Course on Sanctions Against Iran and Libya," Heritage Foundation *Executive Memorandum* No. 756, June 28, 2001, *www.heritage.org/library/execmemo/em756.html*.

Qaeda terrorist network,[4] the perpetrator of the September 11 attacks on U.S. soil.

To varying degrees, international terrorists threaten virtually all contemporary societies. A form of low-intensity warfare, terrorism is a persistent threat to U.S. economic, political, and security interests. Key concerns include the following:

1. **State support of terrorist groups is an insidious part of the global struggle for power.** Hostile states, such as the Soviet Union during the Cold War and Iran, Iraq, and North Korea today, have employed terrorism as a form of warfare to advance their interests at the expense of the West and other democracies. State support helped the terrorist groups to become better organized and equipped to conduct their lethal brand of war against innocent people. In particular, the state sponsors provide money, weapons, training, communications equipment, false passports, and safe haven to their client terrorist groups.

   Confronting state sponsors of terrorism is difficult for several reasons. Such states normally seek some measure of "plausible deniability" when sponsoring terrorist groups. Financial support, for example, is funneled to the groups through indirect channels. Sometimes, taking strong actions against state sponsors may conflict with other U.S. foreign policy objectives. In 1991, for example, Washington allowed Syria to join the U.S.-led coalition against Iraq even though Damascus had long been a sponsor of international terrorism.

   U.S. policymakers frequently resort to economic sanctions to punish state sponsors of international terrorism. Not all states are equally vulnerable to such measures, however. Additional trade sanctions against North Korea, for example, probably would have little effect, given Pyongyang's commitment to economic autarky. Other countries, such as Libya, have proven to be more vulnerable to U.S.-backed sanctions.

2. **The proliferation of weapons of mass destruction (WMD), particularly among states that sponsor terrorism, threatens to raise the potential cost of terrorism dramatically.** The use

---

4. See James Phillips, "Defusing Terrorism at Ground Zero: Why a New U.S. Policy Is Needed for Afghanistan," Heritage Foundation *Backgrounder* No. 1383, July 12, 2000, at *www.heritage.org/library/backgrounder/bg1383.html*.

of chemical, biological, radiologic, or nuclear (CBRN) weapons is an increasingly plausible nightmare scenario.[5] Exercises like "Dark Winter"[6] that simulate such attacks have shown how deadly chemical and biological weapons would be. The September–October 2001 anthrax-letter terrorist attacks that killed five Americans were graphic examples of how disruptive such attacks are to society. Terrorists seek massive casualties to dramatize their causes and capture public attention.

Individual terrorists may have access to lethal weaponry even if they are not part of an established terrorist group or backed by a state sponsor. The Unabomber is the most striking example thus far of the freelance terrorist phenomenon. The interconnected nature of the global economy makes efforts to counter the proliferation of WMD and related technologies increasingly difficult. The formulation of an effective counterterrorism policy is now a moral and strategic imperative.

3. **Making concessions to terrorists will not solve the problem.** Although international terrorism probably never will be totally eradicated, raising its costs and lowering its benefits can reduce terrorist activity. Making concessions to terrorists merely rewards their illegal actions and invites future attacks. The taking of hostages by Philippine terrorists in the past few years was rewarded by paying ransom, which only increased the incidence of abduction and caused the terrorists to raise their ransom demands.

   The United States must resolutely rule out this approach. When hostages are taken, the United States also should limit presidential involvement as much as possible. The reason: Allowing the President to become personally involved in a hostage crisis drives up the perceived value of the hostages and makes the President, in effect, also a hostage. The United States must pay no ransom and must take decisive action against terrorist groups.

---

5. See Jack Spencer and Michael Scardaville, "Understanding the Bioterrorist Threat: Facts and Figures," Heritage Foundation *Backgrounder* No. 1488, October 11, 2001, at *www.heritage.org/library/backgrounder/bg1488.html*.
6. For details on this exercise, see *http://www.homelandsecurity.org/darkwinter/index.cfm*.

4. **Intelligence plays a key role in disrupting terrorist networks.** Taking effective action against terrorists, their ideological allies, and their state sponsors requires accurate and timely intelligence. Without such information, it is difficult to link state sponsors to specific acts of terrorism or anticipate potential terrorist attacks against U.S. interests. Accurate intelligence also is essential for the United States to have any reasonable expectation of targeting specific vulnerabilities of states that sponsor international terrorism. Without it, the United States cannot hope to disrupt terrorist networks or anticipate attacks. Analysts responsible for producing intelligence estimates must be free of political pressures.

5. **An effective antiterrorism policy requires a balance of offensive and defensive measures.** As the war on terrorism demonstrates, the best defense against terrorism is strong offensive action to kill or capture the terrorists, disrupt their networks, and destroy their financing. Where possible, the United States should move to destroy the terrorists' networks and keep them off balance. This means targeting terrorist groups and training bases for military attack. In some cases, especially where terrorists may have access to weapons of mass destruction, the United States must consider preemptive strikes to protect vital security interests. Defensive measures aimed at protecting U.S. citizens and property from terrorists fall under the rubric of antiterrorism. Examples of such measures include hardening U.S. embassies and military bases against possible terrorist strikes. Providing military and diplomatic personnel with terrorist threat briefings is another defensive measure that can reduce the risk of attack.

THE FACTS

FACT: The September 11 terrorist attacks showed that international terrorists pose a clear and deadly threat to Americans.

- Americans remain a prime target of international terrorists. From 1995 to 2000, 77 Americans were killed as a result of international terrorist attacks—an average of 13 per year.[7]

- With disturbing frequency, terrorists have resorted to inflicting mass casualties. Although the number of international terrorist attacks declined from a peak of 665 in 1987 to 273 in 1998 before rising to 423 in 2000, the number of casualties has climbed as terrorists have launched increasingly lethal attacks.
- In February 1993, terrorists bombed New York's World Trade Center, killing six people and wounding over 1,000. Had the terrorists succeeded in bringing down the entire building—as America saw on September 11, 2001—the death toll would have numbered in the thousands.
- In June 1996, terrorists bombed the Khobar Towers in Saudi Arabia and killed 19 U.S. Air Force personnel and injured 500 more. This attack reportedly was launched by Saudi Hezballah, a Shiite terrorist group with close links to Iran.
- In August 1998, the terrorist attacks on the U.S. embassies in Nairobi, Kenya, and Dar es Salaam, Tanzania, killed 224 people, including 12 Americans, and wounded more than 5,000.

FACT: The threat posed by international terrorists is often amplified by state sponsorship.

The U.S. Department of State's list of states that sponsor terrorism includes Cuba, Iran, Iraq, Libya, North Korea, Sudan, and Syria. These state sponsors of terrorism are often aided by countries like China that export weapons or chemicals in violation of international agreements. State sponsors back terrorist acts to drive the United States out of strategically important regions, humiliate its military forces, and undermine its allies and friendly governments and political movements. Countries that assist the terror-sponsoring states do so for similar reasons—to weaken the United States and the effectiveness of its foreign policy.

FACT: Five of the seven state sponsors of terrorism as listed by the State Department are seeking to acquire weapons of mass destruction and missiles to deliver them.

Iran, Iraq, Libya, North Korea, and Syria have established missile programs and are developing chemical, biological, or nuclear

7. Center for Data Analysis, "Facts and Figures About Terrorism," Heritage Foundation *Web Memo*, 2001, at *www.heritage.org/shorts/20010914terror.htm*.

weapons. North Korea and Iran have entered into a strategic alliance, with the North Koreans selling missile technology to Iran in exchange for cash and Iranian oil.

FACT: Iran is the world's most active sponsor of international terrorism.

Iran supports a wide range of terrorist groups, including Hezballah (Party of God), Hamas, and Palestine Islamic Jihad. Iran also has supported many terrorist attacks against Americans: the 444-day hostage crisis of 1979–1981; the 1983 bombing of the Marine barracks in Beirut, Lebanon; and the kidnapping of 15 Americans held hostage in Lebanon between 1984 and 1991. The Iranian-supported terrorist group Saudi Hezballah is believed to be responsible for the deadly June 1996 bombing of the Khobar Towers in Saudi Arabia. Iranian hit teams also have assassinated scores of Iranian dissidents outside Iran. Late in 1998, Tehran announced that a cell of rogue Iranian intelligence agents had assassinated five political activists and writers living inside Iran.

FACT: Terrorist groups also show growing interest in acquiring chemical, biological, and nuclear weapons.

- Osama bin Laden's al-Qaeda terrorist network made concerted efforts to acquire nuclear, chemical, and biological weapons. Bin Laden already may have a "dirty bomb"—one that mixes radioactive material with high explosives to contaminate an area.

- In March 1995, the Aum Shin Rikyo religious cult launched a nerve gas attack in the Tokyo subway that killed 12 people and injured 5,500, many of whom suffered severe nerve damage. A malfunction in the terrorists' delivery system is believed to have prevented tens of thousands of additional casualties.

- The revolution in communications technology has made it more difficult to stem the proliferation of terrorist know-how. For example, recipes for sarin, the World War II nerve gas used in the 1995 Tokyo subway attack, can be downloaded from the Internet. This means the United States is likely to face threats from more Unabomber-style self-taught terrorists.

WHAT TO DO IN 2003

To protect Americans against the threat of international terrorism, Washington must maintain relentless pressure against terrorist groups and the states that support them. In addition to seeking the arrest and punishment of terrorists such as Osama bin Laden, the United States must use diplomatic, economic, and military pressure to penalize the states that support terrorists and their networks.

Punish the state sponsors of terrorism on as many fronts as possible.

Some states rely heavily on terrorism because it is a cost-effective adjunct to their foreign policies. The United States should work with its allies and other concerned states to raise the diplomatic, economic, political, and military costs of supporting terrorism to such high levels that the costs outweigh the strategic benefits. Candidates for office can call attention to this approach by suggesting the following as ways to raise the cost of conducting and sponsoring terrorism:

- **Diplomatic measures.** Countries victimized by terrorism have broken relations or reduced the size of the diplomatic mission of the state sponsor. This helped limit the threat of terrorism to some degree because much of it has been directed, supported, and financed by intelligence personnel operating under diplomatic cover, but diplomatic sanctions usually have been unilateral, ad hoc responses that have had little effect on terrorist states.

  Washington should propose an agreement among the Group of 7 industrial countries and with its NATO allies that requires all of them to expel large numbers of diplomats from—if not break diplomatic relations with—states that support terrorist attacks. Moreover, diplomatic personnel of these states should be expelled for each confirmed terrorist attack by a surrogate terrorist group. This approach would raise the public uproar over terrorism and increase the cost of an attack. It also might give pause to some terrorist states, particularly those such as Iran and Sudan that want the West to bail them out of dire economic predicaments. At a minimum, reducing the diplomatic presence of terrorist states will make it harder for them to support terrorism out of their embassies. This approach greatly undermined Iraq's ability to export terrorism during the 1991 Gulf War.

- **Economic measures.** Washington should persuade its allies to participate in developing a multilateral version of the State Department's list of states that support terrorism. A terrorist state placed on the list would be denied economic assistance, arms sales, and preferential trade privileges from all participating states. Further, the allies would be committed to voting against financial aid for that state from such international financial institutions as the World Bank.

  Such a united front by Western Europe, Japan, and the United States in threatening to impose sanctions would have a sobering effect on the seven states that the State Department lists as state sponsors of terrorism. All, with the possible exception of Libya, will require Western or Japanese economic assistance, loans, or refinancing of existing loans in the near future. The United States should convince its allies to take advantage of their financial leverage and elevate counterterrorism to the forefront of decisions about economic aid and loan refinancing.

- **Financial actions.** The banking and international financial community should work with international law enforcement agencies to identify the accounts of groups engaging in terrorism and to seize or block the use of that money.[8]

- **Raising the domestic political cost of terrorism in the sponsoring states.** The United States should drive up the prospective political costs of state-sponsored terrorism by supporting opposition groups in countries that engage in international terrorism. The war in Afghanistan graphically illustrates the benefits of supporting the Northern Alliance, the major opposition to the ruling Taliban.[9] All

8. See Gerald P. O'Driscoll, Jr., Brett D. Schaefer, and John C. Hulsman, "Stopping Terrorism: Follow the Money," Heritage Foundation *Backgrounder* No. 1479, September 25, 2001, at *www.heritage.org/library/backgrounder/bg1479.html*.

9. See James Phillips, "Uproot Bin Laden's Terrorist Network and Taliban Allies in Afghanistan," Heritage Foundation *Executive Memorandum* No. 776, September 17, 2001, at *www.heritage.org/library/execmemo/em776.html*.

of the states that support terrorism are repressive regimes that generate domestic opposition. Washington should provide diplomatic, economic, and even military support to the most viable opposition groups in each terrorist state. The Iraqi National Congress and the Kurds in Iraq, the resistance movements in southern Sudan, pro-Western exile groups in Iran, and Libyan dissidents all merit increased U.S. and other Western support.

The United States can also bolster the domestic political costs of supporting terrorism by informing the populations of terrorist states about how much money their governments lavish on terrorist groups and how economic sanctions provoked by terrorism lower their standard of living. Many Iranians, for example, may disagree with their government's decision to allocate considerable resources to maintain its extensive terrorist network rather than improve the living standards of the Iranian people.

Retaliate decisively against terrorists, acting independently when necessary.

The credible, decisive use of military force is essential for punishing and deterring state-sponsored terrorism. The military response should be designed to raise the cost of terrorism above the price a terrorist state is willing to pay. The United States should not get bogged down in a tit-for-tat exchange by limiting its attacks merely to terrorist training camps. Instead, it should strike targets that the terrorist state highly values, such as its internal security forces and secret police.

A sharp and decisive military reprisal not only can have a deterrent effect on the terrorist state attacked, but also can have a strong effect on other states that support terrorism. For example, the April 1986 U.S. air strikes against Libya had a significant impact on Syria as well. According to the State Department, Libya reduced its involvement in international terrorism from 19 incidents in 1986 to six in 1987, while Syrian involvement fell from 34 in 1985 to six in 1986 and one in 1987.

Special Operations forces are an important option for fighting terrorists close to innocent civilians, in hostage rescue operations, and in efforts to apprehend terrorist leaders. Special Operations forces also play an important role in attacking regimes that support terrorism, as they did in Afghanistan where they assisted Afghan opposition forces in overthrowing the Taliban regime.

The Pentagon must make an effort to maintain the strength and readiness of the Special Operations Command, which includes the elite Delta Force, Army Special Operations Forces, Navy Seals, Marine Reconnaissance teams, and a special assault unit from the 101st Air Assault Division. These forces should be dispatched periodically on anti-terrorism training exercises in friendly countries in regions where they may be asked to operate against terrorists, particularly the Middle East.

When necessary, the United States should not hesitate to use covert or clandestine action to attack terrorists.

Press allies and other states to increase their involvement in the war against terrorism.

The United States must lead a comprehensive campaign against state sponsors of terrorism that includes diplomatic, economic, intelligence, and military measures. To the maximum extent practical, multinational efforts should include sharing intelligence on terrorist groups, joint counterterrorist training exercises, concerted actions to disrupt and impede terrorist logistical support and fundraising networks, and developing contingency plans for allied military and intelligence operations against terrorist groups.

Too often, European states sought to appease terrorist states and cut separate deals with them rather than take a unified stand against terrorism. The United States must drive home to its allies that appeasement of terrorism is a self-defeating policy that only encourages more terrorism.

Washington also should press its allies to establish a high-level central office for coordinating counterterrorism policies. These offices could act as liaisons with allied counterterrorism agencies. Modeled on the U.S. State Department's Office of Counterterrorism, these offices would help raise the profile of counterterrorism as an international issue and make international cooperation more effective and timely. Washington also should lobby all its allies to adopt stiffer penalties for terrorism, including longer jail terms and seizure of the assets of terrorist groups or states. The Europeans, in particular, should be pressed to stop releasing terrorists before their sentences have been completed as part of secret deals with terrorist states.

Washington should press Saudi Arabia to halt the flow of financial aid to radical Islamic movements. Substantial sums of money from private Saudi religious foundations and individuals bankrolled Osama bin Laden, as well as Sheik Abdul Rahman, the spiritual leader of the World Trade Center bombers, and other radical Islamic fundamentalists. Riyadh placed restrictions on the flow of these funds outside the country in 1993, but it needs to control the activities of Islamic foundations more carefully to prevent them from meddling in the internal affairs of other countries.

Strengthen human intelligence (HUMINT) and covert action capabilities.

The September 11 terrorist attacks also underscored the importance of human intelligence in gaining early warning of impending attacks. To improve HUMINT collection, the intelligence community must (1) focus on recruitment, training, and retention of skilled personnel; (2) place more emphasis on language training and understanding of other cultures; (3) assure career advancement for agency officers who are aggressive in recruiting and employing informants and operatives; and (4) allow agency officers to use commonsense criteria in recruiting foreign operatives and informants. Sometimes foreign informants will be unsavory individuals; U.S. intelligence agencies must be able to recruit spies within terrorist organizations in order to neutralize those organizations.

International terrorist groups have profited from cooperation with organized crime networks. For example, the Lebanon-based Hezballah and the Peru-based Shining Path movement financed some of their operations through the production and smuggling of illegal drugs. The United States needs to lead a coordinated international campaign of intelligence and law enforcement agencies against international criminal and terrorist networks, which sometimes overlap.

Provide money to support research, development, and acquisition of better signals intelligence (SIGINT) systems.

The communications means used by terrorists and their sponsors are not purely military in nature, and this makes the detection and interception of their communications more difficult. More money and resources are needed to strengthen the intelligence community's ability to intercept and exploit terrorist command, control, and communications networks.

Pre-empt terrorist attacks decisively, particularly if terrorists are known to have access to weapons of mass destruction.

The Pentagon has placed heavy emphasis on managing the consequences of a terrorist attack involving weapons of mass destruction, but insufficient emphasis on proactive measures to disrupt terrorist activities before they attack. The United States must be prepared to take pre-emptive action if intelligence sources indicate that terrorists are preparing to use weapons of mass destruction. Where the terrorist threat is immediate and overwhelming, pre-emptive strikes are justified on grounds of self-defense.

Strengthen preparedness against terrorist acts involving weapons of mass destruction.

America must improve its civil defense preparedness for a WMD attack by upgrading contingency planning and coordination among federal, state, and local law enforcement authorities. The efforts of other players—including intelligence agencies, medical institutions, and specialized military units trained to detect, disarm, or protect people from nuclear, chemical, and biological weapons—should be coordinated by the National Security Council to achieve unity of effort. The preparedness of America's public health system must be increased by stockpiling medical supplies and vaccines for a CBRN attack. Local first responders as well as federal response teams need to be trained and to develop contingency plans for such attacks.

—James Phillips is a Research Fellow in the Kathryn and Shelby Cullom Davis Institute for International Studies at The Heritage Foundation. Larry M. Wortzel, Ph.D., is Director of the Asian Studies Center at The Heritage Foundation.

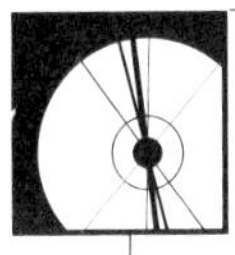

For a complete list and full-text versions of additional studies by Heritage on international terrorism, see the searchable *Issues 2002* companion CD–ROM.

EXPERTS

Heritage Foundation

James Phillips
Research Fellow, Kathryn and Shelby Cullom Davis Institute for International Studies
The Heritage Foundation
214 Massachusetts Avenue, NE
Washington, DC 20002
(202) 608-6119
fax: (202) 675-1758
jim.phillips@heritage.org

Larry M. Wortzel, Ph.D.
Director, Asian Studies Center
The Heritage Foundation
214 Massachusetts Avenue, NE
Washington, DC 20002
(202) 608-6081
fax: (202) 675-1779
larry.wortzel@heritage.org

Daniel W. Fisk
Deputy Director, Kathryn and Shelby Cullom Davis Institute for International Studies
The Heritage Foundation
214 Massachusetts Avenue, NE
Washington, DC 20002
(202) 608-6114
fax: (202) 675-1758
dan.fisk@heritage.org

Ambassador Charles Lichenstein
Distinguished Fellow
The Heritage Foundation
214 Massachusetts Avenue, NE
Washington, DC 20002
(202) 608-6187

Edwin Meese III
Ronald Reagan Distinguished Fellow in Public Policy
Chairman, Center for Legal and Judicial Studies
The Heritage Foundation
214 Massachusetts Avenue, NE
Washington, DC 20002
(202) 608-6181
fax: (202) 547-0641
edwin.meese@heritage.org

Other Experts

Kenneth E. de Graffenreid
Faculty Member in Intelligence Studies
Institute of World Politics
1521 16th Street, NW
Washington, DC 20036
(202) 462-2101
fax: (202) 462-7031
kdeg@nsc-inc.net

Roy Godson
President
National Strategy Information Center
1730 Rhode Island Avenue, NW
Suite 500
Washington, DC 20036
(202) 429-0129
fax: (202) 659-5429
nsic@ix.netcom.com

Christopher Harmon, Ph.D.
Professor of International Relations
Marine Corps Command and Staff College
2076 South Street, MCCDC
Quantico, VA 22134-5068
(703) 784-6855
fax: (703) 784-2628
harmoncc@tecom.usmc.mil

Fred Iklé, Ph.D.
Distinguished Scholar
Center for Strategic and International Studies
1800 K Street, NW
Washington, DC 20006
(301) 951-0176
fax: (301) 951-0286
IkleOfc@csis.org

For continually updated and expanded information on major breaking developments on this issue over the campaign cycle, see *www.heritage.org/issues/terrorism.*

TRADE POLICY

Promoting Prosperity at Home and Abroad

Sara J. Fitzgerald

THE ISSUES

America has benefited significantly from past trade agreements. Today, the United States is the world leader in exports, representing 12.7 percent of global trade. While critics often claim that trade is taking jobs away from thousands of Americans and sending them abroad, the evidence indicates otherwise. The "giant sucking sound" of jobs leaving the United States that Ross Perot predicted never occurred. Rather, lowering trade barriers has brought higher-paying jobs to Americans. Trade has benefited American families, has opened new venues for industry, and has strengthened U.S. diplomatic ties.

1. **The goal of free trade is to open markets by lowering barriers.** America is the world's largest agricultural exporter but faces an average global agricultural tariff rate of 62 percent. Tariffs function as invisible taxes that add to the price of American goods, making them less desirable to foreign consumers. In addition to being subject to tariffs, American exports also face non-tariff barriers in the form of quotas and stringent regulations, making it even more difficult for American products to receive fair treatment in the global marketplace.

   The United States is negotiating a trade agreement with Chile, which already has a bilateral trading arrangement with Canada. Until the U.S.–Chile bilateral agreement is approved, America will continue to lose valuable trade with Chile to Canada. According to U.S. Secretary of Agriculture Ann Veneman, "Canada is now taking market share from us in wheat and potatoes because they have lower tariffs in Chile than we do."[1]

2. **Trade is not just good economic policy; it is also good foreign policy.** Trade can be used as a diplomatic salve. Trade strengthens our allies and engages our potential adversaries, while the absence of trade harms our enemies. Countries that trade with each other are more likely than other countries to iron out their differences in an effective manner in order to remain in good standing. The United States needs to promote free trade as part of a comprehensive foreign policy to promote U.S. interests. Currently, America lags behind the rest of the world in free trade agreements; it is party to only three of the 131 trade and investment agreements that exist.

THE FACTS

FACT: Trade helps the American family.

The lower tariffs and higher incomes that followed the signing of the North American Free Trade Agreement (NAFTA) and the Uruguay Round of the General Agreement on Tariffs and Trade (GATT) resulted in benefits of $1,300 to $2,000 a year for the average American family of four. According to a recent University of Michigan study, a new trade round could deliver an annual benefit of $2,450 for this same family.[2] Trade does not discriminate against the rich or the poor; it elevates all economic levels.

FACT: Trade does not send American jobs overseas; rather, it gives American workers higher-paying jobs.

The U.S. Department of Commerce reports that, on average, jobs tied to exports earn 13 percent to 18 percent more than other jobs earn. In other words, trade brings prosperity and opportunity to workers.

FACT: NAFTA was—and is—good for America.

U.S. Trade Representative Robert Zoellick points out that "U.S. exports to our NAFTA partners increased 104 percent between 1993 and 2000; U.S. trade with the rest of the world grew only half as fast."[3] In the seven years since NAFTA's implementation, U.S. exports to Mexico and Canada have grown to support 2.9 million American jobs today—900,000 more than in 1993.[4]

---

1. See *www.fas.usda.gov/info/factsheets/TPA/sec-062101.html.*
2. See *www.ustr.gov/speech-test/zoellick/zoellick_10.pdf.*
3. See *www.ustr.gov/speech-test/zoellick/zoellick_7.PDF.*

According to the Office of the U.S. Trade Representative, "we trade $1.8 billion a day with our NAFTA partners—that's $1.2 million a minute."[5] As U.S. government data indicate, without NAFTA, the United States would have lower-paying jobs and would export less, and Mexico and the United States would have lower environmental standards.[6]

Farmland Industries of Kansas City, the largest farmer-owned cooperative in North America, sold $50 million in wheat, corn, and soybeans to Mexico before NAFTA. Today, exports have grown to $450 million and include beef and pork.[7]

FACT: Trade improves labor conditions.

Contrary to the claims of critics of free trade, research on developing nations has shown that in countries that have a higher per-capita income, there is a lower incidence of child labor. As World Bank studies have shown, an increase in trade has been correlated with an increase of economic growth in developing countries, and the income of the poor tended to rise at the same rate as overall economic growth.[8]

FACT: Trade is good for the environment.

Studies have shown that countries that open their markets actually spend more money on the environment as a result of gains through trade. Attempts to impose environmental regulations have often been self-defeating because they have stifled the trade necessary for economic growth, which would enable countries to afford to adopt environmental protection policies. The track record of the United States in promoting initiatives to protect the environment provides evidence that environmental freedom and the economic development it engenders are correlated with sound environmental policies.[9]

---

4. *Ibid.*
5. U.S. Trade Representative Robert Zoellick, speech to the Council of the Americas, May 7, 2001.
6. See *www.tpa.gov/factsheets.htm*.
7. See *www.farmland.com/news/sysnews/oldarchive/FEB1999/naftaopens.html*.
8. Aaron Schavey, "Raising Labor Standards Through Trade," Heritage Foundation *Executive Memorandum* No. 785, October 19, 2001, at *www.heritage.org/library/execmemo/em785.html*.
9. Ana I. Eiras and Brett D. Schaefer, "Trade: The Best Way to Protect the Environment," Heritage Foundation *Backgrounder* No. 1480, September 27, 2001, at *www.heritage.org/library/backgrounder/bg1480.html*.

FACT: Free trade agreements will not compromise American sovereignty.

In response to concerns that trade deals may be unconstitutional and could undermine U.S. sovereignty, it should be stressed that the United States will always determine its own domestic laws. Even if future trade agreements allowed some disputes to be submitted to an international tribunal for initial determination, no trade agreement could grant an international organization the power to change U.S. laws.[10]

FACT: Trade agreements foster adherence to the rule of law and protect private property rights.

Free trade forces participating countries to play fair. For example, because of its membership in the World Trade Organization (WTO), China will now have to crack down on software piracy. China has been the world's largest source of pirated compact disks and software. In China last year, software firms lost over $1 billion in profits to piracy, according to the Business Software Alliance.[11] Furthermore, while many criticized China's WTO membership, American industry will benefit because, to comply with agreements of the organization, China now has to lower tariffs and non-tariff barriers.

FACT: The United States needs to negotiate more free trade agreements.

Of the 131 trade and investment agreements that exist throughout the world, the United States is party to only three: specifically, with Jordan, Israel, and the NAFTA countries of Canada and Mexico.

---

10. Edwin Meese III and Todd Gaziano, "Why Trade Promotion Authority Is Constitutional," Heritage Foundation *Legal Memorandum* No. 4, November 28, 2001, at *www.heritage.org/library/legalmemo/lm4.html*.
11. "Microsoft Touts XP in China, Held Back by Pirates," *The New York Times*, November 9, 2001.

The *Index of Economic Freedom* is the preeminent source for measuring the level of freedom and prospects for growth in our global economy. It also is a valuable guide to economic growth for those who want to understand the reasons why some economies flourish and others lag behind. Read the entire book on the *Issues 2002* companion CD–ROM or contact Heritage's Publications office at 1-800-544-4843 to order a copy.

WHAT TO DO IN 2003

Promote greater trade liberalization through the WTO and press for the reduction of the European Union's non-tariff trade barriers.

The United States should continue to promote trade liberalization in the negotiations of the Doha World Trade Round. In addition, while reducing its own subsidies, the United States should continue to pressure the European Union (EU) to reduce its excessive agricultural subsidies, which act as non-tariff barriers to free trade.

Pursue and complete bilateral trade agreements.

The United States should complete the negotiations on a free trade agreement with Chile that are currently in progress. In addition, the United States should complete its trade negotiations with Singapore and actively pursue agreements with Australia and New Zealand.

Promote the creation of a Global Free Trade Association (GFTA).

A Global Free Trade Association, an idea that has generated much interest, would be a trade association in which membership is voluntary, inclusive, and based solely on a country's demonstrated commitment to a liberal trading order.[12] This means that its members would share similar beliefs and market

12. John C. Hulsman, Ph.D., and Aaron Schavey, "The Global Free Trade Association: A New Trade Agenda," Heritage Foundation *Backgrounder* No. 1441, May 16, 2001, at *www.heritage.org/library/backgrounder/bg1441.html.*

institutions. The association would not be limited to a specific geographic region but would be open to any country that qualifies.

In order to qualify for membership, a country would need to meet the following criteria, which would indicate that it is open to trade and investment and maintains a secure rule of law with low levels of regulation.

- **Trade Policy.** To qualify for membership, countries must have an average tariff rate of no more than 9 percent and must maintain minimum non-tariff barriers.
- **Investment.** A qualifying country must have an open investment regime. It should maintain a transparent and open foreign investment code, treat foreign investments impartially, and approve foreign investments efficiently.
- **Property Rights.** A GFTA country must have an established rule of law that protects private property and provides an environment in which business transactions can take place with a high degree of certainty.
- **Regulation.** A country's government regulations should neither deter entrepreneurs from opening a business nor overly burden new businesses with regulation.

Currently, under these criteria, the following countries would qualify for membership in a proposed Global Free Trade Association: Australia, Chile, Denmark, Estonia, Finland, Hong Kong, Iceland, Ireland, Luxembourg, New Zealand, Singapore, the United Kingdom, and the United States. The GFTA would highlight the benefits of liberalized trade among like-minded members—in contrast with past efforts to reduce barriers that made a number of countries perceive compliance with trade agreements as a concession.

—Sara J. Fitzgerald is a Trade Policy Analyst in the Center for International Trade and Economics at The Heritage Foundation.

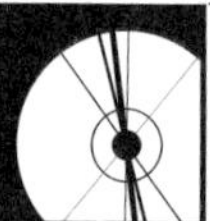

For a complete list and full-text versions of additional studies by Heritage on trade policy, see the searchable *Issues 2002* companion CD–ROM.

EXPERTS

Heritage Foundation

Sara J. Fitzgerald
Trade Policy Analyst
Center for International Trade and Economics
The Heritage Foundation
214 Massachusetts Avenue, NE
Washington, DC 20002
(202) 608-6079
fax: (202) 608-6129
sara.fitzgerald@heritage.org

Aaron Schavey
Policy Analyst
Center for International Trade and Economics
The Heritage Foundation
214 Massachusetts Avenue, NE
Washington, DC 20002
(202) 608-6225
fax: (202) 608-6129
aaron.schavey@heritage.org

Ana I. Eiras
Latin America Policy Analyst
Center for International Trade and Economics
The Heritage Foundation
214 Massachusetts Avenue, NE
Washington, DC 20002
(202) 608-6125
fax: (202) 608-6129
ana.eiras@heritage.org

Brett D. Schaefer
Jay Kingham Fellow in International Regulatory Affairs
Center for International Trade and Economics
The Heritage Foundation
214 Massachusetts Avenue, NE
Washington, DC 20002
(202) 608-6123
fax: (202) 608-6129
brett.schaefer@heritage.org

John C. Hulsman, Ph.D.
Research Fellow in European Affairs
Kathryn and Shelby Cullom Davis Institute for International Studies
The Heritage Foundation
214 Massachusetts Avenue, NE
Washington, DC 20002
(202) 608-6086
fax: (202) 675-1758
john.hulsman@heritage.org

Gerald P. O'Driscoll, Jr., Ph.D.
Director, Center for International Trade and Economics
The Heritage Foundation
214 Massachusetts Avenue, NE
Washington, DC 20002
(202) 608-6185
fax: (202) 608-6129
jerry.odriscoll@heritage.org

Barbara H. Franklin
Visiting Distinguished Fellow
The Heritage Foundation
President, Barbara Franklin Enterprises
2600 Virginia Avenue, NW
Suite 506
Washington, DC 20037
(202) 337-9100
fax: (202) 337-9104
bhfranklin@aol.com

Other Experts

Claude Barfield
American Enterprise Institute
1150 17th Street, NW
Washington, DC 20036
(202) 862-5879
fax: (202) 862-7177
barfield@aei.org

Daniel Griswold
Associate Director, Center for Trade Policy Studies
Cato Institute
1000 Massachusetts Avenue, NW
Washington, DC 20001
(202) 789-5260

fax: (202) 842-3490
dgriswol@cato.org

Brink Lindsey
Director, Center for
Trade Policy Studies
Cato Institute
1000 Massachusetts Avenue, NW
Washington, DC 20001
(202) 789-5228
fax: (202) 842-3490
blindsey@cato.org

For continually updated and expanded information on major breaking developments on this issue over the campaign cycle, see *www.heritage.org/issues/trade.*

THE UNITED NATIONS

Pursuing Reform, Promoting Sound Policies

Brett D. Schaefer

THE ISSUES

A remarkable change in America's relations with the United Nations has occurred during the first year of the Bush Administration. At the beginning of 2001, relations were fairly good. In December 2000, the United States and the U.N. had reached an agreement to reduce America's excessive share of the U.N. regular and peacekeeping budgets; and in February 2001, both houses of Congress passed legislation authorizing the payment of $582 million in arrears to the United Nations that had been linked to the need for serious reforms at the organization.

But the relationship soured rapidly over several key issues, including the Kyoto Protocol on global warming, the International Criminal Court (ICC), and the U.N. Conference on the Illicit Trade in Small Arms and Light Weapons in All Its Aspects. Many pundits interpreted the ejection of the United States from the U.N. Human Rights Commission and the International Narcotics Control Board in May 2001 as punishment for America's opposition to some of these initiatives and other issues, such as the Administration's determination to implement a missile defense system.

This conflict was quickly overshadowed by the September 11 terrorist attacks. Since then, the U.N. has supported America's war on terrorism and has muted its criticism. As U.S. Ambassador to the U.N. John Negroponte has said, "every Security Council resolution adopted since [September 11] has been adopted unanimously, and they do not all have to do with terrorism."[1] This

1. Georgie Anne Geyer, "Negroponte Embraces Evolving Attitudes at the United Nations," Universal Press Syndicate, December 7, 2001.

renewed cooperation does not mean that all issues of contention between the United Nations and the United States have been resolved, however.

1. **The war on terrorism is global, and the U.N.'s continuing support will play a key role.** Winning the global war to eradicate the scourge of terrorism will depend primarily on the willingness of the U.S. government, the American people, and America's allies to persevere over the long term. Beyond diplomacy and better law enforcement at home, the war may require the use of U.S. military force in other regions. The importance of the U.N.'s role in supporting this campaign should not be overlooked.

2. **Proper scrutiny must be given to the U.N.'s attempt to broaden international law and the authority of international bureaucracies through treaties and other agreements.** Some international treaties, conventions, and agreements are in America's interest, but many are of dubious merit and should either be actively discouraged or, at a minimum, not supported by the United States. Examples include the Rome Statute establishing the ICC, the U.N. Framework Convention on Climate Change and the Kyoto Protocol, and the conference agreement on illicit trade in small arms.

3. **Participating in U.N. peacekeeping should not compromise military readiness.** U.N. peacekeeping operations were overly ambitious in the 1990s, resulting in many embarrassing failures, including those in Haiti, Somalia, Sierra Leone, and the former Yugoslavia. These missions also can detract from the readiness of U.S. troops to respond to more urgent contingencies around the globe. According to a Congressional Budget Office study of peacekeeping missions, two-thirds of the surveyed U.S. army officials who had participated in peacekeeping missions felt that the training readiness of their units had declined.[2]

4. **The United Nations still needs to reform.** Great progress followed the demands for reform included in the Consolidated Appropriations Act for FY 2000 (P.L. 106–113), which

---

2. Congressional Budget Office, *Making Peace While Staying Ready for War: The Challenges of U.S. Military Participation in Peacekeeping*, December 1999, Chapter 3, at *www.cbo.gov/showdoc.cfm?index=1809&sequence=0&from=1*.

included the Helms–Biden legislation that tied payments of U.S. arrears to specific U.N. reforms. Much remains to be done, however, as the U.N. remains inefficient, duplicative, and charged with too many mandates for which it is ill-equipped.

THE FACTS

FACT: There are already 12 international treaties and conventions dealing with terrorism.

Terrorism has been listed as an agenda item for each session of the General Assembly since 1972, but the result has been little more than paperwork. Even though 12 international treaties and conventions dealing with terrorism and related activities[3] have been deposited with the U.N. or other relevant international organizations,[4] terrorism has not lessened. In fact, terrorist attacks have increased even as new anti-terrorism treaties have been created. (See Chart 1.)

In October 2001, the General Assembly closed its Plenary Meetings on Measures to Eliminate International Terrorism by urging member states to (1) become parties to international conventions relating to terrorism; (2) conclude negotiations on pending conventions on international terrorism; (3) expedite a report on terrorism from the body's Sixth Committee (Legal); and (4) launch a "dialogue among civilizations" on the fight against terrorism that is "separate from any religion or ethnic group."[5] In other words, the General Assembly recommended more meetings, debates, and international agreements on terrorism while offering no innovative new policies to combat terrorism.

More significant, the United Nations does not even have a definition of what qualifies as terrorism. One of the main recommendations of the Plenary Meetings was to clarify the "definition of terrorism."[6]

---

3. There are also seven Regional Conventions on Terrorism. See United Nations Treaty Collection, "Conventions on Terrorism," at *http://untreaty.un.org/English/Terrorism.asp*.
4. From United Nations Treaty Collection, "Summaries of the Multilateral Treaties Deposited with the Secretary-General," Treaty Event—Multilateral Treaties on Terrorism, at *http://untreaty.un.org/English/tersumen.htm*.
5. Statement by the President of the General Assembly, October 5, 2001, at *www.un.org/terrorism/statements/gapresconclusion.html*.

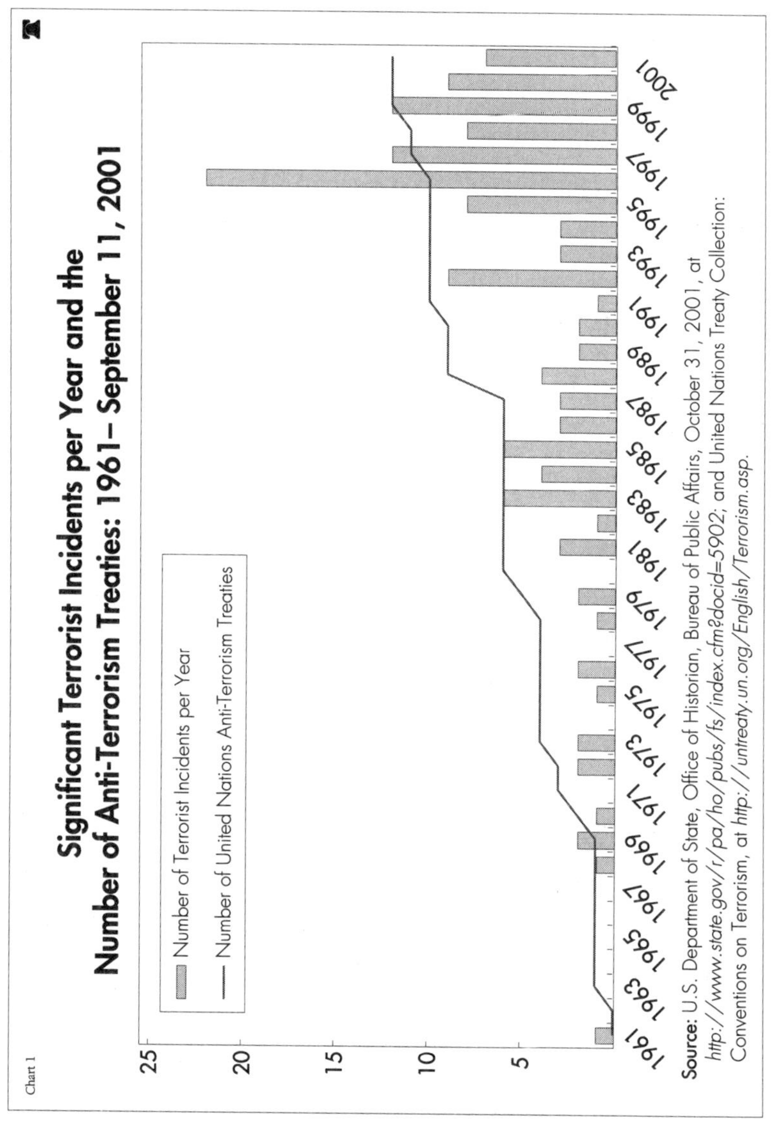

Source: U.S. Department of State, Office of Historian, Bureau of Public Affairs, October 31, 2001, at *http://www.state.gov/r/pa/ho/pubs/fs/index.cfm?docid=5902*; and United Nations Treaty Collection: Conventions on Terrorism, at *http://untreaty.un.org/English/Terrorism.asp.*

FACT: U.N. peacekeeping missions have a poor record of success.

- Of the 54 U.N. peacekeeping operations undertaken since 1948, 36 have been launched just since 1991. The 15 active U.N. peacekeeping operations include the Middle East (1948), India–Pakistan (1949), Cyprus (1964), the Golan Heights (1974), Lebanon (1978), Iraq/Kuwait (1991), Western Sahara (1991), Georgia (1993), Bosnia and Herzegovina (1995), Prevlaka Peninsula (1996), the Democratic Republic of the Congo (1999), East Timor (1999), Sierra Leone (1999), Kosovo (1999), and Ethiopia and Eritrea (2000).[7]

- Many "completed" U.N. peacekeeping operations were immediately followed by new operations in the same country or region with nearly identical mandates, and very few achieved a lasting peace. For instance, three operations that were "completed" took place in Angola, where civil war still rages; five were in the former Yugoslavia, where NATO forces had to take over for the bungled U.N. operation and still remain in place; four were in Haiti, which remains mired in poverty and instability.

- Long-term U.N. peacekeeping operations in the Middle East (53 years), India–Pakistan (52 years), and Cyprus (37 years) without significant results illustrate the U.N.'s inability to impose peace on unwilling nations or populations.

FACT: The U.N. has implemented only partial reforms.

The 106th Congress established a schedule for paying U.S. arrears to the United Nations in the Helms–Biden Act, which instructed the United States to pay $926 million in arrears to the U.N. in three installments after specific reforms had been implemented.

- Congress released the first payment of $100 million in 1999 after the United Nations met the first set of requirements.

---

6. *Ibid.*
7. The acronyms for the missions are as follows: Bosnia and Herzegovina (UNMIBH); Cyprus (UNFICYP); Democratic Republic of the Congo (MONUC); East Timor (UNTAET); Georgia (UNOMIG); Ethiopia and Eritrea (UNMEE); Golan Heights (UNDOF); India–Pakistan (UNMOGIP); Kosovo (UNMIK); Iraq/Kuwait (UNIKOM); Lebanon (UNIFIL); Middle East (UNTSO); Prevlaka Peninsula (UNMOP); Sierra Leone (UNAMSIL); and Western Sahara (MINURSO).

- Congress approved the second payment of $582 million in 2001 after the United Nations reduced America's portion of the regular U.N. budget from 25 percent to 22 percent and reduced its part of the peacekeeping budget from 31.4 percent to 27.58 percent as of July 2001.
- The third arrears payment of $244 million requires the United Nations and U.N. agencies to (1) reduce America's regular budget assessment to 20 percent, 2) establish independent inspectors general, (3) establish new budget procedures, and (4) adopt sunset provisions for U.N. agencies. This last reform is particularly important because it addresses the U.N.'s most vexing problem—redundancy in programs with inappropriate mandates.

FACT: The International Criminal Court has significant flaws that threaten the rights of Americans and legitimate activities of the U.S. military.

The International Criminal Court will be established when the Rome Statute is ratified by 60 countries. As of November 30, 2001, 47 countries had ratified the statute.[8] The United States expressed strong opposition to the Court during the proceedings in Rome for many reasons.

The ICC claims the authority to arrest, prosecute, and punish nationals from any country—even a country that does not sign the treaty—that is accused of such international offenses as war crimes and crimes against humanity. As the statute is now written, Americans who appear before the court would be denied their basic constitutional rights as Americans, such as trial by a jury of one's peers, protection from double jeopardy, and the right to confront one's accusers. That ICC officials would be able to prosecute and punish the nationals of countries that do not sign and ratify the treaty is an astonishing break with the accepted norms of international law.

---

8. For the status of ratification, see *http://untreaty.un.org/ENGLISH/bible/englishinternetbible/partI/chapterXVIII/treaty10.asp*.

WHAT TO DO IN 2003

Candidates should take every opportunity to explain to the American people how the United States should view the United Nations. Specifically, the U.S. government should:

Use the United Nations and international treaties to support the war on terrorism.

U.N. treaties are useful tools in the fight against terrorism but are not, by themselves, sufficient to win the war. The treaties lack enforcement on non-compliant state parties and specific requirements to hinder terrorist activities. Much more effective are Security Council resolutions, such as Security Council Resolution 1373, adopted after the September 11, 2001, attacks,[9] which set binding requirements for U.N. member states on what they must do to fight terrorism.

Make sure that any peacekeeping operation is important for U.S. interests before committing U.S. troops or resources to it.

Not all national interests are equally important, and not all conflicts merit or require U.S. military intervention. The United States must "prioritize where and how it chooses to defend its vital, important, and marginal interests, thereby avoiding both excessive activism that diffuses important resources and isolationism that eschews important opportunities to shape events."[10]

America's ability to meet primary security interests must not be jeopardized by overcommitment to peacekeeping missions. Interventions in areas of marginal security interest only exacerbate the already sizeable strain on U.S. military forces and undermine military readiness.

For this reason, any peacekeeping operations should be entered into and conducted under clearly defined, decisive, attainable, and sustainable military goals and without constraints on actions that are necessary for success. Military interventions should be undertaken to accomplish clearly definable

---

9. United Nations Security Council, Resolution 1373 (2001), S/RES/1373, September 28, 2001, at *www.un.org/Docs/scres/2001/res1373e.pdf*.
10. John Hillen, "American Military Intervention: A User's Guide," Heritage Foundation *Backgrounder* No. 1079, May 2, 1996, p. 2, at *www.heritage.org/library/backgrounder/bg1079.html*.

military goals that are achievable, consistent with overriding political objectives, and supported by enough force to achieve them. Moreover, U.S. military leaders and decisionmakers must be granted the operational freedom and control necessary for success.

Restrict U.S. cooperation with the International Criminal Court.

The American Servicemembers Protection Act (ASPA) entered into law when President Bush signed H.R. 3338 on January 10, 2002.[11] ASPA authorizes the use of military force "to free members of the armed forces of the United States and certain other persons detained or imprisoned by or on behalf of the International Criminal Court." It also restricts U.S. cooperation with the ICC; U.S. military participation in certain U.N. peacekeeping and peace enforcement operations (subject to presidential waiver); the transfer of classified information to the ICC and its parties; and the provision of military assistance to ICC State Parties (also subject to presidential waiver). Codifying such restrictions is a necessary and appropriate step to protect American citizens, troops, and officials and should be enforced.

Continue pressing the U.N. to reform.

As a U.S. General Accounting Office report issued in May 2000 explained:

> [W]hile progress is being made, the overall objectives of the reform have not yet been achieved. Specifically, the United Nations has not yet implemented reforms to focus its programming and budgeting on managing the Secretariat's performance. The initiatives would enable member states to hold the Secretariat accountable for results.[12]

---

11. H.R. 3338, "Making Appropriations for the Department of Defense for the Fiscal Year Ending September 30, 2002, and for Other Purposes," became Public Law No 107–117 on January 10, 2002.
12. "Reforms Are Progressing, But Overall Objectives Have Not Yet Been Achieved," Statement of Harold J. Johnson, Associate Director, International Relations and Trade Issues, U.S. General Accounting Office, National Security and International Affairs Division, before the Subcommittee on International Operations, Committee on Foreign Relations, U.S. Senate, May 10, 2000, GAO/T–NSIAD–00–169.

The Administration should verify that the reforms required in the Helms–Biden act—including budget constraints, reducing the U.S. assessments, and sunsetting U.N. agencies—have not only been implemented, but also are being maintained as specified in the legislation. It should work within the United Nations structure to streamline the organization both to eliminate duplication of effort that wastes resources and to establish clearer lines of responsibility.

—Brett D. Schaefer is Jay Kingham Fellow in International Regulatory Affairs in the Center for International Trade and Economics at The Heritage Foundation.

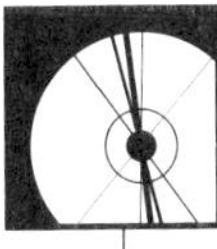

For a complete list and full-text versions of additional studies by Heritage on the United Nations, see the searchable *Issues 2002* companion CD–ROM.

EXPERTS

Heritage Foundation

Brett D. Schaefer
Jay Kingham Fellow in International Regulatory Affairs
Center for International Trade and Economics
The Heritage Foundation
214 Massachusetts Avenue, NE
Washington, DC 20002
(202) 608-6123
fax: (202) 608-6129
brett.schaefer@heritage.org

Ambassador Charles Lichenstein
Distinguished Fellow
The Heritage Foundation
214 Massachusetts Avenue, NE
Washington, DC 20002
(202) 608-6187

Daniel W. Fisk
Deputy Director, Kathryn and Shelby Cullom Davis Institute for International Studies
The Heritage Foundation
214 Massachusetts Avenue, NE
Washington, DC 20002
(202) 608-6114
fax: (202) 675-1758
dan.fisk@heritage.org

Patrick Fagan
William H. G. FitzGerald Research Fellow in Family and Cultural Issues
The Heritage Foundation
214 Massachusetts Avenue, NE
Washington, DC 20002
(202) 608-6207
fax: (202) 544-5421
patrick.fagan@heritage.org

Ambassador Harvey Feldman
Senior Fellow in China Policy
Asian Studies Center
The Heritage Foundation
214 Massachusetts Avenue, NE
Washington, DC 20002
(202) 608-6081
fax: (202) 675-1179
harvey.feldman@heritage.org

Other Experts

Lee A. Casey, J.D.
Baker & Hostetler
Washington Square, Suite 1100
1050 Connecticut Avenue, NW
Washington, DC 20036-5304
(202) 861-1500
fax: (202) 861-1783
LCasey@bakerlaw.com

Ted Galen Carpenter
Vice President for Foreign Policy
and Defense Studies
Cato Institute
1000 Massachusetts Avenue, NW
Washington, DC 20001
(202) 842-0200
fax: (202) 842-3490
tcarpent@cato.org

Dr. Nicholas Eberstadt
Visiting Fellow
American Enterprise Institute
1150 17th Street, NW
Washington, DC 20036
(202) 862-5825
fax: (202) 862-7177
eberstadt@aei.org

Dr. Jeane J. Kirkpatrick
Senior Fellow
Director of Foreign Policy
and Defense Studies
American Enterprise Institute
1150 17th Street, NW
Washington, DC 20036
(202) 862-5814
fax: (202) 862-7177
jkirkpatrick@aei.org

David B. Rivkin, Jr., J.D.
Baker & Hostetler
Washington Square, Suite 1100
1050 Connecticut Avenue, NW
Washington, DC 20036-5304

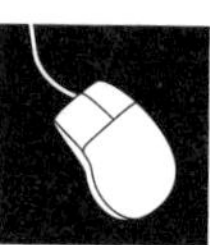

For continually updated and expanded information on major breaking developments on this issue over the campaign cycle, see *www.heritage.org/issues/un*.

EUROPE AND NATO

Strengthening Alliances, Improving Security and Trade

John C. Hulsman, Ph.D.

THE ISSUES

Whether considered militarily, economically, or politically, America's relationship with Europe is still central to U.S. foreign policy. Europe's territorial security remains a paramount U.S. national interest, and the North Atlantic Treaty Organization (NATO) is the linchpin of America's commitment to the continent's security. However, all is not well between the United States and its allies in NATO. The changing dynamics of the post-Cold War era and the intervention in the Balkans reveal that the alliance is in need of reform. One of the most singular events of the post-September 11 world is the fact that the United States chose to act on a bilateral basis with allies such as the United Kingdom (UK) rather than working through the cumbersome NATO decision-making process.

The overall reasons for tension in the alliance are simple: Americans are weary of shouldering more than their fair share of NATO's military burden, while Europeans resent being dominated by the United States. In order to retain its relevance, NATO must rectify burden-sharing inequalities and develop a more flexible decision-making structure in the post-September 11 era to address the following issues.

1. **The United States carries too heavy a military burden for the security of Europe.** Recent attempts to rectify the burden-sharing military imbalance have made little progress. At the NATO summit held in Washington, D.C., in April 1999, member states signed the Defense Capabilities Initiative (DCI). This initiative attempted to build up NATO's military effectiveness by setting specific target goals for military forces that the European allies needed to meet in order to achieve

genuine improvements in overall capability. An internal NATO review has concluded that, even if current spending plans are carried out, the alliance will be able to fulfill less than half of these force goals.[1]

2. **NATO enlargement should proceed with caution.** Until real reforms are made to strengthen the alliance, it would be wise to proceed cautiously in admitting more states to NATO from Central and Eastern Europe. To qualify for membership, applicants should be able to meet all of NATO's criteria for expansion.

3. **U.S. peacekeeping troops in the Balkans should be scaled back.** In return for bearing the brunt of the war against terror, the United States should quickly reduce its force posture in the Balkans—an area that is, at best, only of tertiary national interest to the United States. Such a shift would free American troops from peacekeeping duties, allowing them to lead global efforts against terrorism—by any definition, a primary American national interest.

4. **U.S.–European trade and economic disputes have the potential to erode the foundations of the trans-Atlantic relationship.** To buttress this relationship, a determined American advocacy of free trade policies is imperative. The Bush Administration has inherited a large number of unresolved trade disputes with the EU. Disputes between the world's two largest trading blocs over agricultural policies, investment laws, taxes, and regulatory regimes threaten to stifle the world's most lucrative trading relationship.

5. **The adoption of a common European currency, the euro, could be the first step in creating a centralized federal European state.** On January 1, 2002, the euro was adopted in the form of notes and coins throughout most of the EU economic area.[2] The United States should be wary of both the euro and the process it has set in motion. In a May 1998 meeting in Brussels, 11 of the EU's 15 member states (Greece has since joined) created a European Economic and Monetary Union (EMU), which included Germany, France, and Italy (the EU's

---

1. Michael R. Gordon, "Armies of Europe Failing to Meet Goals, Sapping NATO," *The New York Times*, June 7, 2001.
2. Sweden, Denmark, and the United Kingdom did not adopt the euro.

first, second, and fourth largest economies). These countries agreed to use the euro electronically from January 1, 1999; to jettison their conventional currencies by 2002; and to conform with the macroeconomic policies of a common European Central Bank (ECB), based in Frankfurt, Germany, which would set interest rates for the new "euro zone." In sum, the euro-zone countries have handed over their macroeconomic power to a supranational entity, the ECB. This radical shift in practical political power could well signal the rise of a more centralized EU entity. It may not serve America's interests to support such an entity.

THE FACTS

FACT: For too long, Europe has over-relied on the American military presence on the continent for its defense.

Despite having a slightly larger market share than the United States, the European allies have a defense budget that is only two-thirds that of the United States and a deployable fighting strength that is just one quarter of America's.[3] In 2000, the United States spent 3 percent of its GDP on defense, compared with 2.5 percent in France, 2.25 percent in the UK, 1.9 percent in Italy, 1.5 percent in Germany, and 1.25 percent in Spain.[4]

FACT: As currently constituted, the European Security and Defense Policy (ESDP) will not create a European army; rather, it will create a rapid reaction force designed to serve peacekeeping missions.

At the EU's December 1999 Helsinki summit, European member states declared that by 2003, they would be able, within 60 days of an order, to deploy a force of 60,000 rapid reaction troops that could be sustained in theater for at least a year. In truth, these forces would be activated only for what are known as low-end "Petersburg tasks," which are peacekeeping missions that require only a civil–military police presence rather than that of an army.

---

3. Bruce Clark, "Armies and Arms," *The Economist*, April 24, 1999.
4. "If Only Words Were Guns," *The Economist*, November 24, 2001.

FACT: NATO has clearly defined criteria that need to be met by all candidate states desiring membership.

These criteria include a functioning free-market economy, civilian control of the military, and a sound democratic order. These criteria should function as a yardstick that should be used to measure the qualification of the various Central and Eastern European applicants for NATO membership.

FACT: U.S. military involvement in the Balkans has foundered as separatism, crime, corruption, and economic stagnation have cast doubt on the wisdom of prolonged peacekeeping missions in the region.

The Office of the High Representative in Bosnia reported that around $1 billion in aid has been pilfered by the leadership of various ethnic groups throughout the past six years.[5] Most of the established political parties in all three (Serbian, Croatian, and Muslim) ethnic communities in Bosnia are linked to organized crime. A full 40 percent of the working population in the Muslim–Croat federation had no formal jobs in August 2000, while around 50 percent of the Serbian portion of Bosnia were formally unemployed.[6]

FACT: The equivalent of an entire American Army division has been tied down in Kosovo.

The United States remains the largest overall contributor to the Balkans peacekeeping force. Nearly one in six NATO peacekeepers in the region (9,150 of nearly 60,000) is an American,[7] and this number does not include the forces required for troop rotation or logistical support, which significantly increases the number of troops actually required. For example, while 5,700 American soldiers remain deployed in Kosovo, the operation effectively ties down 17,000 U.S. troops—the equivalent of an Army division—for an indefinite length of time in an open-ended mission.

---

5. "Politics This Week," *The Economist*, August 21, 1999.
6. "The Delicate Balkan Balance," *The Economist*, August 19, 2000.
7. John Hendren, "Rumsfeld Asks NATO to Trim Bosnia Forces to Bolster War on Terrorism," *The Los Angeles Times*, December 19, 2001.

FACT: Trade with Europe is imperiled by the failure of the World Trade Organization (WTO) mechanism to settle disputes.

Both the European and American trade blocs have initiated complaints against each other for use as bargaining chips in unrelated trade disputes or as retaliatory measures to even the score after an adverse WTO ruling. Although the WTO dispute mechanism was intended to provide binding judgments to reach agreements toward a goal of opening markets and liberalizing trade, both blocs have used it to score political points. In self-defeating one-upmanship, both have opted to accept WTO-imposed tariff penalties for non-compliance rather than abiding by its decisions. For example, a case brought against the United States by the EU regarding its Foreign Sales Corporation Tax (FSC) was initiated mainly to retaliate for complaints that the United States had made about the EU's disregard for WTO rulings against its beef ban and banana import regimes.[8] (The WTO ruled that the American stance on taxing the foreign profits of U.S. exporters was an unfair form of preferential treatment.) Such tit-for-tat maneuvers have hurt economies, undermined efforts to expand free trade, and soured relations between the United States and the European Union.

FACT: The euro has greatly depreciated in value because of critical economic structural problems that the EU has failed to address.

The euro was first traded at a rate of $1.18, but its worth has now decreased to approximately $0.86. Since the euro's inception, there has been massive capital flight from the euro zone to the United States. Investors have issued a ringing vote of no confidence regarding Europe's inability to deal with such structural problems as rigid labor regulations, the pension crisis, a lack of productivity, and an overly generous and unaffordable safety net.

8. Editorial, "The FSC Bomb," *Financial Times*, June 28, 2001.

WHAT TO DO IN 2003

Support the Bush Administration policy of favoring European defense integration through ESDP as a means of alleviating the burden-sharing problem within NATO.

The United States should conditionally support ESDP, with the stipulation that NATO retains the right of first refusal in a crisis and ESDP would be activated only after NATO declines to intervene. On the basis of economies of scale alone, the European allies are likely to get a bigger "bang for the buck" through ESDP than the current arrangement provides, and the new arrangement could marginally help to alleviate the burden-sharing imbalance between the United States and its NATO allies.

Support a slow and incremental expansion of NATO to include countries that meet strict criteria.

A large-scale accession to NATO would be premature and dangerous to the health of the alliance. If NATO bypasses established criteria for membership, it will soon be confronting the same problems faced by the other multilateral institutions dealing with Europe.

In addition to the established criteria for NATO membership (a free-market economy, civilian-controlled military, and sound democratic order), two additional requirements should be advocated. New members must commit to modernizing their militaries to make them compatible with current members' troops in manpower and technology, and they should commit to spending at least 2.25 percent of their GDP each year on defense in order to meet their military obligations to the alliance.

Advocate scaling back U.S. troops in the Balkans by using ESDP and the principles embodied in the Combined Joint Task Force mechanism (CJTF).

The CJTF mechanism is an important innovation that was designed to reduce the need to have the United States consistently bear the brunt of NATO's military burden. It allows individual member states to decline to participate actively in a mission if they do not feel their vital interests are engaged but also ensures that such a decision would not stop other NATO members from participating in that intervention. The CJTF offers the use of American communications, logistics, lift, and intelligence-sharing support without requiring that U.S. troops be directly committed to a military operation.

If the principles behind the CJTF mechanism were used in the Balkans, for example, the United States could reduce its involvement to maintaining a small presence in the region, providing intelligence and logistical support for European peacekeeping troops. Such an arrangement would allow the United States to draw down its peacekeeping troops in the Balkans and reassign them to the war against terrorism, where they are desperately needed. While the Europeans may not be able to make a significant material contribution to the war on terrorism, they can help by assigning ESDP forces to tasks that currently occupy U.S. troops in the Balkans.

Accept the WTO ruling against the Foreign Sales Corporation tax and abolish the current corporate tax as a way to end the misuse of the WTO dispute resolution mechanism.

The current system allows the double taxation of income: Profits are taxed first at the national level and then again as personal income when they are distributed to shareholders. Abolishing the corporate tax would not result in a net loss of income for the government. Currently, corporate taxes account for approximately 13 percent of on-budget federal revenue, but studies have revealed that enforcing and collecting the tax costs at least as much as it gathers in revenue.[9]

Ending this tax would provide an immediate economic stimulus—something the American economy, just emerging from recession, desperately needs. For corporations that are burdened with an effective tax rate on profits of more than 50 percent, abolishing the tax would unleash a windfall of capital that companies could reinvest and would generate healthy, long-term growth. In sum, abolishing the tax would enhance American competitiveness. An example of the economic advantages of a low rate of corporate taxation can be seen in Ireland, which accounts for only 1 percent of the euro zone yet is the destination for nearly 40 percent of all North American foreign direct

9. Editorial, "The WTO's Bombshell," *The Wall Street Journal*, September 22, 2001, p. A16.

investment (FDI) in Europe. Such a policy would break the tit-for-tat cycle currently at play in the WTO and change the whole political dynamic in trade negotiations between the U.S. and the EU, refuting the notion that economic liberalization in the guise of adverse WTO rulings is economically disadvantageous.

If it is not possible to abolish the corporate tax immediately, the Administration should consider an interim step of phasing out the FSC while moving toward a "territorial" tax system in which corporations would be subject to income taxes only on their domestic income and not on the profits of their foreign subsidiaries. A territorial tax system (which most of America's trading partners already have) would make U.S. companies immediately more competitive, reduce the hefty compliance costs of the current tax system, and align U.S. tax policy with current WTO policies.

The Administration must revisit its policy of benign neglect regarding the prospect of ever-increasing European integration.

The Clinton Administration continued a long-standing U.S. policy of expressing general, but vague, support for increased European integration. With the advent of the euro, however, Washington's policy of benign neglect must be revisited, since the success or failure of this uniform currency will have profound effects on both Europe and trans-Atlantic relations. Such effects could lead to the possible creation of a European rival that over time might become increasingly inclined to challenge the United States, both politically and economically.

Both the Congress and the White House must change the way they view the EU and recognize it as both an ally and a competitor (just as its member states perceive America). With regard to trade issues, the United States should continue to push for genuine increases in trade liberalization during the Doha World Trade Round, recognizing that the vast majority of European states espouse a more protectionist, statist philosophy. Germany and France, for example, have a market-socialism model that is fundamentally at odds with America's tradition of individualism, deregulation, and free markets.

As such countries decide whether or not to move toward a more market-oriented approach, Washington should encourage countries with similar politico-economic cultures, such as the United Kingdom and Chile, to join a Global Free Trade Association (GFTA). Such an organization could work to lower tariffs and eliminate hidden tariffs, adopt a common accounting scheme, and encourage the free movement of capital between its member states. Moving ahead with like-minded liberalized economies, rather than playing a waiting game with the EU, would change the terms of the debate regarding trade liberalization: A move toward liberalized trade would be seen as politically and economically advantageous rather than as a major international concession.

—John C. Hulsman, Ph.D., is Research Fellow in European Affairs in the Kathryn and Shelby Cullom Davis Institute for International Studies at The Heritage Foundation.

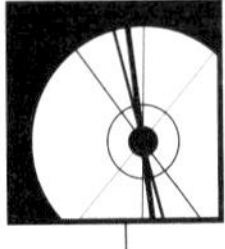

For a complete list and full-text versions of additional studies by Heritage on European security and NATO, see the searchable *Issues 2002* companion CD–ROM.

EXPERTS

Heritage Foundation

John C. Hulsman, Ph.D.
Research Fellow in European Affairs
The Heritage Foundation
214 Massachusetts Avenue, NE
Washington, DC 20002
(202) 608-6086
fax: (202) 675-1758
john.hulsman@heritage.org

Kim R. Holmes, Ph.D.
Vice President
Director, Kathryn and Shelby Cullom Davis Institute for International Studies
The Heritage Foundation
214 Massachusetts Avenue, NE
Washington, DC 20002
(202) 608-6110
fax: (202) 675-1758
kim.holmes@heritage.org

Other Experts

Gary T. Dempsey
Foreign Policy Analyst
Cato Institute
1000 Massachusetts Avenue, NW
Washington, DC 20001
(202) 789-5251
fax: (202) 842-3490
gdempsey@cato.org

Gary L. Geipel, Ph.D.
Vice President and Chief Operating Officer
Hudson Institute
Herman Kahn Center
5395 Emerson Way
Indianapolis, IN 46226
(317) 549-4105
fax: (317) 545-9639
gary@hudson.org

For continually updated and expanded information on major breaking developments on this issue over the campaign cycle, see *www.heritage.org/issues/europeandnato*.

RUSSIA AND EURASIA

Promoting Security, Prosperity, and Freedom

Ariel Cohen, Ph.D.

THE ISSUES

The September 11 terrorist attacks on the United States fundamentally altered U.S.–Russian relations. Russia's support for America's war effort demonstrates that the relationship not only has survived the ups and downs of the 1990s, but also—as President Bush repeatedly stated—has transcended the Cold War. Russia is adjusting to its post–Cold War position as a regional power, but its sales of sophisticated weapons and nuclear technology to states that sponsor terrorism, such as Iran, are destabilizing. In addition, corruption, lack of transparency, difficulty in achieving democratic reform, and the slow pace of market development in the Caucasus and Central Asia are breeding social discontent, swelling ranks of Islamic fundamentalist groups.

Congress should support the Administration's effort to develop a friendlier relationship with Russia and encourage its integration into the global economy and international security system. Specifically:

1. **The United States should convince Russia to abandon its support of the regimes in Iran and Iraq.** From the beginning of the war against terrorism, Russia's support has been significant. In the crucial opening stages of the campaign in Afghanistan, Moscow reassured Central Asian countries, especially Uzbekistan and Tajikistan, that it would support their cooperation with the United States, including the use of military bases and airspace. Both Russia and its Central Asian allies followed through and provided air corridors for U.S. military access to Central Asia. Russia also re-supplied the Northern Alliance, allowing it to bear the brunt of the surface operations.

But more cooperation from Russia—especially ending its support of Saddam Hussein's regime in Iraq and its military cooperation with Iran—will greatly increase the chances for success in the global war against terrorism. The rapid growth of radical Islamic terrorism may be forcing Moscow to recognize the danger of continuing those alliances. The United States should offer to coordinate measures with Moscow to isolate and ultimately remove Saddam from power, and to help end Tehran's support for terrorism and its attempts to acquire weapons of mass destruction. Russia's cooperation also would help quiet European criticism of America's war effort.

2. **The United States should encourage Russia's continued cooperation with NATO.** Russia is currently cooperating on making cuts in its offensive strategic weapons from a level of nearly 6,000 to the 1,500–2,000 range, but it wants a binding treaty to finalize these cuts. During their November 2001 summit in Crawford, Texas, Russian President Vladimir Putin promised President Bush that, regardless of what happens in U.S.–Russia relations, the Cold War–era hostility would not re-emerge; that promise seems to be holding.

   In the long run, Putin wants Russia to be the West's security partner and ally. He has indicated a desire for greater cooperation between Russia and NATO, but the specifics of such cooperation have not been formulated. Putin would like to expand Russia's military ties to the Western alliance, both to reduce the threat from the West that many in the Russian military still perceive and to speed up military reform. Closer cooperation with NATO could facilitate that reform by convincing the Russian military that a smaller force is more effective (and more cost-effective).

   The Kremlin has toned down its opposition to NATO enlargement and for several reasons is not likely to react strongly to the expansion of the alliance to include the Baltic states. Senior officials in Moscow understand that Russia cannot stop NATO enlargement and that the Baltic countries' membership in the alliance would pose no military threat to Russia.

   Moscow is in the process of abandoning its Soviet-era superpower ambitions, which in the past led to global competition with the United States. Moscow should be assured by the West that it can do so in safety and security. According to documents on its national security doctrine, Russia's main military challenge lies in the highly unstable south.[1] China, with its dynamic economy and growing population of 1.2 billion, is also becoming a source of concern.

3. **The United States must convince Russia that its sales of sophisticated weapons and technology to states that sponsor terrorism is a threat to global security.** Russia remains the primary source of weapons for Iran and continues to supply the radical Islamic regime in Tehran with large amounts of sophisticated conventional weapons—including submarines; state-of-the-art, surface-to-air and surface-to-surface naval missiles; and ballistic missile technology and know-how—and is involved in civilian nuclear cooperation. It is also providing two light-water nuclear reactors at Bushehr, which may be the centerpiece of Iran's nuclear weapons program.

   Regarding Iraq, Russia provided diplomatic support for Saddam Hussein in the United Nations Security Council. It negotiated with the United States to end sanctions against Baghdad by summer 2002, providing that Iraq allows the return of the U.N. weapons inspectors. Russia hoped that such support may allow Moscow to recoup a $10 billion Soviet-era debt from Iraq, develop a $20 billion oil field project in Western Qurna, Iraq, and receive multibillion-dollar orders to rebuild the Iraqi military. The U.S. should not allow that to happen as long as Saddam's regime is in power.

   Both Iran and Iraq are on the U.S. State Department's list of state sponsors of terrorism and pose significant threats to regional and national security interests.

1. Nikolay Sokov, "Overview: An Assessment of the Draft Russian Military Doctrine," Center for Non-Proliferation Studies, Monterey Institute for International Studies, at *http://cns.miis.edu/pubs/reports/sokov.htm*; see also Celeste A. Wallander, "Russian National Security Policy in 2000," Program on New Approaches to Russian Security Policy (PONARS), Memo No. 102, 2000, at *www.fas.harvard.edu/~ponars/POLICY%20MEMOS/Wallander102.html*. This is also a conclusion expressed by senior Central European diplomats interviewed in Washington, D.C., in January–February 2002.

THE FACTS

FACT: Following the terrorist strikes on America, Russia shared intelligence on Osama bin Laden and the Taliban.

At the outbreak of the war on terrorism, Russian human intelligence networks in Afghanistan—some of which remain from the 1979–1989 Soviet occupation of that country, and others that were developed through cooperation with the Northern Alliance—were superior to those of the United States, which had to rely on intelligence from Pakistan, the Taliban's main sponsor until September 11.

FACT: Russia joined other members of the U.N. Security Council to pass U.N. Security Council Resolutions 1368 and 1373.[2]

These resolutions authorized the use of force in defense against terrorism and demanded that all countries shut down monetary flows supporting terrorist organizations.

FACT: Russia responded without its usual acrimony to the Bush Administration's announcement of America's withdrawal from the old ABM Treaty.

When the United States announced its withdrawal from the 1972 Anti-Ballistic Missile (ABM) Treaty last year, Moscow refrained from reacting in a manner that would have created a crisis in U.S.–Russian relations. President Putin did call the decision a "mistake," but he also announced that it was not a security threat to Russia. Putin indicated to the Russian military that he would not tolerate the sort of bellicose rhetoric that its leaders have used in the past, including threats to increase the proliferation of ballistic missiles and nuclear technology, withdraw from arms control treaties, or put multiple re-entry vehicles (MIRVs) on strategic missiles.

FACT: Russia and NATO have intensified high-level contacts to expand cooperation.

Putin's allies in the State Duma have indicated in private conversations that Russia would like to join NATO's Political Council and that, if Russia and NATO were to enter a new phase of coop-

---

2. "Security Council Unanimously Adopts Wide Ranging Anti-Terrorism Resolution," at *www.un.org/News/Press/docs/2001/sc7158.doc.htm*; see also *www.un.org/Docs/scres/2001/sc2001.htm*.

eration leading to an alliance, Moscow would have fewer reasons to object to NATO enlargement, which might include the three Baltic states.

FACT: Moscow has announced that it would shut down its electronic intelligence-gathering facility in Lourdes, Cuba, and a naval base in Cam Ran Bay, Vietnam.

The facility in Lourdes was a particular irritant in U.S.–Russian relations. It allowed Moscow to listen to nearly all unclassified communications in the Eastern United States.[3]

FACT: Moscow has initiated peaceful contacts with senior representatives of the Chechen separatists.

The talks between Colonel–General (ret.) Alexander Kazantsev, the former Russian commander in Chechnya, and Akhmad Zakaev, deputy to President Aslan Maskhadov, the secessionist leader of Chechnya who was popularly elected in 1996, could go a long way toward developing a permanent solution to Chechnya's sufferings.[4]

FACT: Resistance to economic and democratic reform in the Caucasus and Central Asia threatens security and stifles growth.

The governments in this region, including Uzbekistan and Turkmenistan, tolerate and encourage corruption, maintain harsh and oppressive regimes, and are reluctant to reform their Soviet-style economies. This stance threatens security and stifles growth. Most of the countries in the region have not conducted democratic elections that international organizations recognize as free and fair.[5] There is a severe "democracy deficit," and there are barriers to the development of civil society. Corruption and the concentration of wealth in the hands of authoritarian rulers and their cronies fuel support for the Islamist forces. Islamic fundamentalists also benefit from the drug trade from Afghanistan and local

---

3. "Rossia ukhodit s voennykh baz v Kamrani i Lurdese" ("Russia is leaving military bases in Cam Ran and Lourdes"), *Gazeta.ru.*, October 17, 2001, at *www.games2000.ru/2001/10/17/na1003319340.shtml.*
4. Ilya Maksakov, "Putin predlozhil Chechnye 'mirnuyu zhizn'" ("Putin offered Chechnya a 'peaceful life'"), *Nezavisimaya Gazeta*, September 26, 2001, at *www.ng.ru/events/2001-09-26/1_pacificlife.html.*
5. Georgia and Armenia have the best track record as far as the conduct of elections and free press are concerned.

suppliers, which thrives because of government corruption and poverty. The war in Afghanistan has increased U.S. influence in Central Asia. The United States should work with its allies in Central Asia to help them fight corruption, increase transparency, expand markets, and boost economic development.

WHAT TO DO IN 2003

Invite President Putin to join the next stage of the anti-terrorism war beyond Afghanistan.

The United States should provide Russia with incentives to remain in the anti-terrorist coalition. If the target in the next stage of the war is Iraq, Russia may face a number of financial concerns, but they can be resolved in a mutually satisfactory manner. Iraq has an outstanding 1980s debt to Russia of approximately $7 billion (now worth as much as $10 billion–$12 billion, including compound interest).

Russia is also concerned about the future of the license to develop the West Qurna oil field in Iraq, which Saddam Hussein's regime granted to two Russian oil companies. West Qurna reportedly is the largest Iraqi oil field, as well as one of the largest in the world, and can generate up to $20 billion over its lifetime. President Bush should assure President Putin that, in exchange for Russia's cooperation and support regarding Iraq in the U.N. Security Council and elsewhere, the United States will honor Russian claims in Iraq and will work to ensure that they will be recognized by the future government of Iraq.

Develop security cooperation with Russia that includes intelligence sharing, anti-terrorism operations, and counter-proliferation initiatives.

The United States and Russia should continue the cooperation that began during the Afghan campaign. Russia's strategic realignment with the West may be a long and difficult process, but if successful, this policy will fundamentally change the geopolitical map of the 21st century. It might eventually distance Russia from China and Iran, and could also disengage Russia from its radical Soviet-era Middle Eastern clients such as Iraq, Syria, and Libya.

The two countries should expand cooperation between their foreign and domestic security services—specifically, between Russia's Foreign Intelligence Service (SVR) and the Central Intelligence Agency in Central Asia and the Middle East, and between the Federal Security Service (FSB) and the Federal Bureau of Investigation—on domestic terrorist threats, drug trafficking, and money laundering. They should conduct exercises and combined training to ensure that their special forces can work together cohesively in anti-terrorism operations. Both the United States and Russia should develop a common understanding of how command and control, rules of engagement, weapons employment, and tactics work in each of the armed forces. U.S. and Russian special forces would learn how to provide immediate threat or battlefield information (tactical intelligence) to each other. And they should continue cooperative threat-reduction efforts in monitoring and providing maximum security for Russia's nuclear, chemical, and biological stockpiles.

Develop a road map for Russian cooperation with NATO enlargement that goes beyond the Partnership for Peace (PFP), which Russia joined in 1994.

This effort should include cooperation in areas that are important to U.S. security, including such anti-terrorist activities as intelligence sharing; special forces inter-operability; counter-proliferation initiatives; joint peacekeeping operations; and assistance with comprehensive military reform—which Russian leaders, including President Putin and Defense Minister Ivanov, would welcome. This should include technical assistance in strengthening civilian control of Russia's armed forces, furthering the professionalization of the military, and promoting increased transparency of its military budget.

Support an invitation to President Putin to address NATO at the summit in Prague.

Inviting President Putin to address the Prague NATO summit in November 2002 could launch a new initiative of alliance-building between Russia and NATO, such as the 19-plus-one formula.[6] As Russia–NATO cooperation develops, both Russia and NATO will greatly benefit from joint activities, which would expand the security envelope throughout the Northern Hemisphere. The United States must be aware that a full alliance relationship would require Russia's commitment to Article 5 of the NATO Charter, which could include providing military forces for mutual defense. Neither Russia nor the NATO allies are ready for Article 5 guarantees at this time.

Encourage Russia's peaceful initiatives in Chechnya, which could lead to peace and broad autonomy for the Chechen Republic within the Russian Federation.

After the September 11 attacks, Putin initiated a dialogue with the Chechen rebel leadership headed by President Aslan Maskhadov. President Bush should express support for this effort to develop a political solution to the situation in Chechnya and should encourage the Russian–Chechen dialogue. The radical Islamist wing of the Chechen separatists, with its transnational terrorist links, represents a real danger to Russia's national security and a threat to the stability of neighboring Georgia. A peaceful resolution of the conflict in Chechnya will be important not only for Russia and Chechnya, but also for the other Muslim autonomous republics of the Northern Caucasus, for Russia's neighbors in the South Caucasus, and for the stability of the region.

Support Russian economic integration with the West, including membership in the World Trade Organization (WTO).

Putin understands that only the West has the capacity to become Russia's principal investor and trading partner, especially as a market for Russia's energy resources. He and Prime Minister Mikhail Kasyanov have stated that Russia will become a reliable energy partner for the West regardless of what may happen to Middle Eastern oil supplies. President Putin has also declared that Russia will not require any special deals from the WTO, so standard criteria should apply for its membership.[7] However, Russia is worried about its automotive, aircraft manufacturing, and agricultural sectors. President Bush should support the recent statement of Russian Finance Minister Alexei Kudrin and call for Russia's accession to WTO in the

---

6. Peter Finn and Peter Baker, "NATO and Russia Reinventing Relationship," *The Washington Post*, November 15, 2001, at *www.ncsj.org/AuxPages/111501NATO.shtml.*

7. "Putin obeshchayet zastavit' VTO uvazhat' interesy Rossii" ("Putin promises to force the WTO to respect Russia's interests"), *Gazeta.ru*, October 30, 2001, at *www.rambler.ru/db/news/msg.html?mid=2019035&s=10315.*

year 2004, provided negotiations with the WTO in all sectors are completed successfully. The U.S. government should also encourage cooperation in energy, aerospace, and high-tech areas.

Lift restrictions of the Jackson–Vanik Amendment in Title IV of the Trade Act of 1974 that apply to Russia.[8]

The Jackson–Vanik Amendment, which denies Russia most favored nation status, is a relic of the Cold War. It was passed in 1974 when the Soviet Union had a policy severely limiting emigration. The U.S. Congress has recognized that the amendment has become an instrument of U.S. policy for assessing certain countries' observance of basic human rights and the protection of minorities, and suspended its application to Russia since the collapse of the Soviet Union. Lifting the restrictions of Jackson–Vanik which still apply to Russia can now be achieved by attaching an amendment to a trade legislation bill.

Support democratic and market initiatives in Central Asia and the Caucasus.

Economic growth and democratic development in Central Asia and the Caucasus are in the interest of the United States because they would be likely to discourage the growth of radical Islamist forces, separatism, and political extremism. The United States should encourage the regimes in the region to implement free-market reforms; promote the rule of law, property rights, and transparency in the government; fight corruption; expand democratic freedoms; and support the development of democratic institutions.

—Ariel Cohen, Ph.D., is Research Fellow in Russian and Eurasian Studies in the Kathryn and Shelby Cullom Davis Institute for International Studies at The Heritage Foundation.

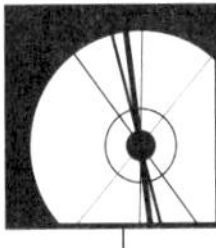

For a complete list and full-text versions of additional studies by Heritage on Russia and Eurasia, see the searchable *Issues 2002* companion CD–ROM.

8. Public Law 93–618, 19 U.S.C. 2432.

EXPERTS

Heritage Foundation

Ariel Cohen, Ph.D.
Research Fellow, Kathryn and Shelby Cullom Davis Institute for International Studies
The Heritage Foundation
214 Massachusetts Avenue, NE
Washington, DC 20002
(202) 608-6117
fax: (202) 675-1758
ariel.cohen@heritage.org

Kim R. Holmes, Ph.D.
Vice President
Director, Kathryn and Shelby Cullom Davis Institute for International Studies
The Heritage Foundation
214 Massachusetts Avenue, NE
Washington, DC 20002
(202) 608-6110
fax: (202) 675-1758
kim.holmes@heritage.org

Other Experts

Stephen Blank
National Security Research Professor
Strategic Studies Institute
U.S. Army War College
Carlisle Barracks, PA 17013
(717) 245-4085
fax: (717) 245-3820
stephen.blank@carlisle.army.mil

Svante Cornell
Editor, CACI Analyst
Central Asia and Caucasus Institute
Paul H. Nitze School of Advanced International Studies
Johns Hopkins University
1619 Massachusetts Avenue, NW
Washington, DC 20036
(202) 663-7712
fax: (202) 663-5782
svante.cornell@pcr.uu.se

Jacob W. Kipp
Adjunct Professor of Russian History
Russian and East European Studies Center
University of Kansas
Lawrence, KS 66044
(785) 841-2856
jacobkipp@cs.com

For continually updated and expanded information on major breaking developments on this issue over the campaign cycle, see *www.heritage.org/issues/russiaandeurasia*.

ASIAN SECURITY

Helping to Assure Peace in the Pacific

John J. Tkacik, Balbina Hwang, and Dana R. Dillon

THE ISSUES

The war on terrorism has not eclipsed East Asia's importance to the United States. China continues to expand its influence in the region, using the threat of force as a tool of coercion. The Korean Peninsula remains a volatile flashpoint. In his 2002 State of the Union Address, President George W. Bush identified North Korea as a member of a terrorist "axis of evil" because it starves its citizens as it continues to develop weapons of mass destruction (WMD). On the economic front, Japan's failing economy threatens to drag down the entire region and with it possibly the rest of the world.

America's interests in Asia are many and include trade and economic policies, alliances, and democratic reforms; but assuring peace in that region is the most important. Thus, a policy framework for U.S.–Asia relations should be based on the following key realities:

1. **China's efforts to expand its influence in the Asia–Pacific require firm U.S. responses to protect U.S. interests.** China's military buildup, quiet encroachment into the South China Sea, and threats against Taiwan convinced the U.S. Department of Defense to address this expansionism in its 2001 Quadrennial Defense Review. The President's firm resolve in dealing with the April 2001 collision of a Chinese fighter jet into a U.S. EP–3 aircraft was the right way to respond to Beijing's coercive behavior. His refusal to accept responsibility for the incident and his restatement of America's commitment to Taiwan discredited hawkish nationalists in Beijing. Furthermore, China's smooth accession to the World Trade Organization (WTO) helped moderates gain political momentum

for the upcoming leadership succession to be held in October 2002.

2. **Reciprocal engagement is the best way to deal with North Korea.** North Korea has tried to blackmail the United States, Japan, and South Korea with threats of war and a refusal to renounce its ballistic missile program. Yet despite receiving millions of dollars in aid, North Korea adamantly refuses to move toward a permanent reconciliation with the South. In this light, President Bush's decision to engage North Korea only on condition that it takes verifiable steps to end its missile program, reduces the military threat on the border with South Korea, and restarts negotiations with Seoul is a wise posture.

3. **Free trade and open market policies will help revive Asian economies.** Burdened with non-performing loans and a failed Keynesian fiscal stimulus model, Japan's deteriorating economy threatens economic stability in Asia. Already weak from the global economic downturn, the traditional engines of growth—Hong Kong, Singapore, South Korea, and Taiwan—could fall into recession if Japan collapses. The United States and Japan should coordinate efforts to avert this scenario. Another way for the United States to inoculate Asia against financial contagion would be to adopt free trade agreements with its open markets—such as Australia, New Zealand, Singapore, South Korea, and Taiwan.

4. **A cooperative effort between the United States and its friends and allies in Asia will suppress terrorism.** Al-Qaeda's links in Southeast Asia have proven more sinister than first anticipated. North Korea remains on the U.S. list of states that sponsor terrorism. Fortunately, America's long-standing alliances and friendships in Asia have made it easier for the United States to encourage local governments to fight terrorism and to offer these countries counterterrorism assistance. This is further proof that a strong, focused, and committed U.S. security and economic presence is the major, if not sole, force for stability in the Asia–Pacific region.

THE FACTS

CHINA AND TAIWAN

The People's Republic of China is an emerging world power. It exercises considerable political influence as the world's most populous nation and seventh largest economy, with the most powerful military in Asia. China is also a permanent member of the United Nations Security Council capable of vetoing any proposed security measure. As America's fourth largest trading partner, China exported over $104 billion to the United States in 2001. Nevertheless, the United States and China have competing interests in Asia that complicate U.S.–China relations.

FACT: Washington's "one China" policy does not mean the United States recognizes Beijing's claim of sovereignty over Taiwan.

The "one China" policy simply means that the United States recognizes the People's Republic of China as the "sole legal government of China." It does not recognize any Chinese claim over Taiwan. On the contrary, on July 14, 1982, President Ronald Reagan gave separate assurances to Taiwan that the United States did not accept China's claim to sovereignty over the island.[1]

FACT: The United States has a major stake in the survival and success of democracy in Taiwan.

Taiwan is America's eighth largest trading partner and sixth largest export market. The United States exported over $24 billion in U.S. goods to Taiwan in 2000—some 50 percent more than it exported to China ($16 billion). And despite a severe economic downturn in Taiwan, it imported $14 billion from the United States from January to September 2001—more than China did at $13.9 billion.

Taiwan is the most vibrant and dynamic democracy in Asia. In 2000, Taiwan elected an opposition party to power for the first time in its history. Taiwan's political leaders acknowledge that the

---

1. Harvey Feldman, "A Primer on U.S. Policy Toward the 'One China' Issue: Questions and Answers," Heritage Foundation *Backgrounder* No. 1429, April 12, 2001, at *www.heritage.org/library/backgrounder/bg1429.html*, and Larry M. Wortzel, Ph.D., "Why the Administration Should Reaffirm the 'Six Assurances' to Taiwan," Heritage Foundation *Backgrounder* No. 1352, March 16, 2000, at *www.heritge.org/library/backgrounder/bg1352.html*.

success of Taiwan's democracy owes much to persistent encouragement and, when necessary, pressure from the United States.[2] America should be proud of its defense commitment, codified in the 1979 Taiwan Relations Act (TRA),[3] that fostered the survival and success of Taiwan's democracy over the past two decades.

FACT: China's missile buildup along the Taiwan Strait justifies the development of a robust missile defense infrastructure in Taiwan.

China's deployment of short-range missiles along the Taiwan Strait has increased from 50 in 1998 to over 300 by early 2001. U.S. intelligence sources project that there will be between 600 and 1,000 missiles in place in the next several years.[4] The United States, in abiding by the terms of the TRA, has delivered to Taiwan updated versions of the Patriot PAC–2 anti-missile system and is considering selling Taiwan some Aegis-equipped destroyers to help it expand its missile defenses.

FACT: China's missile development is part of its strategy to nullify U.S. forces in the Pacific.

For the past 15 years, China has been developing medium-range ballistic missiles (MRBMs) to countervail U.S. forces in Asia, and intercontinental ballistic missiles (ICBMs) to threaten American cities and deter U.S. action. China is in the process of deploying a road-mobile DF–31 designed to hold U.S. forces in the Pacific at risk in case of a conflict over Taiwan or in the South China sea.[5] China also has up to 200 MRBMs deployed against Russia, India,

---

2. See Lee Teng-hui, *The Road to Democracy, Taiwan's Pursuit of Identity* (Tokyo: PHP Institute Press, 1999), pp. 127–135. From 1979 through 1988, Congress held a number of hearings on human rights and political development in Taiwan, including hearings on the Kaohsiung Incident trials, the death of Professor Chen Wen-cheng, and the murder of Taiwan author Henry Liu (Jiang Nan). See Jay Taylor, *The Generalissimo's Son* (Cambridge, Mass.: Harvard University Press, 2000).
3. Public Law 98–8.
4. Michael R. Gordon, "China Buildup Has Taiwan on Edge," *The New York Times*, April 8, 2001, p. 3. See also Bill Gertz, "China Adding Missiles Aimed Toward Taiwan," *The Washington Times*, February 5, 2001, p. A12.
5. See "Zhonggong Zhanshi Xinxing Dongfeng 31 Zhouji Daodan" ("PRC Puts New Version of Dongfeng 31 ICBM on Display"), *China Times*, June 10, 2001. See also Shirley A. Kan, "China: Ballistic and Cruise Missiles," Congressional Research Service *CRS Report for Congress* No. 97–391–F, August 10, 2000, p. 14, and Bill Gertz and Rowan Scarborough, "Inside the Ring," *The Washington Times*, August 17, 2001, p. A7.

and Japan, which is perhaps one reason these countries have acquiesced to America's decision to continue research and development of ballistic missile defenses.

China has also begun to replace its silo-based DF–5 ICBM with the more mobile DF–41, which can be deployed from road, rail, or river-based launchers. This new missile will be capable of delivering a 1,760 lb. nuclear warhead to anywhere in the United States. More disturbingly, China's military leaders have displayed the willingness to use their nuclear arsenal. In December 1995, a senior Chinese general asserted that China could act militarily against Taiwan without fear because U.S. leaders "care more about Los Angeles than they do about Taiwan."[6] This statement—a clear but implicit nuclear threat—characterizes the mentality of the Chinese military leadership.

FACT: China's ballistic missile buildup has nothing to do with America's recent decision to withdraw from the Anti-Ballistic Missile (ABM) Treaty.

On December 13, President Bush announced his intention to withdraw from the 1972 Cold War–era ABM Treaty, which prevented America from developing a missile defense system. Concerns that this would spark an arms race with China are unfounded. China began its ballistic missile modernization program long before the Bush Administration announced its intention to withdraw from the treaty, which received a muted official Chinese reaction: President Jiang Zemin indicated that China would turn its attention to "safeguarding international arms control."[7]

FACT: China's tepid support for America's war on terror does not mean that Beijing intends to curb its expansionist behavior in Asia.

China has offered little substantive assistance to the U.S.-led international coalition against terrorism—declining, for example, to offer overflight rights to U.S. aircraft for the campaign in

6. Patrick E. Tyler, "As China Threatens Taiwan, It Makes Sure U.S. Listens," *The New York Times*, January 24, 1996, p. A1.
7. See "Jiang Says Arms Control Key After US Drops ABM," Reuters, December 14, 2001; China's foreign ministry echoed these comments in *Zhongguo Xinwen She*, December 13, 2001, as transcribed by the Foreign Broadcast Information Service (FBIS).

Afghanistan.[8] Instead, Chinese think tanks and media outlets continue to express suspicions that increasing the U.S. presence in Central Asia is a "pretext" for a sinister American strategy to "contain" China.[9] And despite media reports that "China was instrumental in delivering Pakistan to Washington's war effort, assuring Islamabad that decades of unwavering Chinese support would continue," it is clear that China's diplomacy in Pakistan was solely to protect its own interests in the region, not to further the war against terrorism.[10]

FACT: China's territorial claims over the South China Sea are a threat to freedom of navigation in that strategic waterway.

Six countries on the South China Sea littoral have legitimate claims to various portions of the 1 million square miles of the South China Sea.[11] China claims virtually the entire area as Chinese territorial waters. In February 1992, China passed a Territorial Sea Law that asserts sovereignty over all islets and reefs in the South China Sea and requires that all foreign states obtain advance approval or give prior notification for the passage of war-

---

8. John J. Tkacik, Dana R. Dillon, Balbina Hwang, and Sara J. Fitzgerald, "Preparing for the APEC Summit: Mobilizing Asian Allies for War," Heritage Foundation *Backgrounder* No. 1487, October 4, 2001, at *www.heritage.org/library/backgrounder/bg1487.html*. China has offered to share intelligence, but Administration sources say that its intelligence is of limited value at best. China's foreign minister indicated that China would assist in "rescue" efforts shortly after the September 11 attacks but declined to pursue the matter in later meetings with the State Department. Chinese support has been limited to various anti-terror resolutions in the United Nations and permitting Hong Kong to cooperate with U.S. financial and transportation intelligence collection efforts.
9. Ba Ren, "The United States Meddles with Afghanistan to Kill Three Birds with One Stone—On the White House's Military Deployment and Variable of Central Asian Strategic Patterns," in *Ta Kung Pao*, September 24, 2001, in Daily FBIS–CHI–2001–0924; see also Yi Yangsheng, "Bush Acts with Hidden Motives in Central Asia," Hong Kong *Kuang Chiao Ching*, No. 349, October 16, 2001, pp. 20–22. In the FBIS translations, the source is described as "Hong Kong Kuang Chiao Ching in Chinese—non-PRC-owned monthly magazine ('Wide Angle'); reputed in Hong Kong to have close ties to the PRC military establishment."
10. Charles Hutzler, "China's Quiet, Crucial Role in the War," *The Wall Street Journal*, December 18, 2001, p. A10. Hutzler's characterizations are belied by the facts of the article, which indicate that China's only contribution is to lobby the U.S. for more aid to Pakistan and to contribute $1.2 million of its own aid.
11. The countries are Brunei, the People's Republic of China, the Republic of China (Taiwan), Malaysia, the Philippines, and Vietnam.

ships through the area. The United States does not, and should not, provide such notification.

China's sweeping territorial claims over the South China Sea, coupled with its skewed interpretation of the U.N. Convention on the Law of the Sea, are an explicit threat to the freedom of navigation of any country that uses the strategic waterway.[12] Washington has wisely refused to entangle itself in a legal dispute. However, Washington must make it clear to Beijing that the United States will not tolerate the use of force to resolve conflicting claims and will oppose any extreme claim that would interfere with the freedom of navigation in the South China Sea.

THE KOREAN PENINSULA

South Korea has been a key U.S. ally since 1954 when the United States and the Republic of Korea (ROK) signed the Mutual Cooperation and Security Treaty. Washington's security commitments to Seoul, particularly the 37,000 American troops stationed in Korea, are the most visible signs of support. While the U.S.–ROK relationship remains generally strong, however, there are some obstacles.

FACT: The Bush Administration is not responsible for the impasse in the North–South dialogue.

The Bush Administration fully supports President Kim Dae-jung's "Sunshine Policy" of South Korean engagement with the North.[13] South Korea is taking the lead in establishing a permanent peace with the North and is designing an architecture for stable reunification. The United States should take a supporting role in these efforts but ensure that key national security interests are met. It should continue to press the North to cooperate fully with global efforts to eradicate terrorism, to halt its arms sales and proliferation of weapons of mass destruction, and to reduce its threatening posture on the Korean Peninsula.

12. Dana R. Dillon, "How the Bush Administration Should Handle China and South China Sea Maritime Territorial Disputes," Heritage Foundation *Backgrounder* No. 1470, September 5, 2001, at *www.heritage.org/library/backgrounder/bg1470.html.*

13. Balbina Hwang, "The Bush Administration's Cautious Approach to North Korea," Heritage Foundation *Backgrounder* No. 1455, July 6, 2001, at *www.heritage.org/library/backgrounder/bg1455.html.*

The Bush Administration has stated that the United States is willing to meet with North Korea at any place and at any time to work toward improving bilateral relations. Pyongyang has continually rebuffed U.S. efforts at engagement. The United States should not make concessions to North Korea unless Pyongyang credibly demonstrates that it can function as a responsible member of the international community.

FACT: North Korea is a state sponsor of terrorism.

Since 1988, the State Department has placed North Korea on its list of state sponsors of terrorism. Although the North has not been held responsible for terrorist acts outside the Korean Peninsula since then, the same totalitarian regime controls Pyongyang today and has continued to send saboteurs and un-uniformed agents into South Korea to commit terrorist acts. The most recent attack on South Korea was a 1998 raid of un-uniformed commandos who entered the South's waters aboard a midget submarine. Like the Taliban, North Korea also is guilty of harboring fugitive terrorists.[14]

Even more disturbing, the North has active programs to develop and proliferate weapons of mass destruction, including biological, chemical, and nuclear materials. It actively sells weapons, including ballistic missile technology, to other rogue states like Libya, Iraq, Iran and Syria. And it continues to pose a serious conventional military threat to America's ally, South Korea, and U.S. troops stationed there.

JAPAN

FACT: Japan is a critical American ally in Asia.

As the world's second largest economy, Japan needs to refocus its energy and political will in revitalizing its moribund economy in order to avert a possible worldwide recession. Japan is also America's "northern pillar" of security in Asia. The importance of this relationship was made clear with Japan's strong show of support for the war on terrorism by passing an Anti-Terrorism Special Measure Law. The law is significant; it enables Japan to contribute as a more active U.S. military as well as political partner. It is an

---

14. Balbina Hwang, "North Korea Deserves to Remain on U.S. List of Sponsors of Terrorism," Heritage Foundation *Backgrounder* No. 1503, November 19, 2001, at *www.heritage.org/library/backgrounder/bg1503.html.*

important step in assuming a leadership role in Asia and providing the basis for security and stability in the region.

Japan must reform its economic and financial sectors. It must take strong action to reverse its decade-long economic stagnation. As the anchor of economic stability in the region, Japan must continue the difficult economic reforms initiated by Prime Minister Junichiro Koizumi. These must include major government spending cuts and reform of the financial sector, including the need for banks to write off bad debt. Such efforts will require close coordination with U.S. economic planners to ensure that the effects of a global recession are mitigated.

FACT: The missile threat to Japan is growing.

In August 1998, North Korea test-fired a multi-stage ballistic missile over the Sea of Japan. The Taepo Dong–1, the first three-stage missile tested by Pyongyang, is capable of carrying a nuclear warhead. Japan needs to recognize the vicissitudes of the Asian security environment and seek to anticipate problems rather than just respond to them. Among the most worrisome is the threat of ballistic missile attack. The United States should work with Tokyo to build upon the 1999 agreement to cooperate on developing a ballistic missile defense infrastructure.[15]

SOUTHEAST AND SOUTH ASIA

FACT: The problem of terrorism in Southeast Asia is more sinister than first anticipated.

Among the most notorious terrorist organizations in Southeast Asia is the Philippine-based Abu Sayyaf. Recent intelligence reports reveal credible linkages between these terrorists and the

15. On April 17, 1996, President Clinton and Prime Minister Hashimoto signed the U.S.–Japan Joint Declaration on Security, which reaffirmed both countries' continuing commitment to their security alliance. In September 1997, both countries adopted the "Guidelines for U.S.–Japan Defense Cooperation," and in May 1999, the Japanese Diet passed legislation to implement the Guidelines in law. When fully implemented, the Guidelines will provide greater Japanese support for U.S. operations in a regional contingency. In August 1999, the United States and Japan signed a Memorandum of Understanding to begin technical research on joint theater missile defense (TMD), focusing on sea-based defenses. See *www.defenselink.mil /pubs/ allied_contrib2000/allied2000.pdf*.

al-Qaeda network based in Afghanistan. More disturbing, like-minded organizations exist throughout the region and are beginning to work in concert with one another.

The Philippine government has stepped up military operations to hunt down the Abu Sayyaf. At the request of Manila, Washington sent 600 troops to help train Philippine soldiers in counterterrorism tactics. The United States has also provided $100 million in weapons and sophisticated communications. Additionally, Philippine President Gloria Macapagal Arroyo called for the formation of a region-wide anti-terrorist coalition.

FACT: U.S. policy prohibiting U.S. participation in any multilateral forum that includes Indonesian officers may undermine America's ability to work with Indonesia to crack down on terrorism.

This policy was a response to the Indonesian military's human rights abuses in its campaigns against separatists in East Timor, Aceh, and the Moluccas. However, the Indonesian armed forces are the only institution in that country that can act effectively against terrorist camps or forces. Limited U.S.–Indonesian military engagement that addresses regional security issues and Indonesia's external defense would promote U.S. security goals in the region. They would also provide opportunities, through appropriately crafted programs, to influence the behavior of the Indonesian military.

FACT: Hindu–Muslim animosities in South Asia are dangerous.

The December 2001 attack on India's parliament building by Pakistani Muslim terrorists, killing 14, threatens to undo whatever progress had been made toward easing Indo–Pakistani tensions. India contends that the Pakistani intelligence service sponsored the attack, while Pakistan denies the charge and accuses India of avoiding talks over Kashmir. A government spokesman in Islamabad said on December 19 that if the option of war "is exercised by India, then it will be paid back in the same coin." Such hostile rhetoric fuels concerns about whether these nuclear-capable states would use their weapons against each other. The United States wisely cautioned against war but avoided acting as the negotiator between the two sides.

WHAT TO DO IN 2003

Stand firm when China takes coercive actions.

The United States seeks good relations with China. In some areas, such as pursuing free trade and seeking stability in the Korean Peninsula, the United States and China share common interests. China's economic growth relies heavily on trade with the United States. However, the United States and China also have opposing interests; the United States seeks freedom of navigation in the South China Sea and democracy in Taiwan, while China seeks to expand its influence, by force if necessary. Washington must not allow its desire for good relations to compromise its key strategic, political, and economic interests in Asia.

Urge North Korea to honor its commitments to the South toward reconciliation.

In June 2000, North Korean leader Kim Jong-il met with his South Korean counterpart Kim Dae-jung in a historic summit that was supposed to restart reconciliation efforts. Promises made during that summit—which include a return visit to South Korea, continuation of the stalled family reunion program, and construction of the North Korean half of the trans-Korean Sinuiju railroad—have not been kept. North Korea also needs to open its nuclear facilities to International Atomic Energy Agency inspectors in order to fulfill its obligations under the Agreed Framework it signed 1994.

Encourage Pyongyang to extend its moratorium on missile flight testing.

In February 2000, Kim Jong-il announced a three-year moratorium on flight testing of North Korea's long-range missile, apparently in an effort to induce several European countries to establish diplomatic relations with Pyongyang. That moratorium runs out in February 2003. At a minimum, Washington should make continued engagement with Pyongyang conditional on the extension of that moratorium. Further missile testing by North Korea should result in the immediate cessation of U.S. engagement with the North.

Support Japan's efforts to reform its economy.

In reforming the financial sector to revive Japan's economy, Prime Minister Koizumi will face a series of extremely painful decisions. Major government spending cuts are needed, and banks should be encouraged to write off bad loans within five years and cut equity shareholdings across the board immediately. This will require close coordination with U.S. economic planners to ensure that the effects of these actions on the global economy are mitigated.

Pursue free trade agreements with countries committed to free-market competition.

Several countries in the Asia–Pacific region—Australia, New Zealand, Singapore, South Korea, and Taiwan—are ready and willing to conclude bilateral free trade agreements with the United States.[16] Furthermore, congressional approval of trade promotion authority (TPA), known previously as fast-track negotiating authority, will enable the Administration to expedite the negotiation process. The Bush Administration has vowed to promote "free trade globally, regionally, and bilaterally" and to "reward good performers."[17] TPA would make these policies easier to achieve.

Encourage regional efforts to combat terrorism, and extend and broaden security cooperation with South Asia.

A Southeast Asian anti-terrorism coalition is in its formative stages. Although such a coalition should include as many countries committed to eradicating the problem of terrorism as possible, a core group consisting of Indonesia, Malaysia, the Philippines, Singapore, and Thailand would give it a solid foundation. U.S. diplomatic efforts should help the process along. In addressing homeland security, the United States has developed strategies and protocols that may prove useful to Southeast Asia; it should offer its expertise in this area to countries in this coalition.

---

16. John C. Hulsman, Ph.D. and Aaron Schavey, "The Global Free Trade Association: A New Trade Agenda," Heritage Foundation *Backgrounder* No. 1441, May 16, 2001, at *www.heritage.org/library/backgrounder/bg1441.html*.
17. Testimony of Robert Zoellick, U.S. Trade Representative, before the Subcommittee on Trade, Committee on Ways and Means, U.S. House of Representatives, 107th Cong., 1st Sess., May 8, 2001.

Since September 11, both Pakistan and India have provided considerable assistance to the United States in the campaign against terrorism, especially in Afghanistan. This activity presents a great opportunity to expand the security relationship. Washington should continue to build on and broaden this new relationship.[18]

Avoid getting involved in the Kashmir dispute.

The December 13 attacks on the Indian parliament and the ensuing military standoff have once again focused attention on Kashmir, a battleground of religious and ethnic hatreds between Hindu and Muslim that has raged for over half a century. So long as the conflict can be kept from escalating into a nuclear exchange, peace will require formal partition, billions in development aid, a massive international peacekeeping force, or—more likely—a combination of all three. In any case, the cost to the United States of leading any mediation effort promises to be high, since the United States would be asked to pay for a substantial portion, if not all, of the program. The cost certainly would be far higher than is warranted by U.S. interests in the region.[19]

Engage the Indonesian military where it serves U.S. interests.

Indonesia, the most populous Muslim nation, may very well be a hornets' nest of al-Qaeda operatives. Recent intelligence reports reveal as much. The only institution in Indonesia capable of dealing with this problem is the military which, plagued by years of corruption, is an imperfect instrument. However, carefully structured security cooperation programs that reinforce professionalism, inculcate the value of the rule of law, and discourage human rights abuses are critical to U.S. interests and should be reconsidered.

—John J. Tkacik is Research Fellow for China, Taiwan, and Mongolia; Balbina Hwang is Policy Analyst for Northeast Asia; and Dana R. Dillon is Senior

18. Dana R. Dillon, "Improving Relations with India Without Compromising U.S. Security," Heritage Foundation *Backgrounder* No. 1402, December 11, 2000, at *www.heritage.org/library/backgrounder/bg1402.html.*
19. Dana R. Dillon and John J. Tkacik, "The United States Should Encourage India and Pakistan to Disengage," Heritage Foundation *Executive Memorandum* No. 799, January 25, 2002, at *www.heritage.org/library/execmemo/em799.html.*

Policy Analyst for South and Southeast Asia in the Asian Studies Center at The Heritage Foundation. Paolo Pasicolan, a Policy Analyst in the Asian Studies Center, also contributed to this chapter.

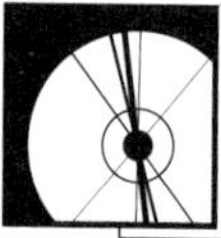

For a complete list and full-text versions of additional studies by Heritage on Asian security, see the searchable *Issues 2002* companion CD–ROM.

EXPERTS

Heritage Foundation

John J. Tkacik
Research Fellow for China, Taiwan, and Mongolia
Asian Studies Center
The Heritage Foundation
214 Massachusetts Avenue, NE
Washington, DC 20002
(202) 608-6103
fax: (202) 675-1779
john.tkacik@heritage.org

Dana R. Dillon
Senior Policy Analyst for South and Southeast Asia
Asian Studies Center
The Heritage Foundation
214 Massachusetts Avenue, NE
Washington, DC 20002
(202) 608-6133
fax (202) 675-1779
dana.dillon@heritage.org

Balbina Hwang
Policy Analyst for Northeast Asia
Asian Studies Center
The Heritage Foundation
214 Massachusetts Avenue, NE
Washington, DC, 20002
(202) 608-6134
fax (202) 675-1779
balbina.hwang@heritage.org

Paolo Pasicolan
Policy Analyst
Asian Studies Center
The Heritage Foundation
214 Massachusetts Avenue, NE
Washington, DC 20002
(202) 608-6132
fax (202) 675-1779
paolo.pasicolan@heritage.org

Larry M. Wortzel, Ph.D.
Director, Asian Studies Center
The Heritage Foundation
214 Massachusetts Avenue, NE
Washington, DC 20002
(202) 608-6081
fax: (202) 675-1779
larry.wortzel@heritage.org

Ambassador Harvey Feldman
Senior Fellow in China Policy
Asian Studies Center
The Heritage Foundation
214 Massachusetts Avenue, NE
Washington, DC 20002
(202) 608-6081
fax: (202) 675-1179
harvey.feldman@heritage.org

Daryl M. Plunk
Senior Fellow
Asian Studies Center
The Heritage Foundation
214 Massachusetts Avenue, NE
Washington, DC 20002
(202) 546-4400
fax (703) 276-8849

Other Experts

Thomas Christensen
Professor
Strategic Studies Program
Massachusetts Institute of Technology
E–38 616 292 Main Street
Cambridge, MA 02139
(617) 258-8431
fax: (617) 452-3975
tjc3@mit.edu

June Teufel Dreyer
Professor
Political Science
University of Miami
Coral Gables, FL 33124
(305) 284-2403
jdreyer@miami.edu

David M. Finkelstein
Director, Project Asia
Center for Strategic Studies
Center for Naval Analysis Corp.
4825 Mark Center Drive
Alexandria, VA 22311-1850
(703) 824-2952
fax: (703) 824-2330
finked@cna.org

Ambassador James R. Lilley
Resident Fellow of Asian Studies
American Enterprise Institute
1150 17th Street, NW
Washington, DC 20036
(202) 862-5949
fax: (202) 862-7178
jlilley@aei.org

James J. Przystup, Ph.D.
Institute for National Strategic Studies
Fort McNair
300 5th Avenue, SW, Room 314B
Washington, DC 20139
(202) 475-1844

Lucian Pye, Ph.D.
Professor Emeritus
Political Science Department
Massachusetts Institute of Technology
77 Massachusetts Avenue
#E53–470
Cambridge, MA 02139-4307
(617) 253-5262
fax: (202) 258-6164
pye@mit.edu

Andrew Scobell
Research Professor
Strategic Studies Institute
U.S. Army War College
Carlisle Barracks, PA 17013
(717) 245-4123
andrew.scobell@carlisle.army.mil

Arthur Waldron
Visiting Scholar
Director of Asian Studies
American Enterprise Institute
1150 17th Street, NW
Washington, DC 20036
(202) 828-6031
fax: (202) 862-5808
awaldron2@aol.com

Ambassador Richard Walker
Richard L. Walker Institute of International Studies
University of South Carolina
Columbia, SC 29208
(803) 777-8180
fax: (803) 787-9308

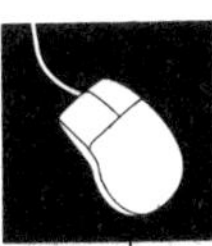

For continually updated and expanded information on major breaking developments on this issue over the campaign cycle, see *www.heritage.org/issues/asia.*

The Middle East

Rooting Out Terrorism and Promoting Peace

James Phillips

THE ISSUES

Even before September 11, 2001, few Americans needed to be reminded that the Middle East is a volatile region. The Bush Administration has done a good job in swiftly and effectively responding to the terrorist attacks launched by Osama bin Laden's terrorist network. The United States attacked al-Qaeda at its headquarters in Afghanistan and ousted the Taliban regime that protected it, literally before the World Trade Center had stopped smoldering. In the process, the Administration bolstered America's prestige and power in the Middle East, which had eroded from its peak following victory in the 1991 Gulf War. Much of the wishful thinking that hampered U.S. policy toward this region during the Clinton Administration has been abandoned for more realistic approaches to the following important issues:

1. **Many of the terrorist networks that threaten American citizens and U.S. interests are based in the Middle East—some with state support.** The al-Qaeda network is but one of many terrorist organizations that have killed Americans in the Middle East. Hezballah, Hamas, Palestine Islamic Jihad, and other terrorist groups continue to enjoy support from states such as Iran, Iraq, Libya, Syria, and Sudan. Terrorist groups have flourished in "failed states" with weak central governments, such as Lebanon and Somalia. The United States must follow up its victory against the international terrorists based in Afghanistan by ratcheting up its diplomatic, economic, and, if

necessary, military pressure on other state sponsors of terrorism. As President Bush has said, "Either you are with us, or you are with the terrorists.[1]

2. **Saddam Hussein's regime in Iraq continues to pose a significant threat to U.S. interests.** Since the expulsion of U.N. weapons inspectors in 1998, Iraq has been free to work on its clandestine programs to build nuclear, chemical, and biological weapons and the long-range missiles to deliver them.[2] Trying to make Saddam "behave" and surrender his weapons of mass destruction (WMD), as the Clinton Administration tried to do, is futile. The only way to end the Iraqi threat to peace and stability in the Middle East is to end Saddam's dictatorship.[3]

3. **Past U.S. policy toward Palestinian leader Yasser Arafat has failed.** The Arab–Israeli peace process has collapsed because of the continuing Palestinian terrorist attacks against Israeli citizens. Arafat has been going through the motions of negotiating with the Israelis, but he has failed to abide by his past commitments to halt terrorism. He has failed to move from being a revolutionary leader steeped in terrorism to being the leader of a national movement prepared to make hard sacrifices for peace, as the Israelis gambled he would after the 1993 Oslo peace agreement.[4]

4. **In Afghanistan, the United States has won a victory against terrorism, but more must be done to ensure that terrorism never takes root there again.** The Taliban regime and bin Laden's terrorist network may have been uprooted from Afghanistan, but Washington needs to help the provisional government build stability and secure a lasting peace to keep terrorists from coming back to roost.[5]

---

1. "Address to the Nation by The President of the United States," *Congressional Record*, U.S. House of Representatives, September 20, 2001, p. H5861.
2. Jack Spencer, *Ballistic Missile Threat Handbook* (Washington, D.C.: The Heritage Foundation, 2000).
3. See James Phillips, "Target Iraq's Terrorist Regime, Not Just Bin Laden, to Win War on Terrorism," Heritage Foundation *Executive Memorandum* No. 780, October 2, 2001, at *www.heritage.org/library/execmemo/em780.html*.
4. See James Phillips, "Building Bridges on Sand: Clinton's Dubious Middle East Peace Initiative," Heritage Foundation *Executive Memorandum* No. 709, January 16, 2001, at *www.heritage.org/library/execmemo/em709.html*.

5. **Iran continues to support terrorism.** Though the new government appears to be wavering from its hard-line anti-American stance, Iran's support for terrorism continues. Iranian reformers, led by President Mohammad Khatami, are engaged in an uphill struggle against hard-liners led by the Supreme Guide Ayatollah Ali Khamanei. These hard-liners continue to block efforts to improve relations with the United States.[6]

THE FACTS

FACT: The United States has suffered repeated terrorist attacks from Islamic extremists.

Even before September 11, Americans had been the victims of terrorist attacks at the hands of Islamic militants:

- The 1979–1981 hostage crisis in Iran;
- The 1983 bombing of the Marine barracks in Beirut;
- The 1983 bombing of the U.S. embassy in Lebanon;
- The kidnappings of 15 Americans in Lebanon between 1985 and 1991;
- The 1993 World Trade Center bombing in New York City;
- The June 1996 bombing of the Khobar Towers housing complex in Saudi Arabia; and
- The August 1998 bombings of U.S. embassies in Nairobi, Kenya, and Dar es Salaam, Tanzania.

FACT: Five of the seven states on the U.S. Department of State's list of state sponsors of terrorism are located in the Middle East.[7]

Iran, Iraq, Libya, Syria, and Sudan continue to support terrorism, according to the April 2001 State Department report, along with

---

5. See James Phillips, "Keys to the Endgame in Afghanistan," Heritage Foundation *Backgrounder* No. 1507, December 6, 2001, at *www.heritage.org/library/backgrounder/bg1507.html*.
6. See James Phillips, "The Rise of Iran's Reformers Requires a Cautious U.S. Response," Heritage Foundation *Executive Memorandum* No. 653, February 25, 2000, at *www.heritage.org/library/execmemo/em653.html*.
7. See U.S. Department of State, "Patterns of Global Terrorism, 2000," April 2001, at *www.state.gov/s/ct/rls/pgtrpt/2000/2441.htm*.

Cuba and North Korea. Afghanistan was not put on the list because the United States did not recognize the Taliban regime as a legitimate state authority.

FACT: Saddam Hussein's clandestine weapons programs threaten U.S. interests in the Persian Gulf, the strategic storehouse of roughly 55 percent of the world's oil reserves.

Despite international sanctions, Saddam continues to provoke confrontations in a relentless effort to wear down the resolve of the U.N. coalition that defeated him in the 1991 Gulf War. The United Nations Special Commission (UNSCOM) weapons inspectors charged with finding and destroying Iraq's weapons of mass destruction and long-range missiles were prevented from doing their work at every step. Saddam scored a major victory in late 1998 when he successfully expelled the UNSCOM inspectors from Iraq, leaving him free to resume his clandestine efforts to build missiles and develop chemical, biological, and nuclear weapons.[8]

Saddam's regime used illegal chemical weapons in its 1980–1988 war against Iran and also against rebellious Iraqi Kurds in the town of Halabja in March 1988.

- Baghdad is believed to have hidden supplies of mustard gas, two types of nerve gas, and several types of lethal biological agents, including anthrax and botulin toxins.
- Before they were expelled, the UNSCOM inspection teams discovered that Iraq's nuclear weapons program was more extensive and sophisticated than suspected.
- Iraq today is believed to be two or three years away from building an atomic bomb.

Saddam also continues to press a propaganda offensive to undermine the economic sanctions that the United Nations maintains on Iraq. To counteract Saddam's propaganda, the United Nations Security Council has gradually eased sanctions restricting the sale of Iraqi oil and permitted the sale of increasing amounts of Iraqi oil under the "Oil for Food" program.

---

8. See James Phillips, "Why the United States Should Help the Iraqi Opposition," Heritage Foundation *Executive Memorandum* No. 563, December 14, 1998, at *www.heritage.org/library/execmemo/em563.html*.

No direct Iraqi involvement in the September 11 attacks has been proven, but there are disturbing reports of several Iraqi contacts with Osama bin Laden and his henchmen. According to U.S. intelligence officials, bin Laden was in contact with government officials in Iraq shortly before the attacks took place. In addition, Mohamed Atta, the suspected ringleader of the 19 terrorists who hijacked the four U.S. airliners on September 11, met with an Iraqi intelligence officer in Prague before coming to the United States.[9]

Iraq has a long record of supporting terrorist groups and using terrorism to advance its foreign policy. During the 1991 Gulf War, Baghdad planned a series of attacks against U.S. targets around the world. Most were blocked by the United States with the help of several foreign governments. Iraqi agents were also apprehended in an aborted April 1993 assassination attempt against former President George H. W. Bush on a visit to Kuwait.

Ramzi Yousef, the mastermind of the February 1993 bombing of the World Trade Center, had strong links to Iraq as well as to bin Laden's terrorist network. He flew to the United States using an Iraqi passport and appears to have acquired a false identity with the help of Iraqi authorities. Another suspect in the 1993 bombing, Abdul Yasin, later returned to Iraq and is believed to be living in Baghdad.

FACT: Yasser Arafat has violated his Oslo commitments to suppress terrorism, arrest and jail terrorists, cooperate with Israeli security forces, and halt the incitement of violence.

Palestinian leader Yasser Arafat has built up the Palestinian security forces far beyond the 30,000 men permitted by the Oslo accords.[10] These forces have been involved in numerous terrorist attacks against Israelis, and Palestinian police and security forces have used their weapons—originally issued to them by Israel—against Israelis.

After Arafat failed to obtain all the concessions from Israel that he had demanded at the Camp David summit in July 2000, he gave the green light for a resumption of political violence, the "inti-

9. See Phillips, "Target Iraq's Terrorist Regime."

10. See James Phillips, "Clinton Must Warn Arafat Against Declaring Statehood," Heritage Foundation *Executive Memorandum* No. 579, March 19, 1999, at *www.heritage.org/library/execmemo/em579.html*.

fada," in September 2000. Since then, continued terrorist attacks against Israelis have blocked the resumption of peace negotiations. The Clinton Administration's approach—working to appease the Palestinians with Israeli concessions—has clearly failed.

While talking about peace, Arafat's Palestinian Authority (PA) has been preparing for war. For example, in January 2002, Israeli commandos intercepted a Palestinian ship bearing 50 tons of Iranian-supplied weapons to be smuggled to Palestinian terrorists in the West Bank and Gaza.

FACT: Iran continues to support terrorism, clandestine efforts to develop weapons of mass destruction, and violent opposition to the Arab–Israeli peace negotiations.

Iranian President Mohammad Khatami, elected in May 1997, has called for better relations with the United States, but Iranian hard-liners have blocked Khatami from undertaking concrete actions to demonstrate Iran's intent to halt its openly hostile policies toward the United States. Iran has undertaken an ambitious military buildup and has become the third largest buyer of Russian arms after China and India.[11] Tehran also provides support for terrorist groups such as Hezballah, Hamas, and Palestine Islamic Jihad. As noted above, Iran also was discovered to have provided 50 tons of arms to the Palestinian Authority in January 2002.

WHAT TO DO IN 2003

Conservative candidates for office in 2003 should make clear that U.S. foreign policy toward the Middle East must be pragmatic. The United States should:

Push aggressively for greater international cooperation to blunt the threat of terrorism and punish states that support it.

The United States should press a relentless, multifaceted campaign against the al-Qaeda terrorist network using military, diplomatic, law enforcement, and economic tools. Particular

11. See Ariel Cohen and James Phillips, "Countering Russian–Iranian Military Cooperation," Heritage Foundation *Backgrounder* No. 1425, April 5, 2001, at *www.heritage.org/library/backgrounder/bg1425.html.*

attention should be given to attacking its cells in Somalia, Yemen, the Philippines, and Sudan.

Washington should push more aggressively for greater international cooperation to blunt the threat of other Middle Eastern terrorist groups, such as Hezballah, Hamas, Palestine Islamic Jihad, Egyptian Islamic Jihad, and Algeria's Armed Islamic Group. States that continue to support terrorism, such as Iran, Iraq, Libya, Sudan, and Syria, should be isolated diplomatically, punished with multilateral economic sanctions, and threatened with military reprisals if necessary.

Help Iraqi opposition forces undermine and extinguish Saddam Hussein's brutal dictatorship.

To prevent Iraq from crossing the nuclear threshold and becoming an even more dangerous terrorist state, the United States should consider a full range of military options to disarm and remove the current regime. It should throw its full support behind the Iraqi opposition forces, including the Iraqi National Congress (INC), support for which received only lip service during the Clinton Administration. The opposition now controls only the safe haven in northern Iraq established by the first Bush Administration in 1991 to halt Iraqi attacks on dissident Kurds.

The United States, in close cooperation with Turkey, should cement a political–military alliance between the INC and the Kurds. After INC cadres return to Iraq's northern mountains to establish a provisional government, they should be protected by U.S. air power. The United States also should establish a "no-drive zone" for Saddam's army in the Kurdish safe haven and southern Iraq, and expand the two no-fly zones already imposed on Iraq's air force to cover the entire country. To ferret out Saddam's strongholds, U.S. special forces, in close cooperation with the Iraqi opposition, should help spot targets for U.S. air strikes as they did in Afghanistan.

Iraq's southern oil fields should be seized and oil revenues channeled to a provisional government, with the INC as its nucleus. To increase the incentive for mass defections from

Saddam's regime, U.N. economic sanctions on any territory controlled by this government should be lifted.

Washington also should agree to the lifting of all U.N. sanctions against Iraq as soon as Saddam's regime is replaced by a government that agrees to halt his weapons programs and live peacefully with Iraq's neighbors. The only way to rid Iraq of its prohibited weapons is to end Saddam's regime.

The United States should use military force primarily to weaken Saddam's grip on power, reduce his capabilities to threaten his neighbors, and support opposition forces, not just to enforce sporadic weapons inspections that have failed to disarm Iraq. Washington should avoid agreeing to a diluted U.N. weapons inspection regime that would provide the illusion of arms control without being capable of dismantling Iraq's clandestine programs. Saddam's threatening regime should be put in a coffin, not just a box.

Encourage a decentralized, broad-based, multiethnic government in Afghanistan that gives all Afghan groups strong incentives to avoid factional feuding.

The U.N.-sponsored Bonn agreement has laid the groundwork for building a postwar government, but this fragile consensus could be threatened by political bickering. Empowering the provincial governments and giving them substantial autonomy and access to reconstruction aid would reduce the possibility of an all-out power struggle over the control of state institutions centered in Kabul.

A decentralized government guided by the principles of federalism also would have the beneficial effect of allowing a new generation of Afghan leaders to advance within the power structure through political competition rather than through military domination. Taliban leaders should be brought to justice and excluded from any future government. While the United States must remain engaged in supporting the interim Afghan government led by Hamid Karzai and preventing Afghanistan's neighbors from meddling in its affairs, it should avoid making any open-ended peacekeeping commitment.

Seek diplomatic dialogue with Iran but maintain economic sanctions until Tehran ends its hostile policies.

Although President Khatami may genuinely want to ease tensions with the West, he is opposed by hard-liners led by Ayatollah Ali Khamanei, who succeeded Ayatollah Ruhollah Khomeini as supreme leader. The challenge for U.S. policymakers will be to test the willingness and ability of Khatami to halt Iran's threatening activities while continuing the economic sanctions. Washington should cautiously probe the willingness of Iran to enter into a substantive dialogue on ending its hostile policies and exploring areas of possible cooperation. But U.S. economic sanctions should be firmly maintained until Tehran takes concrete actions to end its support of terrorism, violent opposition to the Arab–Israeli peace process, and WMD programs.

U.S. economic sanctions helped to create the conditions that brought Iranian reformers to power, and sanctions remain a useful tool for helping Iran make the difficult transition to a genuine democracy. If Iran can complete this transition, Iranian–American relations could be normalized and the two countries could cooperate on a wide range of issues, including containing Iraq, stabilizing Afghanistan and Lebanon, and fighting international drug trafficking.

Shift U.S. policy toward the Arab–Israeli peace negotiations from conflict resolution to conflict management.

Palestinian leader Yasser Arafat is not a credible partner for negotiating peace with Israel. Israel's January 3, 2002, capture of a Palestinian ship carrying 50 tons of weapons bought from Iran is yet another reminder that the Palestinian Authority talks about peace while preparing for war. Washington should scale back its ambitions on the Israeli–Palestinian negotiating front to include reducing violence, halting Palestinian terrorism, and ending the intifada.

Washington must fundamentally rethink the flawed appeasement policy that has raised Palestinian expectations, whetted Arafat's appetite for concessions, and led the Oslo negotiating process into a diplomatic dead end. The peace negotiations can be salvaged only by rigorously holding the Palestinian Authority to its Oslo commitments and ending Palestinian terrorism and mob thuggery.

The United States should resist the temptation to gamble its diplomatic capital on a peace plan until the Palestinian Authority has decisively cracked down on terrorism and ended its manipulation of political violence, as specified under the Mitchell Commission report that set forth requirements for reaching a cease-fire and resuming negotiations. If Arafat refuses to end his incitement to violence and support of terrorism, Washington should break relations with the Palestinian Authority, close the PA's office in Washington, and seek to isolate it diplomatically.

Washington should also block any Palestinian efforts to introduce international peacekeepers, which is anathema to Israel. The ineffective U.N. peacekeeping forces stationed in the Sinai peninsula before the 1967 war and in Lebanon after 1978 were a bitter disappointment; they brought a false sense of security but did nothing to ease the conflict. Israelis naturally want to retain responsibility for their own security in the face of continued Palestinian terrorism.

—James Phillips is a Research Fellow in the Kathryn and Shelby Cullom Davis Institute for International Studies at The Heritage Foundation.

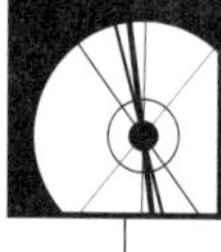

For a complete list and full-text versions of additional studies by Heritage on U.S. policy toward the Middle East and terrorism, see the searchable *Issues 2002* companion CD–ROM.

EXPERTS

Heritage Foundation

James Phillips
Research Fellow, Kathryn and Shelby Cullom Davis Institute for International Studies
The Heritage Foundation
214 Massachusetts Avenue, NE
Washington, DC 20002
(202) 608-6119
fax: (202) 675-1758
jim.phillips@heritage.org

Ambassador Charles Lichenstein
Distinguished Fellow
The Heritage Foundation
214 Massachusetts Avenue, NE
Washington, DC 20002

(202) 608-6187
fax: (202) 547-0641

Other Experts

Dr. Patrick Clawson
Director for Research
Washington Institute
for Near East Policy
1828 L Street, NW
Washington, DC 20036
(202) 452-0650
fax: (202) 223-5364
patrickc@washingtoninstitute.org

Geoffrey Kemp
Director of Regional
Strategic Programs
The Nixon Center
1615 L Street, NW, Suite 1250
Washington, DC 20036
(202) 887-5228
fax: (202) 887-5222
gkemp@nixoncenter.org

Dr. Daniel Pipes
Director, Middle East Forum
1500 Walnut Street, Suite 1050
Philadelphia, PA 19102
(215) 546-5406, ext. 15
fax: (815) 425-2139
meqmef@aol.com

For continually updated and expanded information on major breaking developments on this issue over the campaign cycle, see *www.heritage.org/issues/middleeast* and *www.heritage.org/issues/terrorism*.

LATIN AMERICA

Improving Security, Trade, and Democratic Reform

Stephen Johnson

THE ISSUES

Over the past decade, America's once-strong leadership in the Western Hemisphere has evaporated—jeopardizing the progress many Latin countries had made, both politically and economically—in favor of piecemeal responses to crises as they erupted. But that strategy has failed. Colombia's drug war has become a cancer feeding international crime and terrorism and threatens to infect the entire hemisphere. Democratic progress has retreated in Venezuela and is stalled elsewhere in the region. Free trade with the United States, which could have provided the resources these struggling economies need to strengthen their democratic reforms and defend against growing crime networks, remains a distant goal.

The United States must recognize that, unless it modernizes its outdated security relations with its neighbors to the south and helps to reinvigorate their markets and strengthen democratic institutions, the troubles that afflict Latin America will rapidly become a deluge across the border.

1. **The United States must go beyond narrow counternarcotics efforts to address the growing menace of international crime and terrorism based in Latin America.** Expanded narcotics production in the Andes, Colombia's guerrilla movements, and feeble law enforcement throughout the region have fostered an insidious new threat—a multibillion-dollar transnational crime industry whose smuggling operations reach into every major American city as well as neighboring states and even Europe. Not only are Colombian "rebels" drug traffickers and terrorists themselves, but they have established connections with international terror networks

and now conduct cross-border military operations that could threaten the stability of neighboring governments such as Ecuador's.

2. **Washington needs to reinvigorate its pursuit of free trade in Latin America.** Following congressional approval of the North American Free Trade Agreement with Mexico and Canada in 1994, trade liberalization across the region made plodding progress. The lack of bilateral free trade agreements with other Latin countries has dimmed the once-bright prospects for a hemispheric free trade area and dampened incentives in Latin America for market reforms. Without trade promotion authority (TPA)—or "fast-track" negotiating authority—the Administration is finding it difficult to sign trade agreements with individual countries, which fear that any agreement will get bogged down in Congress. Slow movement on trade agreements both keeps American businesses from pursuing lucrative export and investment opportunities and restricts consumer access to less expensive goods and services.[1]

3. **The United States and Mexico should move forward on urgent security and trade issues.** Vicente Fox is the first Mexican president to come from an opposition party in 71 years, bringing a fresh breeze of democracy across the 2,000-mile border Mexico shares with the United States. But while he has shown his willingness to pursue greater cooperation with the United States, he has proposed ideas that clearly favor his own country, such as facilitating easier migration of low-skilled workers to the United States and Canada to seek work. The Administration has not offered any concrete proposals on migration. Nor has it encouraged homegrown reforms that would help Mexican laborers find work, help reduce corruption, or help Mexico to become an effective partner in stemming the advance of drug trafficking and terror. The United States must develop policies and initiatives on these important issues to protect common markets and borders.

---

1. For additional information on free trade and trade promotion authority, see the chapter on trade.

4. **America has a vested interest in making sure that the democratic gains of the 1980s in Latin America are not rolled back.** America's investment in countering the spread of communism by building democratic institutions and free markets in Latin America lapsed shortly after the Soviet Union imploded. Rather than continuing to solidify and stabilize democratic governance and the rule of law, Washington started spending development money on humanitarian assistance and stopgap programs to slow population growth. Although 34 out of the 35 countries in the hemisphere now choose their leaders by multi-party election, reforms are incomplete. Powerless local governments as well as subservient national legislatures and judiciaries in the region are unable to restrain the excesses of strong presidents or corrupt officials. The United States should target public diplomacy and democracy initiatives to support free and fair elections, the rule of law, transparent and accountable governments, and open debate in civil society.

THE FACTS

FACT: Drugs and insurgency flourish in Latin America despite U.S. assistance to counter them.

While the United States provided narrowly focused counternarcotics assistance to Colombia and other drug-producing Andean states throughout the 1990s, it advised Colombia to address its growing terrorist insurgency by involving the insurgents in an unstructured, objectiveless "peace" dialogue. Not only has that process complicated counternarcotics efforts, but the largest rebel group, the Revolutionary Armed Forces of Colombia (FARC), has spread its operations from 40 percent to 70 percent of the countryside and has nearly doubled in size. Now, heavily financed by drug trafficking, its members murder, kidnap, destroy property and infrastructure, and traffic in arms. The FARC has been aided by the Irish Republican Army (IRA) and is reportedly allied with the Arellano Felix drug cartel in Mexico. Its activities are spilling into neighboring countries, and smuggling connections with regional drug trafficking organizations enable it to reach into major North American cities.

FACT: Terrorism also finds the region a haven of opportunity.

Weak law enforcement and governance over large tracts of territory provide a hospitable environment for the operations of criminals and terrorists. Colombia is an example of a country with open countryside that has fallen prey to the terrorist activities of two formidable guerrilla groups and paramilitary "self-defense" forces that oppose them. Paraguay, Argentina, and Brazil share a poorly governed frontier that also offers haven to terrorist operations and sympathizers linked to the Egyptian Islamic Group (affiliated with Osama bin Laden), the Iranian-backed Hezbollah, and the pro-Palestinian Hamas organization.[2] Cuba has been named by the U.S. Department of State as a state sponsor of terrorism and has its own electronic and biological warfare capabilities. Cuba also has relations with other state sponsors of terrorism, such as Libya and Iraq, and has brokered encounters between such groups as the IRA and the guerrillas targeting Colombia's precarious democratic government.[3]

FACT: The United States has allowed free trade with Latin America to languish.

Despite the Bush Administration's efforts to revive a hemispheric trade agenda, Congress has shied away from promoting free trade with Latin America's $2 trillion economy, citing environmental and labor concerns. This has contributed to America's loss of leadership in the Free Trade Area of the Americas (FTAA) initiative, slated to be finalized by 2005. Moreover, swift U.S. approval of any bilateral free trade accords—for example, with Chile—is not assured. Other countries have leaped ahead of the United States on trade with Latin America. Of the 30 free trade accords in the Western Hemisphere, the United States is party only to NAFTA.

FACT: NAFTA has been a resounding success.

NAFTA is an example of what trade can do to stimulate economies. Since its inception, trade among Canada, Mexico, and the United States has more than doubled, rising from $297 billion in

---

2. See Michael Smith, "Paraguay Suspects Arab Merchants Raised $50 Million for Terrorists," *Bloomberg News*, November 1, 2001; see also the chapter on international terrorism.
3. John Murray Brown and Richard Wolffe, "Havana Says IRA Suspect Is Sinn Fein Frontman," *Financial Times*, August 18, 2001.

1994 to $676 billion in 2000.[4] According to U.S. Trade Representative Robert Zoellick, overall exports from the U.S. to its NAFTA partners support 2.9 million American jobs—900,000 more than in 1993—that typically pay wages that are 13 percent to 18 percent higher than the average American wage.[5]

FACT: U.S. trade with Cuba is blocked by Fidel Castro, who refuses to liberate commerce from his own dictatorial grip.

Some U.S. businessmen and Members of Congress have been eager to pursue commercial ties with communist Cuba and its fickle $5 billion import sector. Fidel Castro, his brother Raul, and the upper echelons of Cuba's armed forces control most of the island's enterprises; they import goods from select countries until Cuba's credit runs out and exploit Cuba's captive labor force, which earns the U.S. equivalent of pennies an hour. Except for self-employment in such occupations as bicycle repair and snack vending, private businesses are prohibited, so trade benefits only the state, which decides how imports will be used or resold.

FACT: Mexico and the United States share important problems that need focused attention.

Despite President Bush's cordial relationship with Mexican President Vicente Fox, Washington's strategy for U.S.–Mexican relations is unclear. Since NAFTA took effect, the area around the U.S.–Mexican border has experienced explosive population growth but without a corresponding investment in infrastructure or security. Informal communities lacking adequate sanitation have increased, mostly on Mexico's side, and water is in short supply on both sides.[6] In fiscal year 2001, 1.2 million aliens were arrested crossing the border illegally; yet the U.S. government has

---

4. From "NAFTA at Seven, Building on a North American Partnership," July 2001, at *www.ustr.gov/naftareport/nafta7_brochure-eng.pdf* (February 11, 2002).
5. Robert B. Zoellick, U.S. Trade Representative, speech before the National Foreign Trade Council, Washington, D.C., July 26, 2001; see also Sara J. Fitzgerald, "The Effects of NAFTA on Exports, Jobs, and the Environment: Myth vs. Reality," Heritage Foundation *Backgrounder* No. 1462, August 1, 2001, p. 2, at *www.heritage.org/library/backgrounder/bg1462.html*.
6. See U.S. General Accounting Office, *U.S.–Mexico Border: Better Planning, Coordination Needed to Handle Growing Commercial Traffic*, GAO/NSIAD–00–25, March 2000, and *U.S.–Mexico Border: Despite Some Progress, Environmental Infrastructure Challenges Remain*, GAO/NSIAD–00–26, March 2000.

not yet decided on a policy either to restrict the flow of illegals or to facilitate the entry of proposed "guest" workers.[7]

President Fox campaigned for office on the need to improve education, establish the rule of law, and enact economic reforms to improve labor skills and boost local employment. Progress on these fronts would help alleviate the flood of illegal migrants, but little has been done to encourage Mexico to implement these measures. A coordinated U.S.–Mexico policy is needed.

FACT: Political stability, democracy, and economic progress are floundering in South America.

Once a region of promise with a wealth of resources, the Andean nations are now in a precarious state. In Colombia, the FARC, a 38-year-old guerrilla movement now funded in part by drug trafficking, is growing in strength and threatening neighboring states. These rebels now operate in northern Ecuador, a fragile democracy that has ousted three presidents in the past six years. Next door, Peruvian President Alejandro Toledo is trying to repair the corrupted government institutions left by his predecessor, Alberto Fujimori. Runaway government spending and bad economic policy have bankrupted Argentina's economy, causing the country to default on its foreign debt, four presidents to resign, and the middle class to take to the streets to regain access to their own bank accounts. Venezuelan President Hugo Chavez, though chosen in a free election, has since tried to create a dictatorship modeled after Cuba's.

FACT: A decade of short-sighted, reactive U.S. policies failed to ensure lasting political and economic reforms in Haiti and Colombia.

In 1994, the Clinton Administration sent 20,000 troops to Haiti and spent about $3 billion to restore ousted president Jean-Bertrand Aristide to office. Since then, Aristide has enriched himself with private business deals while his political opponents have been intimidated and murdered. Now serving a second, non-consecutive term, Aristide is pushing the U.S. Congress to renew

---

7. "Processing Persons Arrested for Illegal Entry into the United States Between Ports of Entry," statement of Michael A. Pearson, Executive Associate Commissioner, Field Operations, Immigration and Naturalization Service, before the Permanent Subcommittee on Investigations, Committee on Governmental Affairs, U.S. Senate, 107th Cong., 1st Sess., November 13, 2001.

direct aid to his corrupt government even though Haiti is no more democratic, stable, or self-sustaining than it was under military rule or the Duvalier dictatorship.[8]

Further south, the U.S. government withheld security assistance from Colombia from 1994 to 1998, facilitating a union between local drug traffickers and the country's two principal guerrilla movements. Despite recent progress, Colombia's security forces have insufficient numbers, training, and equipment to bring the country's drug-fueled rebels and self-styled paramilitary "self-defense" forces who oppose the guerrillas to justice. Thousands have died each year during the past decade.

WHAT TO DO IN 2003

Implement a comprehensive, long-term strategy to improve security, expand free markets, and invigorate democratic institutions in Latin America.

The Clinton-era policy of reacting sporadically to crisis situations should be laid to rest. America needs a comprehensive approach to hemispheric security, prosperity, and a deepening of the democratic experience. Providing development aid alone should not be the objective, as it has been in the past; such assistance should be limited to its use as a tool to leverage durable homegrown reforms to consolidate democratic practices and liberalize markets. What is needed is U.S. leadership and vision to help cultivate the political will to see the reforms through—a prerequisite for firmly establishing the rule of law, decentralizing authority, opening up economies, and fostering long-term stability.

Modernize security partnerships to defeat terrorism and the drug trafficking that supports it.

In the aftermath of September 11, the United States realized that a unified approach utilizing federal, state, and local agencies, the military, and civilian agencies was needed to address the threat of terrorism. Similar analysis should be applied to security throughout the hemisphere. Although the region may not be ready for a NATO-like cooperative defense organization,

8. For a specific illustration of how U.S. tax dollars have been wasted, see U.S. General Accounting Office, *Any Further Aid to Haitian Justice System Should Be Linked to Performance-Related Conditions*, GAO–01–24, October 17, 2000.

bilateral security partnerships should be developed using common protocols and procedures that delineate military and civilian-agency jurisdictions in the event of various kinds of threats, and these partnerships should enhance the sharing of intelligence among cooperating players. Hemispheric defense must be more comprehensive than the current counternarcotics focus of U.S. policy.

Lift the restrictions on the use of U.S.-donated military equipment for anything other than drug interdiction.

The United States should clearly back Colombia's efforts to expand public security sufficiently to eradicate drug trafficking and to protect inhabitants in its poorly governed countryside. This should include efforts to establish the rule of law and reform and decentralize the government in response to the wishes of the majority of its citizens. The Bush Administration should urge the Colombian government to apply the necessary pressure to encourage all illegal armies (including so-called self-defense groups) to lay down their arms and participate in the country's political process. Since narcotics trafficking, transnational crime, and terrorism are now closely intertwined, Congress should lift the restrictions on the use of U.S. training and donated military equipment for purposes other than drug interdiction.

Advance free trade within the hemisphere.

Efforts to protect the U.S. economy from competition will be its downfall. Negotiating free trade agreements in the region must be a priority if the United States is to maintain leadership on international trade matters and help expand markets for American industry. Especially in Latin America, the success of still-fragile democratic reforms depends on the prosperity that only free trade and open markets can provide.[9] Besides the FTAA, Congress should support the free trade agreement now being negotiated with Chile, President Bush's proposal to open free trade with Central America, and liberalized trade with possible partners in South America such as Uruguay.[10]

---

9. For more detailed information on this issue, see the chapter on trade.

Support democrats, not dictators, with friendly ties.

As it rewards democratic countries and those moving toward democracy with trade incentives, the United States should not assist any corrupt, despotic, or even wasteful governments. U.S. lawmakers should not aid Fidel Castro by lifting the U.S. trade embargo on Cuba until the Castro regime guarantees civil liberties to its citizens and establishes a market economy. Although the Cuban state may now purchase U.S. food and medicine on a cash-and-carry basis, American tax dollars should not provide loans to finance such sales. The United States can do more to help Cuban citizens by lifting the U.S.-imposed $100 per month ceiling on remittances—money that American relatives and friends can send back to ordinary Cubans who earn $10 to $15 a month in Cuban pesos.

Improve cooperation with Mexico and Canada on border security.

The United States should protect and enhance its relationship with its leading trade partners, Canada and Mexico. In the aftershock of September 11, fear and tightened security have cut cross-border commerce, particularly with Mexico; layoffs have occurred on both sides of the southwest frontier.

Although the United States should work with its partners to thwart illegal transit and smuggling, it should avoid draconian measures that would harm trade with its NAFTA partners. Both Mexican President Vicente Fox and Canadian Prime Minister Jean Chrétien have, at different times, suggested a "perimeter defense" to address this issue, but that would mean creating a tri-national defense bureaucracy. Instead, the United States should help Mexico improve law enforcement by offering to help train and professionalize Mexican agencies involved in immigration, policing, and counternarcotics, and should promote better coordination of security efforts among all three countries.

---

10. See Ana I. Eiras, "Why the President Should Sign a Free Trade Agreement with Uruguay," Heritage Foundation *Executive Memorandum* No. 800, February 8, 2002, at *www.heritage.org/library/execmemo/em800.html*; see also Ana I. Eiras and Felipe Ward, "Time to Advance Free Trade with Chile," Heritage Foundation *Executive Memorandum* No. 759, July 18, 2001, at *www.heritage.org/library/execmemo/em759.html*.

Establish better oversight to coordinate U.S. agencies at the Mexican border.

Despite the establishment of NAFTA in 1994, proposed steps to develop and enhance the southwest border of the United States have lagged. U.S. agencies such as the Customs Service and the Immigration and Naturalization Service, as well as local police forces, suffer from the lack of coordination. The Administration, governors, and mayors of affected border jurisdictions should work together to solve these problems, with congressional and executive branch oversight to ensure that such efforts are achieving their purpose. Further, because infrastructure has proved inadequate to handle the significant growth in border populations on both sides as new industries have located in that region, the U.S. Department of the Treasury should fulfill its commitments to the North American Development Bank to provide more affordable loans for infrastructure improvements in such basic services as water, sanitation, and sewage.

Target Latin American development dollars where they will have enduring impact and support local efforts to solve problems.

Numerous studies have demonstrated that economic assistance is not necessary for developing countries to achieve economic growth. The most critical component is, in fact, the government's determination to implement economic reform and strengthen the rule of law. Most U.S. assistance dollars in the Western Hemisphere are spent on public health, environmental, and humanitarian relief programs that have little lasting impact and encourage dependence on U.S. largess. If the U.S. government chooses to disburse economic assistance, support should go toward helping implement reforms that are conducive to economic growth and emphasize the role of non-governmental organizations in countries that have committed themselves to democratic principles and true markets.[11]

---

11. See Robert J. Barro, "Rule of Law, Democracy, and Economic Performance," in Gerald P. O'Driscoll, Jr., Kim R. Holmes, and Melanie Kirkpatrick, *2001 Index of Economic Freedom* (Washington, D.C.: The Heritage Foundation and Dow Jones & Company, Inc., 2001), pp. 31–51; see also Richard Roll and John Talbott, "Developing Countries That Aren't," available upon request at *johntalbs@hotmail.com*, November 13, 2001.

Boost the priority of regional public diplomacy programs.

Public diplomacy programs such as civic leader exchanges, forums to discuss political and economic reforms, storefront libraries, and roundtables between U.S. policymakers and the foreign media are affordable: They cost thousands of dollars, not millions. Such initiatives, however, were cut back during the Clinton Administration. This was a mistake; these programs should be revived to help inform local populations of the benefits they can expect from political and economic reforms, as well as to give local civic leaders the informational tools they need to keep progress moving.

—Stephen Johnson is Policy Analyst for Latin America in the Kathryn and Shelby Cullom Davis Institute for International Studies at The Heritage Foundation.

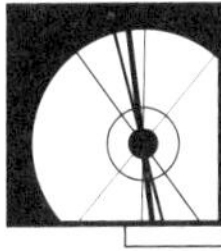

For a complete list and full-text versions of additional studies by Heritage on Latin America, see the searchable *Issues 2002* companion CD–ROM.

EXPERTS

Heritage Foundation

Stephen Johnson
Policy Analyst for Latin America
Kathryn and Shelby Cullom Davis Institute for International Studies
The Heritage Foundation
214 Massachusetts Avenue, NE
Washington, DC 20002
(202) 608-6126
fax: (202) 678-1758
steve.johnson@heritage.org

Daniel W. Fisk
Deputy Director, Kathryn and Shelby Cullom Davis Institute for International Studies
The Heritage Foundation
214 Massachusetts Avenue, NE
Washington, DC 20002
(202) 608-6114
fax: (202) 678-1758
dan.fisk@heritage.org

Gina-Marie Hatheway
Deputy Director of Government Relations, Foreign Policy and Defense
The Heritage Foundation
214 Massachusetts Avenue, NE
Washington, DC 20002
(202) 608-6065
fax: (202) 678-1758
ginamarie.hatheway@heritage.org

Ana I. Eiras
Economic Policy Analyst
Center for International Trade and Economics
The Heritage Foundation
214 Massachusetts Avenue, NE

Washington, DC 20002
(202) 608-6125
fax: (202) 608-1772
ana.eiras@heritage.org

Gerald P. O'Driscoll, Jr.
Director, Center for International Trade and Economics
The Heritage Foundation
214 Massachusetts Avenue, NE
Washington, DC 20002
(202) 608-6185
fax:(202) 608-1772
jerry.odriscoll@heritage.org

Other Experts

Miguel Ceballos
Director, Colombia Program
Georgetown University
3307 M Street NW, Suite 202
Washington, DC 20007
(202) 687-8234
fax: 202-687-2532
ceballom@georgetown.edu

John A. Cope
Senior Fellow
Institute for National Security Studies
National Defense University
Fort Lesley J. McNair
Washington, DC 20319
(202) 685-2373
CopeJ@ndu.edu

Mark Falcoff, Ph.D.
Resident Scholar
American Enterprise Institute
1150 17th Street, NW
Washington, DC 20036
(202) 862-5902
fax: (202) 862-7177
mfalcoff@aei.org

Angel M. Rabasa
Senior Policy Analyst
RAND Corporation
1200 South Hayes Street
Arlington, VA 22202
(703) 413-1100
fax: (703) 413-8111
angel_Rabasa@rand.org

Howard J. Wiarda
Senior Associate
Center for Strategic and International Studies
1800 K Street, NW
Washington, DC 20006
(202) 775-3373
fax: (202) 775-3199

For continually updated and expanded information on major breaking developments on this issue over the campaign cycle, see *www.heritage.org/issues/latinamerica.*

AFRICA

Fostering Development and Stability

Brett D. Schaefer and James Phillips

THE ISSUES

The September 11 attacks on the World Trade Center and the Pentagon affected America's foreign policy around the world. Next to the Middle East, perhaps no regional policy will be more affected by the war on terrorism than U.S. policy toward Africa. To protect American national interests and help Africans to build a prosperous, stable, and secure future, the United States should focus on the following key issues:

1. **America should take its campaign to destroy the al-Qaeda terrorist network to cells in Africa, particularly in Somalia and Sudan, and punish any African regimes or factions that support it.** Osama bin Laden's al-Qaeda network is believed to have a strong presence in Somalia, which has been destabilized by chronic civil war. Terrorists fleeing from Afghanistan may try to regroup there, supported by sympathetic Somali warlords. Bin Laden, who was based in Sudan from 1991 to 1996, may still have supporters operating from that country. Al-Qaeda also has long-standing ties to Islamic extremists in Algeria, Egypt, Kenya, Libya, Tanzania, and Tunisia. Washington must track down these terrorists and uproot the infrastructure that aids them in a broad, determined, and urgent campaign that combines intelligence operations, law enforcement cooperation, diplomatic pressure, covert special operations, and full-fledged military assaults if necessary. Any regime or faction that aids bin Laden should be punished with all the tools at Washington's disposal.

2. **While America cannot solve Africa's problems, U.S. policy can and should promote democracy and stability in that troubled region.** Civil wars have raged in nearly one-third of the 54 countries in Africa during the past decade, and many

governments continue to abuse their citizens. America established the African Crisis Response Initiative (ACRI) to help African nations use regional resources to address humanitarian crises and peacekeeping missions in sub-Saharan Africa. ACRI supports U.S. interests by providing an alternative means for the United States to address the region's political instability and humanitarian crises without diverting U.S. military personnel and resources from other priorities, such as the war on terrorism. Repressive regimes in Africa, like that of President Robert Mugabe in Zimbabwe, should be treated as international outcasts. Governments should be denied assistance and government officials sanctioned until they allow their citizens to express themselves in free and democratic elections.

3. **Washington should address poverty in Africa by promoting economic freedom and trade instead of economic assistance that has proven ineffective.** The average income for the average African in 1995 was roughly equal to the average income of someone living in Western Europe in 1820.[1] The lack of development affects all aspects of society, including education, health, and civil society. Billions of dollars in economic assistance has not helped poor countries develop, and numerous studies have demonstrated no relationship between economic assistance and economic growth. For instance, of the 31 sub-Saharan African countries for which World Bank data are available, a majority (17) have seen a decline in per capita GNP (in constant 1995 U.S. dollars) between 1970 and 1999 despite well over $100 billion in official economic assistance. What do matter are the policies of aid recipients;[2] countries with good policies are more likely to experience positive economic growth regardless of whether or not they receive assistance.[3] If America provides economic assistance, it should maximize its effectiveness by directing economic assistance toward countries with good policy environments, since those with poor economic policies will not experience sustained

1. Angus Maddison, *Monitoring the World Economy: 1820–1992* (Paris: Organisation for Economic Co-operation and Development, 1996).
2. Craig Burnside and David Dollar, "Aid, Policies, and Growth," World Bank, Policy Research Department, Macroeconomic and Growth Division, June 1997, cover.

economic growth no matter how much assistance they receive.[4]

THE FACTS

FACT: Terrorism based in Africa has frequently been targeted at American citizens and U.S. organizations.

- In August 1998, al-Qaeda terrorists bombed the U.S. embassies in Kenya and Tanzania, killing 224 people, including 12 Americans. In June 1999, the U.S. embassies in Ghana, Madagascar, Nigeria, and Senegal were closed temporarily following intelligence reports of possible terrorism.

- Libya has long been a supporter of terrorism. Muammar Qadhafi's support for a wide variety of international terrorist groups led the U.S. Department of State in 1979 to put Libya on the list of state sponsors of terrorism. Qadhafi's regime was involved in the 1988 bombing of Pan Am flight 103 over Lockerbie, Scotland, which claimed the lives of 270 people, including many students from a university in upstate New York. The Libyan bombing of a West Berlin disco in April 1986 killed two U.S. servicemen and triggered retaliatory U.S. air strikes.

- Sudan also has a long history of supporting terrorism. Sudan harbors members of such terrorist organizations as Hamas, Palestine Islamic Jihad, Egypt's Islamic Group, and Egyptian Islamic Jihad. Osama bin Laden lived in Sudan between 1991

---

3. See Robert J. Barro, "Rule of Law, Democracy, and Economic Performance," and Alejandro A. Chafuen and Eugenio Guzmán, "Economic Freedom and Corruption," in Gerald P. O'Driscoll, Jr., Kim R. Holmes, and Melanie Kirkpatrick, *2000 Index of Economic Freedom* (Washington, D.C.: The Heritage Foundation and Dow Jones & Company, Inc., 2000); William W. Beach and Gareth G. Davis, "The Institutional Setting of Economic Growth," in Bryan T. Johnson, Kim R. Holmes, and Melanie Kirkpatrick, *1999 Index of Economic Freedom* (Washington, D.C.: The Heritage Foundation and Dow Jones & Company, Inc., 1999); David Dollar and Aart Kraay, "Growth Is Good for the Poor," World Bank, Development Research Group, March 2001, and "Trade, Growth, and Poverty," World Bank, Development Research Group, March 2001; and Richard Roll and John Talbott, "Why Many Developing Countries Just Aren't," unpublished document available upon request, November 13, 2001.
4. David Dollar and Lant Pritchett, *Assessing Aid: What Works, What Doesn't and Why*, World Bank *Policy Research Report*, 1998, p. 2.

and 1996, and some members of his terrorist network are believed to be living there today.

- Somalia also has been a hotbed of support for bin Laden. Al-Qaeda personnel trained some of the Somali fighters that killed 18 U.S. Special Forces soldiers in an aborted raid in October 1993. The Somalia-based Al Barakaat financial network, according to the Bush Administration, is one of many businesses and groups that transmitted funds, intelligence, and instructions to Osama bin Laden's terrorist cells.[5]

FACT: Millions of people have lost their lives due to the ongoing civil wars and interstate conflicts that plague the region.

Wars have raged in nearly one-third of the 54 countries in Africa in the past decade. Ethiopia and Eritrea recently resolved their bloody war over disputed territory, but the news is not so promising for many other countries.

- Sudan's 18-year-old civil war—the longest-running internal conflict in the world today—has claimed the lives of more than 2 million people, displaced about 5 million people inside the country, and sent another half million into exile. The conflict pits the government, dominated by Muslim Arabs from northern Sudan, against an opposition coalition composed predominantly of black Christians and animists living in the south. In recent years, Sudan's radical Islamic regime has escalated the onslaught to systematic bombing of civilians, starvation, slavery, ethnic cleansing, religious persecution, and other human rights abuses.
- The Democratic Republic of the Congo is a battleground involving troops from at least five countries. Uganda and Rwanda are fighting rebel groups in the eastern part of the DRC, despite protests from President Joseph Kabila, who is supported by troops from Angola and Zimbabwe.
- Zimbabwe is on the brink of anarchy, with President Robert Mugabe and the legislature supporting the outright theft of white-owned farms and refraining from restraining those who have committed numerous murders.

---

5. White House, Office of the Press Secretary, "Terrorist Financial Network Fact Sheet: Shutting Down the Terrorist Financial Network," November 7, 2001, at *www.whitehouse.gov/news/releases/2001/11/20011107-6.html*.

- The long-term inability of peacekeeping missions to put an end to civil and interstate wars is testimony to the need for a new strategy to deal with conflicts in Africa. Two of the U.N.'s most embarrassing peacekeeping debacles occurred in Africa (Somalia and Sierra Leone). The horrible failure of its Somalia mission and the shocking deaths of U.S. soldiers in Mogadishu street battles remain fresh in the minds of Americans. Less well-known is the utter incompetence shown by the U.N. in resolving the conflict in Sierra Leone—a humiliation that culminated in 500 peacekeepers being captured and held hostage by rebels, eventually requiring the United Kingdom to intervene on the U.N.'s behalf. The U.N. also stood by ineptly when an estimated 1 million people were slaughtered in Rwanda in the mid-1990s. In Angola, the U.N. has "completed" three operations, yet civil war still rages.

FACT: Despite billions of dollars in foreign aid, political corruption and turmoil compound ineffective policies to prevent Africa from shedding its place as the world's poorest and least developed region.

Billions of dollars in economic assistance from the United States has not helped African countries develop.[6] The region remains the world's least economically free region.

- Sub-Saharan Africa and the Middle East are virtually tied as the least economically free regions of the world. According to the *Index of Economic Freedom*, neither region has a "free" economy.[7]
- Relatively free countries, such as Botswana, Israel, Jordan, and Mozambique, have consistently outperformed their less economically free neighbors.[8]

Though studies indicate that geography has an impact on economic growth,[9] tropical countries are not "prisoners of geography" doomed to a life of poverty. There is significant variation in

6. See Brett D. Schaefer, "The Keys to an African Economic Renaissance," Heritage Foundation *Backgrounder* No. 1369, May 10, 2000, at *www.heritage.org/library/backgrounder/bg1369.html*.
7. See Gerald P. O'Driscoll, Jr., Kim R. Holmes, and Mary Anastasia O'Grady, *2002 Index of Economic Freedom* (Washington, D.C.: The Heritage Foundation and Dow Jones & Company, Inc., 2002).
8. *Ibid.*

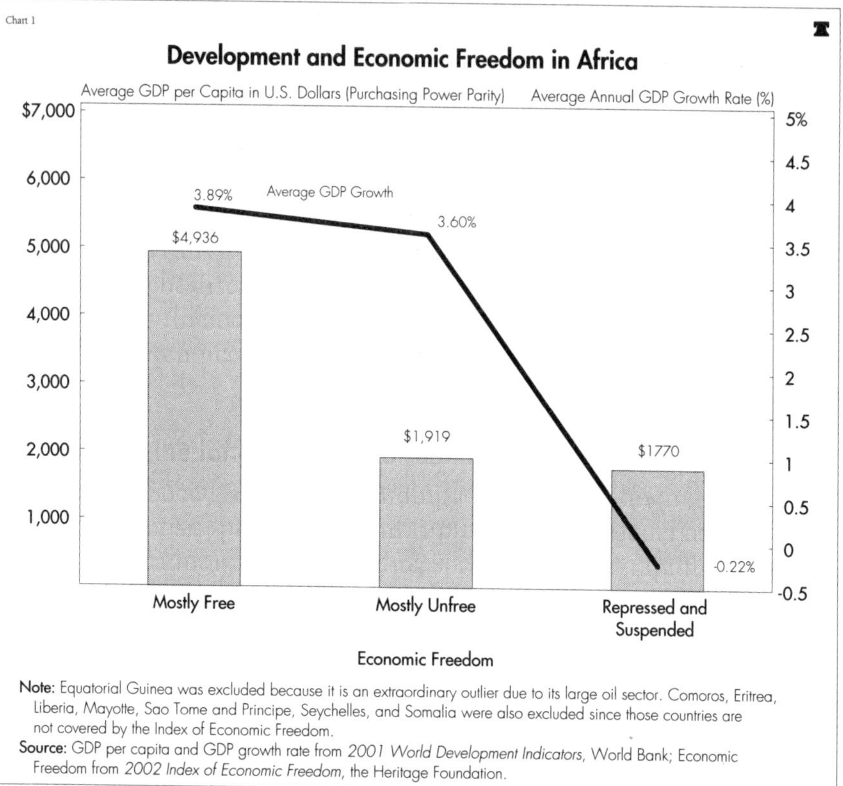

economic growth among African countries. (See Chart 1.) A critical factor in growth is economic liberalization. As long as development assistance continues to flow without any requirement for meaningful reforms, little will change in the poorest countries of Africa.

Many poor nations have accumulated debt burdens beyond their ability to repay. Nearly all of this debt is owed to official lenders (governments or international financial institutions) and was extended at concessional interest rates as foreign aid to promote development. The fact that these loans must now be forgiven demonstrates that they failed to generate economic growth.

9. See John Luke Gallup, Jeffrey D. Sachs, and Andrew D. Meelinger, "Geography and Economic Development," National Bureau of Economic Research Working Paper Series, *Working Paper* No. 6849, December 1998, pp. 30–31, at *www.nber.org/papers/w6849*; Ricardo Hausmann, "Prisoners of Geography," *Foreign Policy*, January/February 2001, p. 47; and Jared Diamond, *Guns, Germs, and Steel: The Fates of Human Societies* (New York: W. W. Norton & Company, 1999).

Chart 2

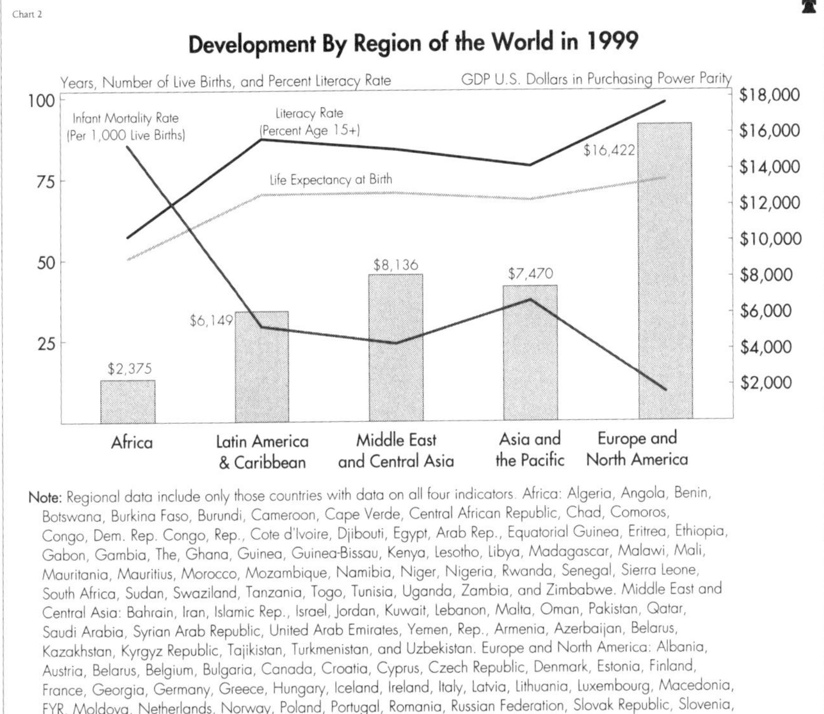

Note: Regional data include only those countries with data on all four indicators. Africa: Algeria, Angola, Benin, Botswana, Burkina Faso, Burundi, Cameroon, Cape Verde, Central African Republic, Chad, Comoros, Congo, Dem. Rep. Congo, Rep., Cote d'Ivoire, Djibouti, Egypt, Arab Rep., Equatorial Guinea, Eritrea, Ethiopia, Gabon, Gambia, The, Ghana, Guinea, Guinea-Bissau, Kenya, Lesotho, Libya, Madagascar, Malawi, Mali, Mauritania, Mauritius, Morocco, Mozambique, Namibia, Niger, Nigeria, Rwanda, Senegal, Sierra Leone, South Africa, Sudan, Swaziland, Tanzania, Togo, Tunisia, Uganda, Zambia, and Zimbabwe. Middle East and Central Asia: Bahrain, Iran, Islamic Rep., Israel, Jordan, Kuwait, Lebanon, Malta, Oman, Pakistan, Qatar, Saudi Arabia, Syrian Arab Republic, United Arab Emirates, Yemen, Rep., Armenia, Azerbaijan, Belarus, Kazakhstan, Kyrgyz Republic, Tajikistan, Turkmenistan, and Uzbekistan. Europe and North America: Albania, Austria, Belarus, Belgium, Bulgaria, Canada, Croatia, Cyprus, Czech Republic, Denmark, Estonia, Finland, France, Georgia, Germany, Greece, Hungary, Iceland, Ireland, Italy, Latvia, Lithuania, Luxembourg, Macedonia, FYR, Moldova, Netherlands, Norway, Poland, Portugal, Romania, Russian Federation, Slovak Republic, Slovenia, Spain, Sweden, Switzerland, Turkey, Ukraine, United Kingdom, and United States. Asia and the Pacific: Australia, Bangladesh, Bhutan, Brunei, Burma, Cambodia, China, Fiji, Hong Kong, China, India, Indonesia, Japan, Korea, Rep., Lao PDR, Malaysia, Mongolia, Nepal, New Zealand, Papua New Guinea, Philippines, Samoa, Singapore, Sri Lanka, Thailand, and Vietnam. Latin America and the Caribbean: Argentina, Bahamas, The, Barbados, Belize, Bolivia, Brazil, Chile, Colombia, Costa Rica, Dominican Republic, Ecuador, El Salvador, Guatemala, Guyana, Haiti, Honduras, Jamaica, Mexico, Nicaragua, Panama, Paraguay, Peru, Suriname, Trinidad and Tobago, Uruguay, and Venezuela.

Source: *Human Development Report 2001: Making New Technologies Work for Human Development*, United Nations Development Program, (New York, NY: Oxford University Press, Inc., 2001), available at *http://www.undp.org/hdr2001/* and *World Development Indicators 2001* (Washington, D.C.: World Bank Group, 2001) on CD-ROM.

Donor nations have agreed to forgive most of the bilateral debt to these countries and fund debt reduction for the debt owed to international financial institutions through the Heavily Indebted Poor Countries (HIPC) initiative.

All but eight of the 42 countries potentially eligible for HIPC debt relief are located in Africa. Forgiving debt to these nations is necessary—and a recognition of reality, as most of them are incapable of paying it—but should be accompanied by reform of bilateral and multilateral foreign aid policy.[10]

As observed by David Dollar of the World Bank,[11] the ineffectiveness of past and existing debt relief proposals lies more with the refusal of official creditors, both bilateral and multilateral, to reform lending policies and tendencies than in an unwillingness to forgive debt. Unless the lending philosophy of official creditors is reformed, debt relief efforts are doomed to failure, and "in 15 years you have another debt crisis."[12]

FACT: Expanding trade opportunities with Africa will help both Africa and America.

- In 2000, 2.3 percent of all U.S. imports were African in origin (1.9 percent from sub-Saharan Africa), and 1.4 percent of U.S. exports went to Africa (0.8 percent to sub-Saharan Africa).

- Africa is an important source of minerals including cobalt, industrial diamonds, and crude oil. The region supplies 15.7 percent of America's oil imports (13.4 percent from sub-Saharan Africa), a share that is expected to grow significantly over the next decade.

- Although the African Growth and Opportunities Act,[13] a trade agreement with sub-Saharan Africa, did not take effect until December 2000, total imports from sub-Saharan Africa in calendar year 2000 had already increased 63 percent to $2 billion in nominal terms. This included a 165 percent increase in imported precious stones and metals, a 68 percent increase in fuel and oil imports, a 49 percent increase in imported knit apparel, and a 17 percent increase in woven

---

10. See *Report of the International Financial Institution Advisory Commission*, March 2000, at *www.house.gov/jec/imf/meltzer.htm*; Brett D. Schaefer, "Debt in Developing Countries: History, Structure, and Efforts to Address Unsustainable External Debt Burdens," paper presented to the International Financial Institution Advisory Commission, January 4, 2000; Brett D. Schaefer, "Real Help for Poor Nations: President Bush's World Bank Grant Proposal," Heritage Foundation *Backgrounder* No. 1466, August 17, 2001, at *www.heritage.org/library/backgrounder/bg1466.html*; and Brett D. Schaefer, "The Bretton Woods Institutions: History and Reform Proposals," Heritage Foundation *Economic Freedom Project Report* No. EFP00–01, April 2000.
11. Dollar and Pritchett, *Assessing Aid: What Works, What Doesn't and Why*.
12. Andrew Broman, "Poor-Nation Debt Relief Ineffective, Experts Say; More Control Sought Over How Savings Spent," *Houston Chronicle*, October 10, 1999, p. A20.
13. Public Law 106–200, signed into law on May 18, 2000, as Title I of the Trade and Development Act of 2000.

apparel.[14] The U.S. Trade Representative attributes this increase to investment in anticipation of AGOA.

FACT: Tropical diseases exact an enormous toll in terms of medical costs and labor lost due to sickness.[15]

- In seven African nations, over 20 percent of the adult population is infected with the HIV/AIDS virus. An estimated 300 million to 500 million people are infected each year with malaria, which kills more people than any other communicable disease except tuberculosis. People are often not treated or immunized against disease in Africa because countries lack access to effective, sufficient, convenient, or affordable medical services.
- The impact of tropical disease on economic growth is significant. A recent study found that from 1965 to 1990, countries with severe malaria experienced 2 percent less economic growth per year than countries without malaria.[16]
- Calls to expropriate drug patents belonging to Western pharmaceutical manufacturers are misguided. Pharmaceutical companies invest vast sums to develop new drugs and often do not recoup that investment for many years. Expropriating drug patents removes the ability of these companies to see a return on their investments, and thus undermines their incentives to invest large sums to develop new drugs. Overriding a patent to allow generic brands to proliferate may provide short-term relief,[17] but is not in the long-term health interests of any nation, most of all poor nations.

---

14. "U.S. Trade and Investment Policy Toward Sub-Saharan Africa and Implementation of the African Growth and Opportunity Act," A Report Submitted by the President of the United States to the United States Congress, Prepared by the Office of the United States Trade Representative, May 2001, p. 106, at *www.ustr.gov/regions/africa/repo_2001.pdf*.
15. Major tropical diseases include African trypanosomiasis (sleeping sickness), Dengue, Leishmaniasis (kala azar), Lymphatic filariasis, Malaria, Onchocerciasis (river blindness), and Schistosomiasis (bilharzia). See "Travelers' Health," National Center for Infectious Diseases, at *www.cdc.gov/travel/*.
16. See Gallup *et al.*, "Geography and Economic Development," p. 40.

WHAT TO DO IN 2003

African security, as well as U.S. security, is threatened by international terrorism. Africa's long-term economic security is also threatened—by the ongoing legacy of a socialist development model that encourages such economically devastating policies as price controls, prohibitions on trade not authorized by the state, and roadblocks to external trade while nationalizing farming and restricting the movement of people within and across borders.[18] Such policies have crippled the development of markets and retarded economic development. To protect American interests and help African nations attain greater security, economic growth, and political stability, the United States should:

Eliminate Osama bin Laden's terrorist network wherever it has taken root.

The United States must lead a relentless campaign to eradicate the al-Qaeda terrorist network throughout the African continent, but particularly in Somalia, where it has flourished due to civil war. Washington must mobilize the full capabilities of U.S. intelligence, law enforcement, and military organizations and bring them to bear, in cooperation with America's friends and allies if possible, on the urgent task of crushing al-Qaeda. The Central Intelligence Agency (CIA) should recruit and deploy Somali spies, special forces, and tribal militias to locate and attack al-Qaeda forces and those who support them. The CIA also should deploy paramilitary forces, backed by U.S. Special Forces and precision U.S. air strikes, to target al-Qaeda bases and leaders. The United States should assist Somali factions that cooperate in hunting down bin Laden's terrorists by giving them arms, economic aid, and political support.

---

17. This is questionable, however. Many countries do not enforce patents, leaving little benefit to rejecting patent rights. These countries are already able to take advantage of drugs produced in violation of the patent. In addition, many poor countries lack a health infrastructure capable of using drugs effectively even if supplied at no cost. See Amir Attaran, D.Phil, LLB, and Lee Gillespie White, LLB, "Do Patents for Antiretroviral Drugs Constrain Access to AIDS Treatment in Africa?" reprint, *JAMA*, Vol. 286, No. 15 (October 17, 2001), and Robert Block, "Despite Cheap Drugs, South Africa Stumbles in Tuberculosis Fight," *The Wall Street Journal*, April 26, 2001, p. A1.
18. George Ayittey, "Promoting Economic Freedom in Africa," paper presented at Association of Private Enterprise Education Conference, Crystal City, Virginia, April 10, 2001, p. 7.

Press Libya and Sudan to halt their support for terrorism.

Maximum diplomatic and economic pressure should be put on Libya and Sudan to end their support of terrorism and expel members of terrorist organizations that have found sanctuary there. If these two countries fail to respond appropriately, Washington should offer direct support to their opposition movements to overthrow those regimes and should also consider military strikes against terrorist groups within their borders.

End the jihad in Sudan.

The Bush Administration has tried to broker a settlement of the Sudanese civil war by dispatching former Senator John Danforth to Sudan as a special envoy. Sudanese dictator Omar Bashir paid lip service to Danforth's diplomatic efforts while continuing the onslaught against the Sudanese opposition movement in the south. Washington should set a six-month deadline for diplomatic efforts to end the fighting. If the Khartoum regime fails to halt its bombing of the south and continues to drag its feet on a political settlement past this deadline, the United States should provide military support and economic aid to the opposition and work to overthrow Bashir's regime.

Reorient aid to facilitate economic development.

Since 1945, the United States has committed approximately $500 billion in bilateral assistance to promote development in developing countries, including the countries of Africa. This investment has had no definitive impact on their economic growth.[19] A more immediate link should be established between economic development assistance and the policies of recipient governments that are conducive to economic growth—specifically, by expanding economic freedom and strengthening the rule of law.

---

19. The Senate Foreign Relations Committee estimates that the United States spent $450 billion on development assistance between 1946 and 1996. See Report 104–99 accompanying the Foreign Aid Reduction Act of 1995 (S. 961), p. 12.

Continue to work to lower developed country trade barriers to goods from this region and encourage economic reforms that would secure access to its resources.

The barriers developed countries maintain against developing countries often apply to sectors that play only a minor role in their own economies, such as the textile and apparel and agricultural sectors, but a major role in the economies of the developing world. Lowering those barriers will allow trade and exports to increase, and African countries can become more proficient in producing the goods for which they have a competitive advantage, acquire the technologies or capital goods they are lacking, and increase their foreign exchange reserves. By gaining access to the world's wealthiest markets, they would be able to increase the level of employment, personal income, and capital available for investment.[20] America began this process with the African Growth and Opportunity Act (AGOA), but barriers to important African products remain in effect and should be eliminated.

Support the African Crisis Response Initiative (ACRI).

America established the African Crisis Response Initiative to help African nations use regional resources to address humanitarian crises and peacekeeping missions in sub-Saharan Africa. With approximately $20 million per year, ACRI has helped train and equip over 6,000 peacekeepers from six African nations.[21] It provides an alternative means for the United States to address the region's political instability and humanitarian crises without diverting military personnel and resources from other priorities, like the war on terrorism. America should expand ACRI funding and training—provided African countries are willing and able—to increase Africa's ability to respond to regional crises.

---

20. Denise H. Froning and Aaron Schavey, "Breaking Up a Triple Play on Poor Countries: Changing U.S. Policy in Trade, Aid, and Debt Relief," Heritage Foundation *Backgrounder* No. 1359, April 13, 2000, at *www.heritage.org/library/backgrounder/bg1359.html.*

21. U.S. Department of State, "Summary of the African Crisis Response Initiative," International Information Programs, at *http://usinfo.state.gov/regional/af/acri/acrisumm.htm.*

Use market incentives to develop vaccines and treatments for tropical diseases rather than trampling on intellectual property rights.

Because people in developing countries often cannot afford to pay for existing medicine, much less expensive new treatments or cures for diseases predominantly affecting developing nations, the incentive for pharmaceutical companies to devote resources to find cures for tropical diseases is very small or nonexistent. The low incentive is further undermined by the lack of adequate intellectual property protection in many developing nations, which leads many pharmaceutical companies to conclude that new drug patents will not be honored. The United States should help stimulate this market by devoting some of the existing foreign aid budget to the purchase of pharmaceuticals, treatments, and vaccines for tropical diseases while encouraging developing countries to increase protection of intellectual property.

—Brett D. Schaefer is Jay Kingham Fellow in International Regulatory Affairs in the Center for International Trade and Economics, and James Phillips is a Research Fellow in the Kathryn and Shelby Cullom Davis Institute for International Studies, at The Heritage Foundation.

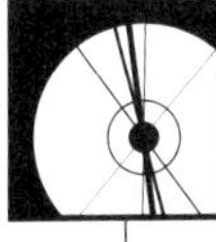

For a complete list and full-text versions of additional studies by Heritage on Africa, see the searchable *Issues 2002* companion CD–ROM.

EXPERTS

Heritage Foundation

Brett D. Schaefer
Jay Kingham Fellow in International Regulatory Affairs
Center for International Trade and Economics
The Heritage Foundation
214 Massachusetts Avenue, NE
Washington, DC 20002
(202) 608-6123
fax: (202) 608-6129
brett.schaefer@heritage.org

James Phillips
Research Fellow, Kathryn and Shelby Cullom Davis Institute for International Studies
The Heritage Foundation
214 Massachusetts Avenue, NE
Washington, DC 20002
(202) 608-6119
fax: (202) 675-1758
jim.phillips@heritage.org

Other Experts

George B. N. Ayittey, Ph.D.
American University
4400 Massachusetts Avenue, NE
Washington, DC 20016
(202) 885-3779
ayittey@american.edu

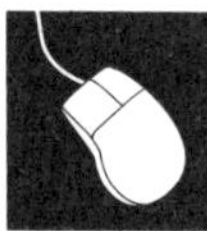

For continually updated and expanded information on major breaking developments on this issue over the campaign cycle, see *www.heritage.org/issues/africa.*

Contact Information

For additional information about The Heritage Foundation and the information that we may provide, please contact the following individuals in our Government Relations department:

Mike Franc 202-608-6064
Vice President, Government Relations

Senate

Tripp Baird 202-608-6070
Director, U.S. Senate Relations
tripp.baird@heritage.org

Doug Stamps 202-608-6062
Deputy Director, U.S. Senate Relations
doug.stamps@heritage.org

House

Lauren Noyes 202-608-6030
Director, U.S. Senate Relations
lauren.noyes@heritage.org

Kara Dougherty 202-608-6073
Deputy Director, U.S. House Relations
kara.dougherty@heritage.org

To schedule an individualized candidate briefing, please contact:

Crystal Gibson 202-608-6078
Manager, Candidate Education Project
crystal.gibson@heritage.org